Sexism, Racism and Oppression

Sexism, Racism and Oppression

Arthur Brittan and Mary Maynard

BASIL BLACKWELL

© Arthur Brittan and Mary Maynard, 1984

First published 1984

Basil Blackwell Publisher Ltd
108 Cowley Road, Oxford OX4 1JF, UK

Basil Blackwell Inc.
432 Park Avenue South, Suite 1505
New York, NY 10016, USA

British Library Cataloguing in Publication Data

Brittan, Arthur
Sexism, racism and oppression.
1. Sexism 2. Racism
I. Title II. Maynard, Mary
305.3   HQ1075

ISBN 0–85520–674–8
ISBN 0–85520–675–6 Pbk

Library of Congress Cataloging in Publication Data

Brittan, Arthur.
Sexism, racism and oppression.

Includes index.
1. Sex discrimination against women.   2. Race discrimination.   3. Oppression (Psychology)
I. Maynard, Mary.   II. Title.
HQ1154.B833   1984   305   84–12483
ISBN 0–85520–674–8
ISBN 0–85520–675–6 (pbk.)

Typeset by Oxford Publishing Services, Oxford
Printed in Great Britain by Page Bros, Norwich

For
Eileen and Ethel

Contents

Preface

Throughout this book we have used the term 'women' to refer to the objects of sexist practices. Although there are problems with this usage in that it implies that white, black and third world women share a common form of oppression, the difficulties are not so formidable as those encountered in devising an appropriate way of talking about racism. Consequently we have chosen to employ terms like 'out-group', 'ethnic-group' and 'migrants' interchangeably. While we realize this is not really satisfactory we do not believe that there is any viable alternative, given the degree of confusion about 'race' in the literature. We would have preferred to use the term 'oppressed group', but this would be to beg the question.

We would like to express our thanks to Bob Coles for all his help and encouragement, as well as to Sue Plummer who spent a great amount of time attempting to come to grips with our respective styles.

1 Primary and Secondary Oppression

Our aim in this book is to examine the way in which both feminism and anti-racism have challenged traditional accounts of 'oppression'. In this respect we do not believe that oppression can be understood in terms of any one explanatory scheme; we do not believe that we can explain 'oppression' by reducing it to some deep underlying cause, some hidden mechanism which allows us to define it in simple and unambiguous terms. Accordingly, this opening chapter will be devoted to a consideration of a number of biological, cultural, psychological, and other viewpoints which have all tended to reduce racism and sexism to a primary level of causation.

It is, of course, notoriously difficult to define oppression. Minimally, it would seem to imply that those who are oppressed are coerced by others. Their freedom of action is limited by the superior power of those who are in a position to ensure their compliance.

> The root of the word 'oppression' is the element 'press'. The press of the crowd; pressed into military service; to press a pair of pants; printing press; press the button. Presses are used to mold things or flatten them or reduce them in bulk, sometimes to reduce them by squeezing out the gasses or liquids in them. Something pressed is something caught between or among forces and barriers which are so related to each other that jointly they restrain, restrict or prevent the thing's motion or mobility. Mold. Immobilise. Reduce. (Frye, 1983, p.2)

It is the nature of the moulding and pressing forces that constitutes the difficulty. The temptation is to look for the source of oppression in a primary biological or social reality. Hence, both racism and sexism are often treated as if they were surface or secondary characteristics of far more fundamental kinds of oppression. In other words, a distinction may be made between primary and secondary oppression.

Primary oppression refers to those direct consequences of the unequal possession of biological capacities, and/or economic, cultural, and social resources. In the case of biology, for example, the oppression of women and out-groups is attributed to their assumed inferior or different genetic endowment. In contrast with their oppressors, they are supposed to be deficient in respect to qualitites such as aggressiveness and intelligence. Thus, the oppression of women and out-groups is described as being unavoidable — or, to put it another way, inequality is justified in terms of biological power. In the case of social and economic oppression, the main argument is usually based on the assumption that the 'mode of production' and 'class' are the ultimate determinants of all other kinds of oppression. Hence, racism and sexism are not explained in their own terms, but are seen as being dependent upon the class antagonisms of this or that society. Primary oppression, in this sense, makes no claims about inevitability. In principle, the economic and political arrangements that structure inequality can be changed, so that sexual and racial oppression may be modified or eliminated.

Secondary oppression is always something other than it appears to be to the naive consciousness of the oppressed person. When migrants encounter racism in housing, employment, and at the interpersonal level, they find that social scientists often translate these experiences into the language of reductionism. Despite this, migrants know what racism and discrimination are without the benefit of the sophisticated analytical language of social and political theory. They might be very aware that racism is intimately connected with the severity of economic crisis, but this knowledge is almost irrelevant when they are the victims of racist attack. Put more strongly, secondary oppression is not considered to be secondary by those unfortunate enough to be at its receiving end.

The problem as we see it is that in reducing all oppression to primary processes, there is a danger of completely missing critical dimensions of personal and social experience. Take the phenomenon of wife battering. In crude terms, it may be claimed that this is a consequence of high unemployment and economic insecurity. Certainly, these factors are relevant, but is this the sum total of our understanding of wife battering? Questions like this have been taken up by contemporary femininist theorists. Instead of male violence being explained by the mode of production, they have argued that we need an entirely different way of formulating the power relations of personal and domestic life. The oppression of women is not reducible to class oppression; it cannot be explained by traditional essentialist and reductionist accounts.

So this chapter will not be concerned with the search for a general theory of oppression incorporating 'race', gender, and class. We do not subscribe to the view that such a theory exists, or even is desirable. Accordingly, we find it difficult to reduce racism and sexism to class. While we are very much aware that we are likely to find racism and sexism in a society in which the mode of production implies specific economic relationships, we cannot go all the way with those practitioners who want to use the 'last instance' as a final arbiter of this or that form of oppression. (Hopefully, the reason why we cannot subscribe to a 'last instance' argument will become clearer over the following few chapters). Nor for that matter can we subscribe to a general eclecticism in which oppression is seen as the sum total of a host of sub-oppressions which together make up a grand totality. If we talk about oppression in Chile or Afghanistan, it is obvious that certain kinds of explanation are more plausible than others. Or, if we try to understand the advent of National Socialism in Germany in the 1920s and 1930s, we cannot ignore the fact that sexism, racism, and economic exploitation are so closely entwined in this context that it does not make sense to treat them independently. It would be very difficult, for instance, to conceive Nazism as having no relationship with capitalism. On the other hand, we cannot account for German anti-Semitism simply as an effect of economic crisis, high unemployment, etc.

What we assert in this text is that the distinction between primary and secondary oppression is problematic. We do so by discussing aspects of oppression which, in the past, have not normally been considered to be significant, namely, sexual relationships, the family, and personal relationships. In other words, we have taken on board the feminist argument that the traditional emphasis on the state, the economy, and other institutions as being critical sources of oppression ignores power and oppression in a host of other situations. We will, therefore (by implication at least), point to the site of oppression as being particularly crucial. By looking at a multiplicity of sites where oppressive relationships obtain, we can perhaps dis-

cern the operation of forms of power which are ruled out by macro-
theory. For example, the classic conceptualization of the family in
radical analyis has been to see its power relationships as being
determined by the political sphere. The implication of this was to
assume that an alteration in the balance of power of classes or elites
in the outside world would automatically influence the balance of
power in the family. The more democratic the society, the more
open its class structure (so the argument goes), then the more likely
that family relationships will be open and democratic. Feminist
writing has repudiated this peculiarly monocausal image of power.
It has done so by subjecting the entire range of personal relationships to critical scrutiny. And it is precisely in these relationships that the operation of gender oppression can be discerned.
But it is not only in the family site that oppression can be discovered
— it can be discovered in the minutiae of everyday life. Everywhere
men and women engage in sexual and social interaction this oppression is reaffirmed and reproduced. Hence, all encounters between
men and women provide a possible site for the expression of power
relationships.

But it is not only women who encounter oppression at the personal level. Homosexuals, lesbians, Jews, blacks, gypsies, Pakistanis, and countless others, face in their everyday encounters a constant barrage of insults and abuse, not only from work-mates,
bureaucrats and 'general members of the public', but also from
those whom they may define as friends or intimate acquaintances.
The discourse of racism is so prevalent in our society that we more
often that not do not see it for what it is. When someone says 'one of
my best friends is a Jew, or a West Indian', this is not a harmless
game — it is a way of hurting the listener, even though there may be
no conscious intention of doing so. And if we realize that this kind of
remark is translated into the countless interaction episodes that
constitute social life, then we come to grips with racism in its most
generalized aspect. The point here is that the occasions for racism
are generalized; every encounter can be a site for the expression of
racist language, and every site may therefore be the occasion of
oppression. In its starkest and simplest form, oppression can be seen
at work in the look that a publican directs at one of his black
customers. Racism in this sense is not something out there — it is
present in personal and mundane circumstances.

We are so used to talking about power and oppression in terms of the functioning of monolithic institutions, that it becomes almost impossible to examine the evidence of the oppressed, and even when that evidence is considered, it is often treated with the greatest suspicion. When, for example, a woman complains to the police that her husband has struck her, this testimony is frequently not taken very seriously, because the police do not consider family violence as being very important or serious, despite their protestations to the contrary:

> It is still true that for a woman to be brutally or systematically assaulted she must usually enter our most sacred institution, the family. It is within marriage that a woman is most likely to be slapped and shoved about, severely assaulted, killed or raped. Thus, it is impossible to understand violence against women without also understanding the nature of the marriage relationship in which it occurs and to which it is inextricably related. (Dobash and Dobash, 1980, p.75)

The family is, by this token, the most likely location for the expression of male violence. However, oppression does not necessarily have to have an institutional base — it can be sited anywhere. Nevertheless, in focusing on the family as the site for the oppression of women, we can counter the tendency of traditional social analysis which defines oppression as belonging to the public domain only.

In the presentation of this introductory discussion we will examine claims made by those who see inequality as being culturally determined or genetically programmed. We will simultaneously look at the parallels between the kinds of arguments used to explain racism and sexism. We will not conclude, however, that parallel kinds of explanation necessarily indicate that all oppression can be subsumed under one explanatory scheme. Because there are cultural explanations for both racism and sexism does not mean that they deal with the same phenomenon. Yet, there are certainly similarities in the mechanisms of oppression that are manifest in racist and sexist practice. For example, some of the ways in which gender is socially constructed are reminiscent of the ways in which 'race' is constructed. In both cases, social objects are given life by the purposes and behaviour of those who make the constructions. In both cases, certain groups of people benefit from these constructions, but this does not entitle us to assume that we are, in fact, uncovering a common source of oppression. The search for parallels might be a fruitless exercise because it could be that each form of oppression has a different history and a different set of social consequences. To quote Carby:

> Much contemporary debate has posed the question of the relation between race and gender, in terms which attempt to parallel race and gender divisions. It can be argued that as processes, racism and sexism are similar. Ideologically, for example, they both construct commonsense through reference to 'natural' and 'biological' differences. It has also been argued that the categories of race and gender are both socially constructed and that, therefore, they have little internal coherence as concepts. Furthermore, it is possible to parallel racialized and gendered divisions in the sense that the possiblities of amelioration through legislation appear to be equally ineffectual in both cases . . . . We would agree that the construction of such parallels is fruitless and often proves to be little more than a mere academic exercise; but there are other reasons for our dismissal of these kinds of debate. The experience of black women does not enter the parameters of parallelism. The fact that black women are subject to the *simultaneous* oppression of patriarchy, class, and 'race' is the prime reason for not employing parallels that render their position and experience not only marginal but also invisible. (Carby, 1982, pp.212–213)

Accordingly, parallelist arguments about 'race', gender, and class are just as problematic as reductionist arguments; what is left out of both is any real consideration of the complex simultaneous operation of all three forms of oppression. It is this simultaneity which pinpoints the experiential dimension of black and third world women, and it is this which is left out of so much white radical and feminist literature. However, although we may question the use of parallelism, we still have to account for this simultaneity. The fact that black women are oppressed in three different ways is not fortuitous. Hence, we have to ask why it is that these three kinds of oppression, if not reducible to each other, somehow seem to cohere together?

A classic answer to this is that we have to identify the groups of individuals who benefit from oppressing others. In any situation, then, we should unmask the oppressors. This is where the difficulty lies, because in so many cases, it is not all that easy to see who benefits. Take for example the relationship between a black man and a white woman. From one point of view, it is the man who can be seen to be exploiting the woman, and yet it could be equally true that the woman is exploiting the man. In this context, the relative power of each party is shaped by all sorts of factors, not the least of which is whether or not the position of blacks is defined rigidly or not. What each partner brings to the relationship is the burden of their past histories which, in differing ways, have influenced their own responses to oppression. Who benefits from this relationship will, therefore, not be readily apparent. Of course, it might be objected that in taking our example from a particular interpersonal relationship, we are ignoring all those supposedly vast historical forces which have conditioned the participant's present conduct. Obviously, as we have already stated, the 'burden of their past history' enters into the terms of their relationship, but equally, their behaviour is not reduced to this history.

We are suggesting that the terms of oppression are not only dictated by history, culture, and the sexual and social division of labour. They are also profoundly shaped at the site of oppression, and by the way in which oppressors and oppressed continuously have to renegotiate, reconstruct, and re-establish their relative positions in respect to benefits and power. In the final analysis 'oppression is where you find it', and this is almost everywhere. The point we want to make in the balance of this book is that oppression is not simply the effect of overwhelming social and political forces, but that it is pervasive in the interstices of all human encounters. Moreover, we hope to demonstrate that when we talk about the simultaneous oppression of patriarchy, capitalism and 'race', we are not simply conceiving them as dimensions which, when added together, enable us to explain oppression. Like Foucault, who sees power as coextensive with social relationships, we see oppression as being discoverable in a multiplicity of sites. This does not mean we avoid the task of analysis. It is not enough merely to discover oppression in the most unsuspected places. We also have to account for its possible non-presence in other sites. In other words, we have to be able to say something about power as a historical phenomenon as well as locating it in the routines of everyday life.

It is not our intention to get involved in yet another recapitulation of the controversy surrounding essentialism and reductionism in the social sciences. Our main concern here is to briefly review some of the arguments relating to primary oppression as explanations of racist and sexist practice. In particular, we shall be looking at:

1 biological essentialism;
2 cultural determinism;
3 psychological reductionism and repression.

The question of 'class' and the mode of production as the final determinants of all forms of oppression will be taken up specifically in the following chapter on class.

Biological essentialism

The reduction of human behaviour to biology has had, to say the least, a rather unfortunate history in the social sciences. There is no way in which we can pretend to reproduce this history, nor would we want to. Unfortunately, some of the consequences of this are still with us. After all, it is not so long ago that crude biological theories were employed to provide a spurious scientific justification for Auschwitz and Buchenwald. While some of the cruder formulations of social Darwinism no longer have much scientific respectability, alternative contemporary evolutionary theory has recently been used to explain the naturalness of social and gender differences, and the inevitability of inequality.

It is only in the last two decades that sociobiology has come to dominate biological thinking about animal population behaviour, and it was perhaps not until E. Wilson published *Sociobiology: The New Synthesis* in the mid-seventies that it filtered into academic and popular consciousness. Certainly, before the advent of sociobiology, various kinds of ethological accounts had achieved a degree of public acclaim in most Western contexts. We were treated to media presentations about territoriality and aggression, as well as being bombarded by a number of popularized animal behaviour texts which achieved the status of best-sellers (Ardrey, 1966, and Morris, 1966). Thus, biological views of human nature and behaviour remained very much on the agenda, especially in terms of the way in which they were supposed to illuminate inter-group and gender differences.

To be sure, sociobiology was not originally intended to provide a definitive statement about human culture and social behaviour. Its original purpose was to establish a contemporary evolutionary framework for the understanding of animal behaviour. And in so far as humans are animals, it purported to demonstrate that human behaviour was part of the evolutionary continuum. In principle, sociobiology suggests that the same basic behavioural traits operate for animal populations as for human populations. The fact that a human population may exhibit an apparently infinite variety of behaviours which supposedly are all manifestations of the same trait does not seem to be problematic for sociobiologists. Take, for example, their discussion of ingroup/out-group hostility. This maintains that the hostility breeding populations show toward strangers is determined by some kind of trait that enables members of the population to protect the lives and interests of fellow members, even when this may lead to their death. In sacrificing itself for the good of the group, an individual animal ensures that the group will survive.

This discussion is based on work done on animal populations, the accuracy of which we cannot adequately comment on, but we can comment on its applicability to human groups. Lumped together under the rubric of ingroup/out-group hostility are racism, nationalism, imperialism, war, rivalry between village football teams, the Olympic games, etc. Sociobiology tends to reduce all these highly complex instances to a fundamental trait. As Martin Barker puts it in his critique of Pierre van den Berghe's conversion to sociobiology:

> He argues that all racial dislike has a genetically-based component. He goes through an account of the derivation of racism, ethnocentrism and nationalism, all from the same source: kin altruism. A breeding population over a long span of time develops sufficient genetic closeness and closedness for such 'powerful sentiments' to develop, whose 'blind ferocity' and imperviousness to rational arguments are 'but a few indications of their continued vitality and their primoridiality'. 'As hominids became increasingly formidable competitors and predators to their own and closely related species, there was a strong selection pressure for the formation of larger and more powerful groups.' Thus the creation of 'superfamilies' or nations 'necessarily meant organising *against* other competing

groups and, therefore, maintaining ethnic boundaries.'

Thus is racism rooted in the genes, in the specific style of sociobiology. Limited altruism within a genetic community has its counterpart in open selfishness, hostility and aggression towards competitive outsiders. (Barker, 1981, p.97)

Certainly van den Berghe does not defend racism, but anybody reading his paper would be forced to conclude that racism is some-how natural (van den Berghe, 1978). Indeed, this is precisely the inference that others made in their discovery of sociobiology. It seemed to make sense of racism as a natural phenomenon, as an unavoidable consequence of inter-group contact. In Britain, hostil-ity toward West Indian and Asian immigrants was not anything to be ashamed of; rather, it was seen to be a normal dimension of group relationships. In addition, it made group separation respectable. Nothing that the theorists of 'apartheid' had imagined can equal the rationale for separation that sociobiology has given those who are already racist.

While sociobiology has been used to bolster the practice of racism, it has also been important in the support it gives to gender discrimination. Here the argument is that certain genetic traits give men advantages over women that ensure their continued domi-nation. Male dominance is accounted for in two ways. Firstly, women are supposed to be programmed to be dependent on men because of their central role in reproduction and child rearing. In evolutionary terms, it is apparently adaptive that women 'mother' children. Secondly, male dominance is achieved by a greater propensity for aggression, a propensity which has adaptive and survival value.

From the *reproductive argument,* it is inferred that women can never fully enter into public life. Their reproductive capacities are geared to the needs of child rearing and home building. Consequently, their role in the public sphere can only be achieved at some kind of biological and social cost. Dependency is, therefore, a natural state of affairs. It is natural that women 'invest' in children and domestic-ity. From the *aggression argument* it is inferred that male domi-nance is inevitable, that patriarchy is unavoidable in much the same way as racism is supposed to be inevitable. Of course, there are vulgar and sophisticated versions of these arguments. For example, in Goldberg's *The Inevitability of Patriarchy,* sociobiology is used in the

name of an almost obsessive defence of the biological determination
of patriarchy. Goldberg examines the prevalence of male dominance
in a large number of historical and contemporary societies, and
asserts that this must logically imply that the apparent universality
of patriarchy is a consequence of biological differences in men and
women, differences which determine the sexual division of labour,
and which in turn explain the relative power of each gender.
As we have said Goldberg's defence of patriarchy does not stand
alone. It might be vulgar and doctrinaire, but it is given credibility
by more respectable theorizing. It is, as we have already suggested,
the extrapolation from animal behaviour to human behaviour which
is the bedrock of the sociobiological position. The attempt to find
homologies between animal behavioural traits and specific items of
human behaviour has been the guiding principle in its attempt to
biologize social life. If dominance hierarchies are found among
certain species of primate, then it seems perfectly logical to discover
similar dominance hierarchies among humans. If male baboons
consistently appear to be aggressive, then it is perfectly logical to
assume that the same kind of aggressiveness serves in human males.
   What is problematic in the sociobiological approach, and indeed
in all biological reductive accounts, is the fact that a behavioural
trait which appears to be universal in primate or animal societies is
regarded as being the necessary base for its extrapolation to human
societies. Racism, sexism, economic exploitation are, therefore, seen
as being features of human societies because they have analogues in
other animal settings. It is certainly true that human males exhibit
aggressive behaviour. But can we really say that a man who batters
a woman is replicating the behaviour patterns of a dominant male
baboon? To assent to this would be to assent to the proposition that
there is no way in which male sexual violence could be eliminated in
human societies, except by direct biological intervention like that
proposed by Firestone and Holliday. Indeed, Holliday believes that
male aggression is determined by the particular constitution of male
hormones. Male aggression and dominance then is a function of
male biochemistry, and the only way in which this can be modified
is by various artificial biofeedback procedures (Holliday, 1978).
   Why a man batters a woman cannot be simply correlated with his
supposedly innate aggressiveness. Although rape is found in a wide
number of historical contexts, we cannot presume that this fact is
simply a function of superior male strength. While it is not always

useful to point to cross-cultural evidence, we can certainly argue that male violence against women is not a universal aspect of social relationships. Among the Mbuti, for example, violence is almost unknown. Moreover, it is not sanctioned (Turnbull, 1961). This is not to say that Mbuti males are not capable of violence, but it is to say male violence is only relevant in a given set of circumstances. Thus we agree with those arguments which maintain that violence must be understood concretely, that is, not as an underlying basis of behaviour, but as an element in a social, cultural, and historical context.

Note we are not denying biology. Nor, for that matter, are we suggesting that sociobiology or any other biological discipline is of no relevance to the understanding of human behaviour. This would be the height of presumption. What we are objecting to is the position that sees biological differences as being responsible for hierarchy and inequality. An alternative perspective would see oppression as the social construction of the body as an object.

For example, discussion about 'race' has proceeded as if 'race' as an object could be found in the real world, that is, certain groups of people are categorized as having physical characteristics which mark them as being essentially different from those who construct the categorization. The perception of phenotypical characteristics like skin-colour, head shape, etc. has dominated popular consciousness. Indeed, 'race' is given reality by the attribution of significance to the phenotype. Put differently, it is the active construction of the meaning of the phenotype that constitutes a group as a 'race'. Initially, this construction was strongly influenced by Social Darwinism in the nineteenth century, and later sedimented in everyday consciousness. Today, popular categorizations and constructions are echoed in the academic attention paid to 'race', despite the fact that the weight of opinion among geneticists is that 'race' has no significance, except in so far as a given population has a given distribution of genes. The point here is that the differences in a population are often greater than the differences between populations (Bodmer and Cavalli-Sforza, 1976).

Nevertheless, this has not prevented various practitioners from conducting their research on the assumption that 'race' is what they are researching. Everybody pays lip service to the distinction between genotypes and phenotypes, and yet this does not hinder the emergence of the study of race relations as a body of knowledge about 'race'. But this knowledge is not something that exists about the so-called object; its existence depends on the power of the attribution process, that is, on the historical actors who give reality to the idea of 'race'. In Britain, 'race' does not exist, but racism does. There are Jews, Jamaicans, Pakistanis, Indians, Chinese, etc. but no races. However, political discourse proceeds as if the reality of 'race' was self-evident. Parliament legislates on 'race'. The media discuss 'race'. Politicians discover 'race' as an important dimension of their appeal to the electorate. For a non-existent object, 'race' has a very pervasive hold on the behaviour of a large number of people. Thus, despite the demonstration that 'race' has no scientific validity, those who label groups as races, and those who are so labelled, come to believe in the reality of the label, or the category.

The social construction of 'race' obviously is not simply a matter of the perception of phenotypical differences. Perception by itself does not constitute the ground on which the 'race' construction is built. The construction will have no power unless there are strong forces at work which coerce the construction. This is what we mean when we talk about the body as an object of coercion. A person who is treated and classified as a 'race' object comes to define her/his body as 'racialized'. Racism is successful when it forces its victims to define themselves in terms of phenotypical characteristics. To use a term from phenomenology, 'lived experience' of the body is subverted by 'objective' forces.

Similarly, when we talk about sexual objectification, we are talking about the gendered body. A woman's body is a gendered body. While she has her own feelings, perceptions, pain, her 'lived experience' is mediated and worked upon by social and cultural powers which 'objectify' her sense of bodily reality. Her existence is shaped by the structures of male domination. As a body, she exists for men, and as such her 'sexed subjectivity' is rooted in taken-for-granted heterosexual relationships.

We have so far briefly examined some of the sociobiological claims about the naturalness of racism and sexism. We have argued that these claims are based on the assumption that a generalized behavioural trait among animal populations can be extrapolated to human populations. We believe it is impossible to derive the multiplicity of racist events from such an underlying trait. Thus, we strongly disagree with John Rex's endorsement of van den Berghe's 'principle of nepotism' (Rex, 1983, pp.xix–xx). Inter-group hostility

does not, in our view, depend upon a 'genetically determined trait'.
Nor can we accept the sociobiological claim that male dominance is
genetically programmed. Sociobiology ignores history; it ignores
multiplicity and it ignores the contextuality of meaning. There is no
way that we can point to a particular racist or sexist act and say of it,
that it is a manifestation of a predisposing genetic trait. When we
look at the diversity of acts and beliefs subsumed under the rubric of
racism, it is impossible to classify them in terms of some master
biological mechanism. What connects anti-Semitism in Germany in
the 1930s, racist abuse of Jamaicans in a contemporary London
setting, a lynching in the *ante bellum* South of the United States of
America, the conviction in South Africa of a black woman for not
possessing a pass, is not the fact they are instances of 'natural
nepotism', but that they all are oppressive practices. Human beings
oppress each other historically. Oppression exists in history. Racism
and sexism do not exist outside history. While it may be tempting to
see male baboon dominance behaviour in terms of oppression, we do
not normally do so. Animals do not oppress each other.

Again, we must emphasize that we are not rejecting biological
explanations of human behaviour. What we are rejecting is the
assumption that biology explains oppression.

But, if we reject biological essentialism, do we do so in the name of
culture? Do we oppose culture to nature and thereby presume that it
is in culture that oppression is located? When we say that 'oppression exists in history', we do not thereby mean that history is outside
biology. We agree with those practitioners who argue that the social
and cultural sciences have been so involved in the construction of
the autonomy of culture and the social, that they have lost contact
with bodily reality. By ignoring the limits which the body imposes
upon behaviour, some social scientists live in a fantasy world in
which human beings almost seem to assume the status of disembo-
died cultural essences. In this respect, Trigg writes:

> This typically sociological way of looking at things gives a
> social meaning to just about every human activity and identi-
> fies activities in terms of the social roles they are deemed to
> have. As a result, there is no way of picking one out without
> already prejudicing the issue in favour of one cultural
> interpretation rather than another. The approach can easily
> produce the conclusion that culture is all-important and

human nature so malleable that it is nothing until given a distinct form in a particular culture. Writers may concede that biology places 'natural limits' on human functioning, but the limits may be thought so wide as to be of little importance in explaining human culture. It is then easy to hold that the differences between cultures in different places far outweighs any similarities. An appeal to our common humanity is thought empty and irrelevant . . . Marxists will invoke economic structures as an explanation, but they are usually very reluctant to go deeper and admit that biology is also relevant. One difficulty is that if human beings are all subject to the same biological constraints, these constraints can easily be overlooked merely because they cannot explain (at least on their own) the *differences* between societies . . . and out similarities can be ignored. (Trigg, 1982, pp. 66–7

Granted that social scientists have tended to concentrate on the cultural differences between societies, and granted that biology is usually ignored in their formulations, this does not entail the opposite conclusion, namely that biology can explain the differences. The trouble is that once we start talking about differences it is easy enough to lapse into an either/or fundamentalism. Either differences between groups and genders are explained by differential genetic endowment, or they are seen in terms of unique cultural histories. Both explanations do violence to human reality by their insistence that this reality can be reduced to basic causal mechanisms. By saying that 'history is not outside biology', we are merely restating a point made earlier, namely, that the human body may be conceived of as the object of oppression. So, in a sense, we could define the history of oppression as the history of the objectification process (a point we shall be taking up in chapter 6). Human bodies live in history. They make history, and history repays the compliment by 'living' in the human body.

Cultural determinism

The previous discussion has partly pre-empted our consideration of culture as a prime causative factor in the genesis of racism and sexism. Nevertheless, we must look at culture more closely. Cultural racism in Britain (and other European societies) is often explained

16 *Primary and secondary oppression*

by the history of colonial involvements and conquests which left a legacy of bitterness among those who have experienced the 'loss of empire', and who subsequently returned home and contaminated popular consciousness with their stereotypes and images of the colonized which, in turn, gave substance to the hostility that commonwealth and other migrants encountered. The implication of such a position is that racism can be conceived of as a legacy from the past. It spreads from the colonies to the metropolitan society and becomes part and parcel of the general cultural stock in trade of everyday life. In Britain, these stereotypes about Blacks, Pakistanis, Indians and others operate almost automatically to stigmatize and categorize all migrants and 'strangers'. These stereotypes are not necessarily active. They tend to lie dormant until activated by economic and political pressures which bring migrant and host population into confrontation — a confrontation that leads to a further strengthening of racist beliefs.

So it is the beliefs, attitudes, stereotypes implicit in British and Western culture that constitute the seed-bed for racism. Western culture as a whole has some kind of racist potential built into it, especially in terms of its history of colonial conquest. From this point of view, racism is seen as a cultural phenomenon, culture playing the same role as biology did in the previous discussion.

> By 'cultural' we mean that the bases and causes of group oppression are deeply rooted in the traditional way of life of the society in such a way that they affect all or nearly all aspects of that way of life. We can isolate, for example, economic causes of group oppression, but there are also causes which include other aspects of the society and culture. These other causes include psychological, political, religious and philosophical causes. But there are more than all of these. *Cultural causes are related to and underlie all of these particular causes.* We call them 'cultural' because they are a facet of nearly all aspects of the society. They are part of the society's traditional way of life. We are not arguing that the particular causes which have been previously isolated and discussed are not important, but that the bases of and the interrelationships among these particular causes cannot be adequately understood until the cultural causes discussed here are also understood. (Hodge, Stuckmann, and Trost, 1975 p.x, our emphasis)

Western culture, therefore, contains within it tendencies which express themselves in racism, but which also simultaneously express themselves in other cultural forms, such as sexism and patterns of socio-economic exploitation. In Western societies the sexism and racism derive from common cultural resources. Where there is a complex of racist beliefs (so the argument goes), then there will also be accompanying sexist beliefs. The justification for the oppression of out-groups will echo the justification for the oppression of women. Certainly, as we have noted, the manner in which biological evidence is used for both 'race' and sex categorization, supports the contention that there may be similar categorization forces at work. But what are these forces? How do we identify them in Western society? To say that they are a set of values and beliefs is pretty weak. We have to identify the particular ideas, values, and attitudes which function to structure racist and sexist practice. Moreover, we have to discover how these oppressive values are reproduced over time.

Cultural relativism and socialization

In the case of sexism, the answer to these questions is often located in the socialization process. More appositely, it is the family which is seen as the site in which male domination is continuously reproduced and maintained. The socialization into gender roles provides cultural ammunition for the belief in the natural sexual division of labour. Not only are men socialized into accepting their dominant status, but women (it is suggested) come to accept the appropriateness of their own roles.

There are certainly countless cross-cultural studies of childrearing and education practices which document the privileged treatment that male children receive from their families, as well as from the public sphere. Yet, as has been pointed out by a number of commentators, there is a great deal of variation from culture to culture in the way in which this privilege and domination is achieved. In addition, the inevitability of male domination is not so clear-cut as some people argue. In this respect, Leacock's work among the Montagnais Naskapi of Labrador strongly indicates that women were not subordinate to men, and that there were strong egalitarian pressures at work in their society (Leacock, 1981, pp. 33–

81). In other words, the socialization argument can be turned on its head. Different socialization practices might operate to construct entirely different kinds of gender relations. In principle, if one were to accept the socialization argument, there is no reason to believe that male dominance cannot be subverted by the expedient of simply choosing to change child-rearing practices.

One of the problems with the socialization argument is that it situates gender in an abstract symbolic world of values and expectations. Male dominance is seen as a central value of Western society and, because of this, the assumption is that boys and girls will somehow internalize the expectations associated with this value. Gender, from this point of view, becomes a matter of learning the appropriate expectations linked with each specific sex role. To acquire gender is to acquire the blueprints of a definite identity which has no existence outside role definitions. Put more succinctly, to be a man or a woman, is to be labelled masculine or feminine. Accordingly, the *cultural* 'gender script' determines the sexual division of labour in addition to securing male dominance.

Of course, it is absurd to say that culture secures male dominance unless one points to the reason why this should be so. To assert that Western culture is sexist and racist does not lead us very far. The question is, why is Western culture (and other culture) sexist and racist? The answer to this question cannot simply be stated in terms of the significance of certain key values for Western culture, because to do so is to be guilty of tautology.

To summarize, the cultural argument asserts that racism and sexism can be explained by the presence or non-presence of certain values in a particular society. These values are mediated and reproduced through socialization. In practice, cultural theorists cannot be so naive as to explicate racism and sexism exclusively in terms of the reproduction of certain values. For instance, if we ask why do men oppress women, we cannot answer in terms of the paramountcy of dominant male values, because this tells us nothing. We know that where there is sexual oppression, then there will be justifications and rationalizations of that oppression. We also know that these justifications are not *per se* the same thing as the oppression. The housewife who is locked into her domestic work is oppressed, whether or not there is a suitable cultural definition of her oppression. Similarly, cultural definitions and constructions of groups do not constitute 'race' discrimination. The 'host' society's reaction to 'stran-

gers', 'foreigners', 'aliens' is not simply cultural. If discrimination
was merely about one group not understanding or liking another
group's way of life and customs, then there would be no difficulty in
overcoming racism.

Thus it would be absurd to describe the South African racist state,
as though it represented an extreme, but unfortunate case of cultural
misunderstanding on the part of the white minority and black
majority. Similarly, racism in Britain and the United States cannot
be conceived of in terms of a breakdown in communication between
various ethnic groups. Jews did not go to concentration camps
because the Nazis did not interpret Jewish culture correctly. Certainly, in all the above instances ethnicity and culture do play an
important part in inter-group relations, but this does not entail
automatic inter-group hostility. Nor does it guarantee that one
group will try to dominate and oppress another. Even though we are
not denying that 'strangers' and different cultural groups may be
treated with a great deal of circumspection by the host society, we
are denying the claim that this is an inevitable and universal process. Just as we rejected the argument 'that racial dislike has a
genetically based component' (Barker, 1981), so do we reject the
claim that ethnocentrism is implicit in all contacts between different
cultures and ethnic groups. In other words, we do not believe that
'minorities', 'out-groups' etc., are oppressed or discriminated
against because they are perceived to be different from their oppressors. Oppression implies power. We cannot subsume power under
culture. Obviously power has a cultural dimension, but this is not
equivalent to seeing power exclusively as a cultural phenomenon.
Despite this, recent discussions about ethnicity in Britain and the
United States have tended to place emphasis on cultural differences
as the reason for discrimination.

There is another point to consider. If culture is given priority in
the explanation of oppression, then this presumes that oppression is
a symbolic construction. Now, to a certain extent, both racism and
sexism appear to exist primarily at the linguistic level. There is, in
other words, a discourse of oppression. There are rhetorical forms
which mediate oppression. Racist and sexist language can hurt, but
the language itself does not determine the oppression. Calling somebody a 'bloody Jew' does not hurt because the words hurt; it hurts
because of the possibility of violence they presage. The discourse of
oppression is part of the practice of oppression — as such, it can

constitute a form of power, but the power does not lie in the discourse alone. Certainly those who have greater linguistic resources, who have access to discursive strategies which give them an advantage over others, are in a powerful situation to influence and control those who do not. This is not to say that language should be regarded merely as an instrument of domination, but it is to say that language *alone* does not constitute the basis of power.

We realize we are on very tricky ground here, because of the centrality that language and discourse analysis have assumed in social analysis. Despite this we still do not accept the view that language itself shapes social relationships. Sexism is not defined by sexist language, it is sexism which gives sexist language its potency. The labelling of a group in terms of this or that characteristic only has consequences if the label is underpinned or supported by the possibility of force, violence, or other sanctions. Names and labels can do a lot of damage, but only as components, not determinants of domination.

Culture, structure and power

This is not the right context for a consideration of the relationship between culture, power and social structure, but it is essential to realize that when we talk about culture, we are not talking about it as though it has a 'free-floating' reality independent of any structural constraints. Moreover, even when we speak about the 'relative autonomy' of culture, the implication is that it is relative to something other than its own internal dynamics. Values and ideas have no oppressive force, except through the actions of real historical actors. Take, for example, the life of a black woman in South Africa. If she works as a domestic servant in a white household in the suburbs of Johannesburg or Cape Town, she is not only subject to exploitation by her employer, she is also subject to the effects of discriminatory legislation that confines her to particular living quarters, and the necessity of carrying a 'pass' wherever she goes. In addition, she is more than likely to be exposed to the sexism of both white and black males. Her oppression is multi-dimensional. It appears to have a triple source. It has a source in the mechanics of South African capitalism — hence it has an economic dimension; it has a source in the cultural classifications of South African history — hence it has a 'race' dimension; and it has a source in the sexual division of labour — hence it has a gender dimension.

All three dimensions claim priority in the explanation of her situation. They all may be defined as basic or primary. And this is precisely the problem posed earlier about the validity of postulating a primary level of oppression which has precedence over secondary levels. Yet, in looking at South African society, it does not seem to stretch the bounds of possibility to talk about 'white supremacy'. We can talk about parallel working classes in the black and white communities, but obviously, the white working class is in a privileged condition *vis à vis* the black working class. Moreover, we can talk about the relative power of white and black women. A black woman employed as a domestic servant is oppressed and often abused in racist terms by her white woman employer. So what is implied by the term white supremacy? Does it mean the supremacy of the white minority as a class? Or does it entail the domination of the majority cultural group by the minority group? Or does it imply the privileged power and status of white men? These questions seem to be in Eisenstein's mind when she distinguishes between exploitation and oppression:

> Oppression and exploitation are not equivalent concepts, for women or for members of minority races, as they were for Marx and Engels. Exploitation speaks to the economic reality of capitalist class relations for men and women, whereas oppression refers to women and minorities defined within patriarchal, racist and capitalist relations. Exploitation is what happens to men and women workers in the labour force; women's oppression occurs from her exploitation as a wage-labourer but also occurs from the relations that define her existence in the patriarchal sexual hierarchy — as mother, domestic labourer and consumer. Racial oppression locates her within the racist division of society alongside her exploitation and sexual oppression. Oppression is inclusive of exploitation but reflects a more complex reality. Power — or the converse oppression — derives from sex, race, and class, and this is manifested through both the material and ideological dimensions of patriarchy, racism, and capitalism. Oppression reflects the hierarchical relations of the sexual and racial division of labour and society. (Eisenstein, 1979, p.22–3)

For Eisenstein then, the concept oppression encompasses exploitation which refers to class relations. In other words, oppression is a function of the dynamic interaction of three hierarchical systems —

sex, 'race' and class — none of which has any claim to primacy. But does this mean that there really are three hierarchical orders which are analytically separate and autonomous, and whose respective histories have different starting points? In a sense, this would be to argue for a very ahistorical point of view, because the assumption seems to be that all three systems are universal features of all societies. If we claim that gender, 'race', and class are constructed by human beings, then we cannot assume that they are constructed without reference to the lived experience of human beings. Classism, sexism, racism cannot exist in independent conceptual ghettos for the simple reason that in the real world they tend to cohere together.

Reverting to the South African case, a black domestic woman worker does not experience oppression in a compartmentalized way. Her oppression is rooted in the fact that a certain group of people are in a position to ensure the conditions of her subjection. By this we mean that South African society is structured to sustain oppression continuously. Apartheid is an oppressive system which, systematically and simultaneously, exploits and oppresses large sections of its population. Historically, we may be able to account for this oppression by examining the method whereby white Dutch and British colonists imposed a racial stratification system on the indigenous population. We can examine the implications of the role of British capital in fostering a cheap labour policy. We can look at the way in which this cheap labour policy intermeshed with a racist ideology whose history appears to have a different trajectory. And we can also concentrate on how white male domination interacted with black male domination to produce the particular form of oppression experienced by black women.

All these dimensions of South African history and social structure enter into a black woman's experience of oppression. From her point of view, the most obvious aspect is the racial classification system which completely encapsulates her life. But, at the risk of labouring a point, we do not believe that a racist culture exists independently of the institutional structures through which it is expressed. Now this may seem to be a trite sociological observation, but if we maintain that racism has a life of its own, then we are giving it an aura of inevitability. Racism is a historical phenomenon. And, as such, it is intertwined with other forms of domination. However, we must emphasize that we do not believe that racism can be reduced to other forms of domination, only that it is likely that a particular form of domination has implications for other forms of domination (see chapter 6).

Excursus 1

Before we discuss psychological reductionism we need to say two things about the relationship between oppression and reductionism. Firstly, we have not defined oppression. We think we know what we are speaking about when we talk about racism and sexism, but we have not unambiguously defined them. We know that oppression has to do with power, and yet we cannot give power any exact meaning. We can make a distinction between oppression and exploitation in which the latter is conceived of as a specific kind of oppression (in Eisenstein's sense), but if we do so, we still do not come any nearer to catching the essence of oppression. This might be the result of being too obsessed with definitions and ideas rather than with realities. So we could, if we wished, subsume oppression under the concept exploitation, thus giving it a relatively precise connotation. However, to do this would be to assent to the proposition that class relationships are primary in any discussion of oppression.

Secondly, we have appeared to conflate oppression with reductionism. The concept reductionism refers to the tendency in science and social science to look for an underlying causal explanation for natural and social phenomena. Oppression refers to the 'pressing' of individuals and groups into a situation or situations by the superior power of others. In order to understand why oppression occurs, why some people are oppressors and others oppressed, social scientists, philosophers, historians, psychologists, and biologists have searched for a basic mechanism, an ultimate cause which they hoped would enable them to understand what makes oppression possible. We have already looked at biological essentialism and cultural determinism as being examples of this kind of explanation. Obviously, what we mean by reductionism and oppression are two different things, but what is important in this context is the fact that theories of oppression are more often than not associated with reductionist viewpoints. Note we are not saying that reductionist explanations of racism and sexism are not possible, but what we are saying is that too often this kind of explanation completely distorts the evidence. On the other hand, we are not advocating some kind of eclectic view of oppression which describes it as being a little bit of this and a little bit of that. When we speak of the possiblity of three forms of domination, we are not thereby abdicating our responsibility for specifying the way in which these three forms interact, nor for that matter are we ignoring the real possibility that in given circum- stances, one form is more important than others.

Psychological reductionism and repression

We have as yet not come to grips with a concept often used instead of oppression, namely repression. Indeed, we have not used this term at all. The verb 'to repress' is defined in the Longman Lexicon of Contemporary English in the following way: 'to rule by holding back from (natural feelings, actions, etc.)'. (McArthur, 1981, p.114) Repression, therefore, appears to be a form of oppression which acts to contain natural feelings. There is an additional element in this definition which the dictionary version seems to gloss, this is, the possibility that repression may somehow be self-induced. Thus, repression may be seen as that process in which people are encour- aged to deny their feelings, sexuality, and desires. Repression oper- ates to ensure the human body is protected from its desires. From this, the conclusion may be drawn that society needs to repress the natural reservoir of instinct in human beings in order to maintain a viable civilized existence. Hence, repression is justified because it provides the basis for society. For Freud, repression is an absolute necessity. Without it, the pleasure principle would run amock. Re- pression involves costs — it is the price we pay for civilized complex- ity, a price that may be far too high in terms of the damage it does to psychic functioning (Freud, 1977). In the Freudian scheme, it is the family which enables individuals to handle their desires. In this context, they find themselves engaged in a constant state of intra- and inter-psychic war. Accordingly, 'repression' operates to keep the peace, a peace underpinned by anxiety and neurosis. From birth, men and women are locked into an epic struggle with instinct, which inevitably ends up with its repression and the Oedipal resolution.

It is this particular view of repression which causes commentators to register their disagreement. In general, this disagreement is centred on the notion that the Oedipal situation is universal and that repression is an inevitable psychic process. In this respect, Poster writes:

> The main elements of the Oedipal situation are the child's sexual feelings for the parent of the opposite sex, the child's profound feelings of ambivalence toward the parent of the same sex and the child's profound feelings of anxiety in relation to threats against its genitals by the parents. Freud believes that these elements are not rooted in any specific family or social structure. Oedipus is universal. There are two critical questions that must be pursued. (1) Is the Oedipus complex and the resulting psychic structure a consequence of these 'universal' elements or can it be connected with a specific family structure? (2) Is Freud attempting to illuminate a universal aspect of psychic experience with his concept of Oedipus or is he in fact explaining particular psychic experiences? By analysing these questions, it can be demonstrated that Freud's Oedipus complex explains psychic formations specific to a limited family structure and, because he is unable to conceptualize Oedipus from the perspective of social theory, he falsely expands the power of Oedipus to cover all situations, thereby disfiguring a critical concept into an ideological one. (Poster, 1978, p.17)

The debate about the historicity of the Oedipus complex has been ferocious for a long time. Poster's point is about the specificity of a particular family structure, namely, the bourgeois nuclear family. He implies that other family structures reproduce different kinds of power and authority arrangements which, in turn, have different consequences. Accordingly, repression is a relative, not a universal feature of gender. Also, the assumption that Freud and other psychodynamic writers make about the normalcy of heterosexuality is questioned, once we historicize Oedipus. Strangely enough, Freud himself had emphasized human bisexuality as being the foundation on which men and women are somehow forced into their respective gender identifications (Freud, 1977). But he does not make too much of this, because lesbianism and homosexuality assume a deviant status in his attempt to universalize the Oedipus situation.

Authoritarianism and the repression of instinct

Where does this leave repression? In the broadest sense, we may still testify to its reality in our lived experience. This reality is available to us every time we try to handle our sexuality, every time we endeavour to cope with our emotionality and subjectivity. In spite of nearly one hundred years of sexual discussion, in spite of the 'sexual revolution', sexuality is still underscored by guilt and anxiety. Reich, for instance, thought this state of affairs was not specific to capitalism (although he did make this connection in his Marxist days); rather, it was the consequence of the accumulated history of sexual repression embedded in the bodies and psyches of men and women reared in authoritarian families. Repressed sexuality is the way in which all authoritarian structures are able to hold down the potential power of the masses. Hence, repression secures human acquiescence and docility because it imprisons the 'natural' in the 'unnatural'. Sexual liberation, from this viewpoint, is the primary condition for human liberation; repression disappears when sexuality is restored to its natural state, but liberation is dependent upon the dismantling of the patriarchal family, the source of all our discontents (Reich, 1975a). Ironically, behind Reich's celebration of the healing power of sexual liberation, is the assumption that sexuality is ultimately heterosexual, and that therefore homosexuality and lesbianism are unnatural effects of repressive patriarchy. As Barrett argues, such a view is 'essentialist':

> In Reich's work the concept of repression has been extensively used to analyse the character and sexuality of those people raised under fascist ideology (the 'authoritarian personality'). But the notion of repression, especially when used rather loosely in this way, poses the problem of essentialism. It proposes a sexual self, or essence, which is then moulded by the social — for instance by destroying male tenderness or female initiative. (Barrett, 1980, p.51)

The belief that there is a true sexual self buried beneath the veneer of the 'social' is certainly not only to be found in Reich. Ideas like this played an important part in European romantic discourse. What is central to these ideas is the contrast between nature and culture in which the cultural is blamed for distorting sexuality and emotionality. But the cultural does not work in a vacuum, that is, repression must have a site in order for it to be effective. This site is the family, especially the authoritarian patriarchal family. It is this family in its bourgeois form which supposedly does all the damage. It is this family which is the source of bourgeois ideology, and it is this family which continuously produces repressed and alienated people. The bourgeois family is thereby given the credit for the entire range of political and social problems of our society. But we may ask, why only the bourgeois family? Why not the working-class family? Why not the peasant family? Why not any family? If repression is only confined to the bourgeois family, then we are entitled to ask why its absence in other family structures has not resulted in some kind of revolutionary surge from those uncontaminated sites? Moreover,

> Reich was unclear about the precise mechanisms of family structure which generated sexual repression. At times he put the fault with parental negative *attitudes* to sex; at other times with the *institution* of 'marriage and the family'. (Poster, 1978, p.49)

What is certainly true is that parents do attempt to shape their children's sexuality. Even today, masturbation is frowned upon, tolerated, because the text books advise parents to do so, but not ignored. In addition, the different pressures put on boys and girls about appropriate behaviour is not conducted haphazardly. Very few parents give their children absolute freedom in regard to their sexual needs, nor do they encourage them to experiment with alternative gender commitments. So certainly, at this level, we might want to speak of repression, but is this what Reich means? To a certain extent, yes, because in Reich's view all external regulation ends up in the repression of natural feelings. Again, we have the emphasis on the dualism of nature and culture, on the assertion that culture is the enemy of desire.

The critique of psychological and sexual autonomy

Reich, and other sexual radicals, have been criticized for their acceptance of sex as an autonomous and fundamental force which reduces the social to a secondary process. The thrust of these criticisms is that sexuality is so dominated by the social, that it makes no sense to isolate it as libido or energy. The question that Foucault, for example, addresses himself to, is why has the discourse of sexuality been so important for Western social scientists and political practioners? Why have both left and right wing commentators defined sexuality as a potentially explosive force which could, if not repressed, smash the structures of the social order? For Foucault, the discussion of repression is based upon a peculiar definition of power, a definition which assumes a monolithic 'them' versus 'us'. This definition invests sexuality with a significance which may have no real relationship to the sexual at all, but which is important for purposes of social control. Sexual feelings, reproduction, are saturated with a symbolic content which allows various institutional forces to exercise power in sites which were previously thought to be unproblematic. Put more simply, the 'invention' of sexuality in the nineteenth century enabled the family to be demarcated as being subject to external manipulation. It is a site of power relations in which sexuality is used to secure some kind of advantage by all sorts of people, including of course, the members of the family (Foucault, 1979). Commenting on this Coward writes:

> Foucault suggests that a primary means in the controlling of the population was the interrogation, detailing and policing of sexuality. There was no one single discursive production of a sexuality but the production of sexual definitions across discourses around health, education, parenting, and in social policy such as housing, etc. The nuclear family, in fact, was privileged as a solution to the restructuring of the population. It was constructed as an institution crossed by numerous legal, medical, and educational investigations and recommendations about sexuality. But it was not an institution which was the guardian of a single sexuality. Instead, it was crossed by a series of different incitements and prohibitions. For example, sexual satisfaction between the married partners would be positively encouraged, so much so that all sorts of violence against women might be condoned so long as the husband was seen to be receiving sexual satisfaction. Sex between siblings and between generations, however, would be subjected to fairly strict taboos. (Coward, 1983, p.283)

So, instead of a unitary sexual instinct which has to be controlled because of its subversive nature, the construction and invention of sexuality is the means whereby power is exercised. It is not sex which is the hidden force behind history — on the contrary, it is the discursive use of sex which enables some people to be dominated by others. Indeed, over the last few centuries, it is the body which has come to be defined as a suitable venue for repression. Against the argument advanced by psychodynamic theorists that repression is a mechanism which controls desire, Foucault claims that it is a means through which sexuality is used to coerce populations in the name of sexual liberation (Foucault, 1979). What is being questioned here is the belief, the orthodoxy, that defends the autonomy of the psychological. This orthodoxy derives both racism and sexism from the operation of the irrational, from the hidden depths of the human psyche.

Family psychodynamics

The belief in a separate psychological sphere which underpins political, economic and social phenomena is obviously not only Freudian; the psychological viewpoint has had a long history in Western thought. What seems to be evident in the psychodynamic case is its association with the family situation. Accordingly, it could be argued that it is the family which provides the occasion for the unfolding of the autonomous psychological sphere which, in turn, acts back on the family. Certainly, we are all aware of the old claims about the family as the cornerstone of social morality, as the prime unit of social cohesion, as the locus of sexuality, as the core of the reproductive and socialization processes, etc., but here we are concerned with those arguments which suggest that the family drama situation is constitutive of social reality. The psychological dynamics of the family's interior life are projected out into the public sphere where they duplicate the family's pattern of power and authority. Freud saw this pattern as inevitable, because of his insistence on the universality of the Oedipal situation. But one does not need Freud to point to the way in which men exercise power in the family. Indeed, the thrust of the feminist critique of the family has been to demonstrate its oppressive and exploitative nature, not only now, but historically. More generally, their conclusion has been to suggest that oppression and inequality in the family not only reflect the pattern of oppression in the outside world, but are often constitutive of that outside reality. In both cases, the oppression of women originates in family relationships.

In this connection, Christine Delphy's now classic claim that the

family is a distinctive mode of production in which men systematically appropriate the labour of women seems to suggest that women
occupy a class position in relation to men. In other words, the family
is the site of a class struggle which is separate although coterminous
with the classic class struggle (Delphy, 1977). The elimination of
capitalism, therefore, will not end the oppression of women. This
will only end when the men are no longer in a position to appropriate women's labour. Accordingly, it is only when the family is
abolished that we may see the end of all oppression. Now whether or
not women constitute a class is open to debate. What is not in
question is the prevalence of male dominance in most Western, east
European and non-European societies. What has to be established is
the manner in which domination varies from society to society. For
example, in recent discussion about slave families in the *ante bellum*
South, a number of black feminists have spoken about the family as
a centre of resistance to the racism of white slave owners.

> The salient theme emerging from domestic life in the slave
> quarters is one of sexual equality. The labour that slaves
> performed for their own sake and not for the aggrandizement
> of their masters was carried out on terms of equality. Within
> the confines of their family and community life, therefore,
> Black people managed to accomplish a magnificent feat. They
> transformed that negative equality which emanated from the
> equal oppression they suffered as slaves into a positive quality:
> the egalitarianism characterizing their social relations. (Davis,
> 1981, p.18)

Moreover,

> If Black women bore the terrible burden of equality in oppres-
> sion, if they enjoyed equality with their men in their domestic
> environment, then they also asserted their equality aggres-
> sively in challenging the inhuman institution of slavery.
> (Davis, 1981, p. 19)

Davis is suggesting that in the case of the black slave family, it
would be imprecise to talk about the relevance of black male dominance because both men and women saw the family as a focus of
identity and opposition to white racism.

This foray into family theory seems to have taken us away from psychological determinism. The point we are making here is that the notion of a separate psychological sphere as the source of racism and sexism is problematic, because it assumes oppression or domination are simply aspects of the interplay between instinct and repression. Once we start talking about the family as though it was psychologically autonomous, then we give it status as the only source of domination. While recent feminist analysis has given us a great deal of insight into how the family operates as a form of domination, it has also enabled us to appreciate fully some academic cross-cultural information about kinds of kinship relationships. What emerges from this is not the universality of repression, but its variability. If the slave family was a focus of resistance to white domination, then this certainly cannot be construed as exemplifying psychological encapsulation.

Again, we must make the same kind of disclaimer we made earlier in our discussion of biological essentialism. We are not rejecting the reality of the psychological sphere but the claim that it determines oppression. Repression is a form of oppressive practice which has psychological and biological consequences. While both racism and sexism are often strongly imbued with irrationality, this in itself does not explain them. Psychologically, oppression operates as repression. The repression does not explain the oppression. Oppression is what some people do to other people. What men do to women, what whites do to Blacks, what straights do to lesbians and homosexuals, what the powerful do to the powerless. The family is one of a number of sites in which people are oppressed. This does not mean that it is a prototype for all oppression. Nevertheless, there is one important point to be made about the psychology of oppression. It is at the subjective level that oppression is experienced. The psychological sphere is a politicized sphere. The effects of domination are not only collective, they are also intensely personal. It is this that feminist theory has so strikingly illuminated for us. Social theory has always tended to ignore the personal, usually treating it as an epiphenomenon of macro forces. For the first time for a long time women are articulating their oppression in a fashion which taps the real roots of their personal existence. The 'personal is political' is not only a slogan — it reflects the recognition of the 'personal' as the sphere in which male domination has its deepest ideological and material consequences. This last point leads us to a consideration of a more general view of the political nature of the personal in the final section of this chapter.

Excursus 2 and conclusion: The concept of shared oppression

When black women complain about the racism of some of their
feminist and radical allies, they are not merely sloganizing. For
black women in Britain, South Africa, the United States, and elsewhere, it is their confrontation with racism that shapes their everyday existence. *The personal is racist* because the pin-pricks of mundane
existence are racist, from the bus queue to the factory floor, and from
the school to the household. But black women also share oppression
with black men. It is this shared oppression that cannot be reduced
to something else. When Angela Davis writes about the slave
experience and the terrible dehumanizing methods of social control
used by slave owners, she is referring to an extreme case perhaps,
but the implication is the same for other situations.

In addition, there is a very important point to be made. If we take
any society in which racism is sedimented in social consciousness,
and that is almost everywhere in the Western world, we discover
that it is not only white men who stand in an oppressive relation to
Blacks. White women oppress Blacks also, not only black women,
but black men as well. In a naive way, we can see this at work in
South African society. The oppression of the entire Black population
cuts across sex divisions. Racism is not the privilege of the white
male minority — white women also are racist. They, just as much as
white males, engage in both the practice and discourse of racism.

It might be objected that in concentrating on South Africa, we are
looking at an exceptional circumstance, and that it would be wrong
to generalize about racism in other countries. Yet the evidence is
that racism is sex-blind, and also pervasive in groups who ostensibly
are committed to the fight against other kinds of oppression.

> In a discussion of marxism and the woman question, to speak
> of women, all women categorically, is to perpetuate white
> supremacy — white female supremacy — because it is white
> women to whom the comments are addressed, and to whom
> the comments are most appropriate. . . . Marxist analysis
> focuses on the class question and short-changes the woman
> question. To discuss women categorically is to commit a simi-
> lar, parallel error whereby the reality of the operation of race
> relations within the woman question is denied. History clearly
> shows how and why Black women and white women today
> suffer from gender inequality. Writers must recognise,

however, that Black women in American society have at least
as much in common with Black men as with white women.
The shared oppression of Blacks serves as the great equalizer,
and racial oppression wears a crown emblazoned with the
words, 'I am the great equalizer'. (Joseph, 1981, p.95)

For those white radicals who have never been exposed to racism
there is no way in which they can readily empathize, let alone
understand, the direct experience of those who have. The shared
position of men and women in racist societies, in the colonial world,
in their common experience of oppression, is therefore, a 'given' of
their everyday lives. When we attempt to reduce these experiences
to a more basic category, we are in danger of losing sight of their
reality.

Similarly, recent attempts to explain genocide and the
concentration camp experience in terms that reduce it to this or that
kind of explanation are legion. We have had Freudian explanations,
Marxist explanations, cultural theories, historical reconstructions,
etc. The assumption is that it is explainable — it has no special or
privileged situation in the context of human happenings. We certainly know what happened in these camps — we know about the
systematic extermination of Jews, Poles, Russians, homosexuals,
lesbians. We know about the torture and rape; we know about the
histories and biographies of those responsible; we know about the
rationalizations used by functionaries and others; we know about
the ideology which justified and sanctioned the extermination process. We know all these things, and we then attempt to encompass
them in general explanatory schemes which purport to demonstrate
that there is nothing unusual about what happened — unfortunate
yes, but not beyond comprehension. Obviously, genocide is not a
historical aberration. Those who were exterminated in the gas
chambers were not there by accident, but when we suggest that we
can give an exact explanation for genocide which does not take
account of the witness of the victims, then the explanation is nothing
more than an eviscerated abstraction.

Also, the way in which lawyers, politicians, and social scientists
have discussed 'rape' is often from the vantage point of a particular
ideological or theoretical commitment, so that the victim's account
is relegated to the background. Her feelings of humiliation and
disgust are treated as if they are of no importance. It is this failure

to consider seriously the subjective element in the construction of
explanations of oppression which makes it difficult to give credence
to the primacy of any one such explanation.

We are suggesting that the experience of oppression cannot be
encompassed in a theory or theories which do not give the oppressed
a voice. Moreover, as has been pointed out by various feminists and
black writers, most accounts of oppression have been the province of
white male practitioners. Our view of the Third World, racism in
Britain, and elsewhere, are always, or almost always, provided by
white (mostly male) experts who theorize from their own stock of
readily available explanations. It is only recently that black practitioners have provided their own version of their oppression.
Nowhere is this more apparent than in the manner in which black
women have been locked out of history by official accounts. Indeed,
the history of colonialism was often written as though it was something that only concerned black and Asian men — women were
pushed to the margin, as if their 'herstories' were merely peripheral
to the real world of men. The reconstruction of black women's
experience of slavery is now very much on the agenda of black
feminists who reject both the sexism of standard white male histories
of slavery, but also the racism of some white radicals who ignore the
specificity of black oppression (Hooks, 1982).

It might appear from the foregoing that we have retreated into a
'subjectivist' view of oppression. On the contrary, we are merely
restating our view expressed at the beginning of this chapter 'that
the terms of oppression are not only dictated by history, culture and
the sexual and social division of labour' but also profoundly shaped
at the site of oppression. Determinist and reductionist views of
oppression tend to overlook the opposition of the oppressed, they
tend to ignore the power of human intentionality. We do not subscribe to the view that 'over-objectifies' human behaviour.

2 The Class Problem

In their attempt to understand the subordinate position of women and out-groups in society, and the mechanisms through which such subordination is accomplished, many writers have turned to either sociological analyses of stratification or to the work of the major theorist of class oppression, Karl Marx. The critical questions asked are, how far do women and out-groups fit into the existing hierarchical or class structures and, for Marxists, to what extent can their particular positions within these structures be explained by the genesis and continuing development of the capitalist productive system? Now the operative word here seems to be 'fit', since both sociologists and Marxists are concerned to enunciate which adaptations to their theoretical frameworks, if any, will be necessary to accommodate these two potentially analytically disruptive groups. To put it baldly, are 'race' and gender merely complicating factors in the overall discussion of stratification and class, or do they necessitate some kind of reformulation of them? Can racial and gender oppression be subsumed within working class oppression or do they require some other form of explanation? Of course, stratification and class models are seen to be important here since they have been traditionally the vehicle for signifying inequality, discrimination, and the oppression of subordinate groups.

In this chapter we will examine the various ways in which a relationship between gender and class, and 'race' and class might be posited. To do this a distinction will be made between three main groups of writers. Within the first group there is a tendency to render both gender and 'race' as unproblematic. Because neither 'race' nor gender are regarded as independent contributors to an oppressed state, both women and out-groups can, from this perspective, be incorporated into a hierarchical system already defined in *a priori* terms. Neither 'race' nor gender invoke any qualitative changes in that pre-defined system. The second approach, epitomized in the writings of Marxists, reduces the oppression of females, Blacks, and other populations of colour to the capitalist economic system and explains their subordinate position in terms of class relations. Although many neo-Marxists have attempted to escape such reductionism, in our view they can never be completely successful. The third group of writers treat 'race' and gender as analytically independent variables and therefore as constructing a separate class or stratification system. Thus, white/black and female/male oppression are treated as autonomous, as well as distinct from the oppression or exploitation of economic class. Few of these contributions then discuss in any detail the interrelationship between all three component dimensions, that is, between 'race', class, and gender.

The Incorporation of 'Race' and Gender

The sociological literature on women and the class question is very inadequate. Not only is woman's class position considered very infrequently, but the discussions which do take place seldom raise the issue in anything other than a marginal way. Women, as we know, are visible only fleetingly within mainstream sociology, although, of course, there exists a large body of descriptive material which carries the feminist label. Where sociologists *qua* sociologists *do* address themselves to the category 'woman', she is usually unquestioningly accommodated within a pre-existing framework. For example, Westergaard and Resler marginalize the significance of both gender and 'race' when they argue that each simply reinforces class inequality (Westergaard and Resler, 1975). Class divisions are accentuated for women and ethnic groups because gender and 'race' merely emphasize the impact on them of disadvantages experienced by the working class as a whole. Gender and 'race' are just added on to class from this perspective. These additives compound working class females' and Blacks' occupational inequality, making them a particularly disadvantaged sector of this class. The nature of the class structure overall is unaffected by the addition of these extra variables and gender and 'race' themselves are 'dissolved' away to re-emerge as just one particular disadvantage, among many, that some working class members have to endure.

A second sociological approach to woman's class position focuses on the problems raised by using occupation as the unit of analysis for class. Here, the emphasis is on the difficulty of taking a married woman's own occupation into account, when this implies a class location different to that of her husband. Part of the reason for this anomaly is that non-manual clerical and service jobs, where many women are employed, are ranked higher than manual work so that a woman can be placed in a class above that afforded to her husband. Additionally, problems arise when a woman is not in paid employment, for then she is simply put into the class position designated by her husband's occupation. However, as Delphy has cogently argued, the latter is unsatisfactory for two reasons (Delphy, 1981). Firstly, the criterion of marriage, which is totally alien to social stratification theory, is introduced for a specific category of women. They are assigned to a class not on the basis of occupation, but because of their marriage to a specific man. Indeed, in a lot of sociological research, this criterion is used even for women who do have paid employment. Secondly, assigning a woman to her husband's class overlooks the fact that she has an alternative occupation, involving domestic work in the home. Women have jobs as houseworkers.

Several researchers have attempted to redress the problem of the husband and wife whose occupations place them in different classes. For example, Britten and Heath introduce the category of 'cross-class families' where members fall on different sides of the conventional non-manual/manual divide (Britten and Heath, 1983). But the highly significant point that domestic work constitutes an occupation for women, whether they also work outside of the home or not, has been ignored by sociologists as a contributory factor to woman's overall class position and status in society. This means that her position and status *vis à vis* men cannot be considered either. Thus, not only is there merely a small amount of sociological literature which concerns itself with women's class position, the little that exists is mainly empirical or methodological in orientation. The former simply 'adds' women onto the existing male-defined structure. The latter contents itself with trying to sort out the classificatory problems that the 'additive' orientation produces.

Much of the early 'race' literature similarly submerges black populations into the existing white stratification system, thus affording 'race' itself little independent significance in accounting for the subordinate position of Black and Asian peoples. In Britain this was known as the 'immigration perspective' (Patterson, 1965), In America, it was called the 'colour caste approach' (Myrdal, 1944). For Britain it was argued that the initial difficulties in the immigrant-host relationship, caused by status differentials, would eventually disappear as the immigrant culture and mores came to be tolerated and accepted by the indigenous population. Similarly, in the States, it was predicted that northern migration by Blacks and increased industrialization in the south would replace caste by class feelings. Thus, in both countries, racism and racial disadvantage would disappear as the Black populations were increasingly absorbed into the white class system. In Britain, the term 'accommodation', and in America the metaphor of the 'melting pot', suggested that different groups would pool their characteristics to emerge as one nation, with shared values and principles. Clearly, in these perspectives, 'race' itself ceases to have any kind of independent status, the assumption being that the Black groups could be integrated into the existing class structure without any changes in that structure itself. It is, of course, glaringly obvious that on neither side of the Atlantic has such absorption taken place. Nor can such a formulation explain the particularly disadvantaged position in which Afro-Americans, Afro-Caribbeans, Asians and other groups are placed when compared to their white counterparts. Marxists have attempted to explain this disadvantage in class and economic terms. As we shall see, those arguments couched in traditional Marxist terms tend to regard both 'race' and gender as only a secondary and rather insignificant aspect of social class relationships. However, recently, a number of Marxist writers on 'race' and immigration, together with Marxist feminists, have attempted to rescue 'race' and gender respectively from their traditional inconsequential status.

Marxist Approaches to Class and 'Race'

Marxism has played a major role in elucidating the class position of out-groups and in explaining how this position arose and is maintained. However, difficulties arise with both the orthodox and neo-Marxist arguments due to their implicit insistence that the terms of the debate can only be couched from *within* the context of capitalism and its class system. Such an approach immediately opens up the danger of reductionism and indeed some writers have almost mechanistically explained racism (and sexism too), in both its institutionalized and personalized forms, in terms of the needs and interests of capital. The demands of the 'system' are regarded as paramount and almost anything can be reduced to, and thus explained by, the 'system's' requirements. Additionally, to consider from the start the position of out-groups primarily in relation to capitalism and class, precludes the possibility of exploring their relationship to other factors which may lie outside of a capitalism/class framework. Where such extraneous variables *are* introduced they can only be taken into account in a tangential way. We may add here that similar problems have arisen with the Marxist and some Marxist feminist analyses of women.

'Race', Capitalism and Class

The works of O.C. Cox and of Castles and Kosack provide us with two examples of the classic Marxist approach to the genesis of racism and its structural significance within capitalism (Cox, 1970; Castles and Kosack, 1973). Cox's study is usually regarded as the theoretical precursor in the field and is often cited as *the* Marxist text on 'race'. Whereas his focus is on the history of the development of racism, the relationship between slavery and capitalistic exploitation, and the situation of blacks in the United States, Castles and Kosack consider the impact of the arrival of immigrant workers on the class structure of western Europe, including Britain. However, although the nature of the time period and subject matter covered is different, their resulting lines of argument and subsequent explanations are broadly similar.

For our purposes, there are two aspects to Cox's argument which are particularly important. *Firstly*, he argues that racism emerged towards the end of the fifteenth and the beginning of the sixteenth centuries. Racial prejudice is a product of modern times and its origins causally linked to the development of the capitalist mode of production. *Secondly*, racism as an ideology was formulated as a justification for the exploitation of labour power and was, therefore, a direct product of the bourgeoisie. In Cox's terms it was 'propagated among the public by an exploiting class for the purpose of stigmatizing some group as inferior so that the exploitation of either the group itself or its resources or both may be justified.' (Cox,

1970 p.393). Cox supports his arguments in the following ways. He suggests that prior to the discovery of the Americas, Catholicism inhibited the growth of racism because it emphasized that everyone was a creature of God and thus bestowed the status of human being on conquered peoples. Those populations 'discovered' at the time of and after the development of capitalism were not afforded this privilege. By distinguishing between ethnocentrism, intolerance, and race prejudice, Cox claims to be able to site the arrival of racism at this particular historical conjuncture, whereas the other two sets of attitudes have a much more general applicability. Ethnocentrism, defined by Cox as the 'we feeling', has been and still is an important aspect of all group behaviour. It may be present in families and football teams as well as in races or nations. Cox suggests that although ethnocentrism can lead to racism, it need not inevitably do so, and does not necessarily involve aggression or antagonism. Intolerance on the other hand is also as old as human society and refers to an unwillingness on the part of a dominant group to tolerate the beliefs and practices of a subordinate group, leading to the latter's persecution. Race prejudice differs from intolerance because of its emphasis on supposedly inherent racial characteristics, and the designation of some groups as racially inferior, and others as superior and masterful. Such racism arose from the need of the bourgeoisie to exploit labour, initially in the form of slave labour, and gradually intensified to attain full maturity during the latter half of the nineteenth century. According to Cox the difference between intolerance and race prejudice is that 'The dominant group is intolerant of those whom it can define as anti-social, while it holds race prejudice against those whom it can define as sub-social. Persecution and capitalist exploitation are the respective behaviour aspects of these two social attitudes.' (Cox, 1970, p.400).

Because he defines racism narrowly in terms of attributions of innate racial inferiority, Cox is able to assert that forms of prejudice which existed prior to capitalism were not in fact racism. Thus, anti-Semitism, for example, is regarded by him as a manifestation of intolerance and not race prejudice. Additionally, since, as we have seen racism arises from the need of a particular class to exploit labour it must be understood as simply one particular aspect of the proletarianization and exploitation of labour in general, regardless of the colour of the particular workers. For Cox the problems and interests of the black worker are synonymous with those of all labourers since racism is just one part of class conflict. He therefore regards Blacks as structurally located within the working class, arguing that the fight against racism entails the destruction of the capitalist productive system which produced it. In Cox's terms, there is nothing inherent in racism *per se* to justify locating out-groups as being external to the white working class.

A slightly different position is advanced by those analysts who *are* prepared to give analytical and political significance to the specific socio-economic conditions experienced by Blacks. The work of Castles and Kosack serves as an example here (Castles and Kosack, 1973). They claim that although black and white workers together constitute the working class, as objectively defined by their position in the relations of production, two other dimensions divide them. Because migrants generally have lower incomes and poorer social conditions than their white counterparts, they constitute a distinct stratum within the working class. The corollary of Blacks' inferior economic position is that whites comprise a labour aristocracy. This objective division is paralleled by a subjective one, whereby the indigenous workers are highly prejudiced against Blacks and adopt a form of colonial mentality towards them. Thus, the working class is divided and conflict between workers weakens the Labour Movement, to the great advantage of the dominant class. Castles and Kosack see labour migration as one aspect of a neo-colonial system which exploits the Third World, agreeing with Cox that the origin and function of racism emerged with the ideological needs of capitalism. Discrimination is based on economic and social interests and prejudice originates to defend such discrimination. They therefore argue that changes in attitudes would not remove the causes of discrimination. Along with Cox, they claim that if prejudice is a product of specific socio-economic conditions, it is these aspects of the capitalist system that must first be challenged.

Several writers have pointed to a number of conceptual problems arising from the above interpretations of the impact of racism and race discrimination on class structure (Miles, 1980; Gabriel and Ben-Tovim, 1978). Here we are concerned with the political consequences of such approaches, together with the more general criticisms which can be made.

Firstly, historical analysis throws doubt on the claim that racism originated in, and was a product of, capitalism. Winthrop Jordan, for example, very persuasively argues that whites' first contact with

Africans was through foreign travel and expeditions and was not in fact structured by the labour exploitation of slavery (Jordan, 1974). He suggests that there cannot be a simple deterministic relationship between racism and capitalism, since existing western European culture already contained a predisposition to negative evaluations of people with darker skin, via its preoccupation with such things as dirt, sin and the nature of a civilized society. In addition, historical evidence indicates that notions of physical and innate inferiority, usually associated with the beginnings of slavery, did not in fact develop until the late eighteenth century and did not constitute a fully fledged ideology until the nineteenth century (Miles, 1982). In fact, rather than being a simple consequence of the capitalist mode of production, it appears that aspects of racism already had a place in white culture prior to colonialism and slavery.

Following on from this, our second point relates to the 'narrow' definition of racism as referring to theories of inherent inferiority primarily related to blackness. Apart from the fact that this restricts racism to the nineteenth and twentieth centuries, it means that conventional Marxist theory is quite unable to account for anti-Semitism which is clearly not reducible to either colonialism or skin colour. As we have seen, Cox avoids this problem by claiming that prejudice against Jews is a form of intolerance and not race prejudice. However, as Miles has shown, many justifications for racism have attributed significance to both cultural and physical factors, and certainly anti-Semitism has been historically legitimated as protecting gentiles from contamination and degradation by both Jewish culture and Jewish blood (Miles, 1980). Moreover, the 'narrow' definition precludes the evidence that, although discrimination may not be justified on the basis of biologism, its basis still lies in supposed physical difference. For example, the shift in South African ideology, from claiming Africans to be biologically inferior to assertions of their cultural and linguistic distinctness does not alter the fact that appearance is still the foundation upon which apartheid occurs. Similarly, the development of the 'new racism' in Britain, based again on cultural rather than genetic factors, does not alter the viciousness with which the prejudice is expressed, nor the discriminatory consequences which its victims experience (Barker, 1981). We therefore concur with Miles that social differentiation on the basis of supposed physical differences cannot be rigidly or easily distinguished from that based on cultural characteristics. Neither can it be argued that each gives rise to different, and mutually exclusive, types of social relationships (Miles, 1980).

Thirdly, several commentators have remarked on the conspiratorial explanations of the genesis of racist ideology found in the classic Marxist accounts (Gabriel and Ben-Tovim, 1978; Miles, 1980). The implication is that racism is a deliberately contrived plan on the part of the ruling class. Apart from the lack of historical evidence supporting such a view, the supposed reasons behind such a conscious policy are frequently confused. Sometimes an economic motive is advanced. Here the suggestion is that racism aids the dominant class in the super-exploitation of black and migrant workers. Alternatively, the political argument sees racism as a tool developed to divide the working class and prevent class consciousness. However, whether these accounts are advanced separately or together, their advocates commonly fail to explain either the mechanism whereby racism is produced, or the processes through which such prejudice is transmitted to the lower classes. Not only are unwarranted claims made concerning the homogeneity of both interest and purpose within the ruling class, the working class is portrayed as an empty vessel into which bourgeois ideas are poured and their content passively received. The point here is not simply that such a model is extremely mechanistic, if not naive, it also fails to account for the possibility that the working class, (or parts of it), may itself under certain circumstances reject dominant ideas or even generate those of its own. Indeed, the line of reasoning adopted is frequently so deterministic, with the working class portrayed as sheer cultural dopes, that it becomes impossible to envisage any possibility for social change.

Fourthly, if the ruling class is seen as a homogeneous group, both the white working class and its black counterpart are similarly conceived. The different histories, cultures, migration patterns and socio-economic experiences of Afro-Caribbean, Afro-Asian, Asian, black South African and other groups are overlooked, so that black workers are treated as if they constitute a uniform and indistinguishable mass of new proletarians. They are just pawns in an invisible game of which they are completely ignorant and over which they exercise no control.

Finally, the reasoning behind these ways of explaining the relation of racism to capitalism and its class structure is entirely economistic. Of significance here is that racism becomes just another aspect of an ideology conceived as a mere reflection of economic forces. The specific characteristics of racism and its consequences are lost. This is not just an academic point. For example, the outcome of mechanistically reducing racism to an effect of certain forms of economic organization is that such prejudice becomes just a form of false consciousness, the results of which can be understood only in terms of socio-economic disadvantage and inequality. The power relationship between white supremacy and black subordination, which exists on both a material and an ideological level, cannot be considered from within such a framework, because the analysis is centred solely on the exploitation of labour power and the benefits which accrue to capital. Moreover, if racism is a form of false consciousness which divides the working class, the celebration of Blackness has to be seen as similarly false and divisive. But this is to deny the very experience of being Black in white society, and to dismiss the strategies for resistance that Black peoples have developed. Such a view denigrates their histories and cultures and implies that the significance and distinctness of these will disappear on the road to a 'rational' and classless society.

It seems to us, therefore, that the classic Marxist attempts to reduce racism to the capitalist productive system and locate out-groups within the working class have been fairly problematic. Part of the difficulty lies in the economically determinist and mechanistic aspects of their approach. Accordingly, questions are surely necessary concerning the appropriateness of the Marxist framework in general, both as a method for analysing black/white relations and as a means for describing and explaining the forms which those relationships take. Certainly, some Marxists have themselves been highly critical of the kinds of theories which have been described here and have attempted to reformulate the arguments, with the help of various conceptual developments from writers such as Althusser and Poulantzas. For example, some have claimed that migrants constitute a racialized class fraction. Others assert that racism must be seen to have a degree of autonomy from its base within capitalist relations of production. A third group argue that 'race' is the modality in which class relations are experienced, and that it is important to recognize the autonomy of Black struggles at all levels of society. We will consider such formulations fairly briefly before drawing some general conclusions.

Neo-Marxism: Class Fractions

The concept of class fraction has been developed by Phizacklea and Miles both in joint and separate publications (Miles, 1982; Phizacklea and Miles, 1980; Phizacklea, 1982). They argue that 'race' and class are not equivalents, since they do not refer to the same general phenomena. Moreover, because racism and racial discrimination occur within specific contexts, it is necessary to define that context *prior* to a consideration of racism itself. It is essential to commence any analysis by identifying the dominant mode of production within a social formation, since this constitutes the basis for identifying its primary classes. Clearly, therefore, in the context of British migrant labour, the context is capitalism which produces and reproduces the two unambiguous classes of workers and bourgeoisie. Phizacklea and Miles then go on to use the concept of class fraction as a means of identifying the basis of stratification *within* classes. Class fraction is defined as 'an objective position within a class boundary which is, in turn, determined by both economic and politico-ideological relations.' This means that 'class boundaries mark the objectively different structural positions in economic, political and ideological relations, but these relations also have independent effects within these boundaries.' (Phizacklea and Miles, 1980, p.6).

The argument therefore appears to be that the socio-economic determinants of class, structure not only class itself but also the fractions within class. Moreover, migrant labour constitutes a class fraction for the following reasons. Firstly, although immigrants are structurally part of the working class, a systematic patterning of economic disadvantage within that class sets them apart from their white counterparts. That is, they have a specific economic position, within the general economic position of the working class as a whole. Secondly, immigrants also have a particular place in ideological relations. This is because racial categorization or ascription of the 'race' label is used to classify and negatively evaluate them.

Now a superficial reading of Phizacklea and Miles' position might suggest that they are advocating an analysis similar to that of Castles and Kosack who, as we have shown, conceptualize the working class as divided into two distinct strata with immigrants occupying a separate and lower position. However, Phizacklea and Miles themselves dispute such a comparison. Although, like Castles and Kosack, they regard racial categorization as an ideological process, unlike the latter they claim that such ideology is also effective at both the economic and the political levels. Thus, whereas Castles and Kosack situate migrants in terms of their economic relationships alone, Phizacklea and Miles consider that the ideology of 'race' can interact with these material factors. However, in our view, such a formulation does not entirely escape the charge of economic reductionism since, of course, racial categorization is in their terms constructed under certain conditions of production and in the final analysis will be determined by those productive conditions.

Phizacklea and Miles also distinguish their work from that of Castles and Kosack by arguing that, whereas the latter see the working class as divided by 'race' only, the concept of class fraction allows for cleavages along other lines such as gender. They therefore claim that women also constitute a class fraction. This is related to women's dual role in production as both wage and domestic labourers. We will be considering women's relationship to capitalism and class in a later section, so it would be premature to start such a discussion here. Suffice it to say at this juncture that although we applaud the acknowledgement that gender, along with 'race', is a significant issue, we are not convinced that they should be treated in the same kind of way, as is suggested by the class fraction designation. Such a formulation assumes the subordination of women and Blacks is the same kind of subordination and that the processes and mechanisms associated with this are also alike. Additionally, it is not clear to us what form the relationships *between* the various class fractions might take. Some confusion seems to exist here, since not only are female and black labour separately defined in class fraction terms, West Indian women are also seen as occupying a specific fractionalized class position. Of course, the location of all migrant labour as a class fraction runs into the same problem as was identified with classical Marxism, in that it obscures differentiation within the Black population.

Neo-Marxism: Racism as a Relatively Autonomous Ideology

Other writers have couched their neo-Marxist discussion on 'race' as obvious attempts to move away from the class-reductionism and economism of the earlier works. Gabriel and Ben-Tovim, for example, use an Althusserian framework to explain the development and operation of racism as an ideology (Gabriel and Ben-Tovim, 1979). Their model views capitalist society as a complex totality comprising a number of relatively autonomous levels each with its own degree of effectivity and its own conditions of existence, although, in the 'last instance', these latter are set within the context of a specific mode of production. Ideology is just one of a number of relatively autonomous levels, which are not only interconnected but can also have a material influence on the political and economic spheres. Since racism is clearly a specific form of ideology, it can also be seen to have a *degree* of autonomy from its base within the capitalist relations of production. Now this is clearly an improvement on earlier formulations. However, Gabriel and Ben-Tovim do stress that the autonomy of racism is only 'relative' when they write: 'a rigorous specification of the economic and political conditions that enable racist ideology to be reproduced and to have certain effects is an essential complement to the analysis of autonomous determinations.' (Gabriel and Ben-Tovim, 1978, p.146).

Thus, although racism has a certain independence from the social relations of production and cannot simply be reduced to one of its effects, nevertheless the sets of parameters within which it is free to develop must be conditioned by relations of capitalistic production. Further, class analysis *per se* seems to have disappeared completely from this approach so that racism in particular, and ideology in general, are no longer ascribed by class, but take on a free-floating form which is simply articulated by particular classes at appropriate points in time. From our point of view, the concrete day-to-day oppression of blacks seems to vanish here to be supplanted by an understanding of 'race' as simply an ideological or cultural issue. Part of this difficulty stems from a failure to consider or elucidate the material relationships between the black and white populations, and the class system.

We would argue, therefore, that the major attempts to revise the Marxist understanding of the relationship between Black oppression, social class, and capitalism have not been able to escape some of the problems faced by their more orthodox counterparts. The two approaches discussed offer challenging, complex and very different analyses of racism and capitalism but neither is entirely satisfactory.

Both appear to retain a degree of reductionism in their arguments. For Phizacklea and Miles this is economic; for Gabriel and Ben-Tovim it takes a form of neo-idealism. One view which appears to escape these sorts of difficulties can be found in the writings of the Birmingham Centre for Contemporary Cultural Studies. For example, Gilroy, arguing that Black consciousness of class and 'race' cannot be empirically separated, talks about 'race' as the modality in which class relations are experienced (Gilroy, 1982). Class should not be regarded as a continuous historical subject which, once formed, continues its development in a linear way. Rather it exhibits many contradictions and divisions of which those of gender and 'race' are the most obvious. Gilroy goes further than most other writers in acknowledging the significance of patriarchal and racist oppression as having autonomous political significance and status. Moreover, he stresses the danger of going too far in emphasizing the parallels between them. If such parallels do exist, they must be analytically and empirically displayed. But, although Gilroy stresses the autonomy of the Black struggle, he identifies this as primarily a *class* struggle expressed in Black terms. It is a 'class struggle in and through race' (Gilroy, 1982, p.283). Thus, class and 'race' are collapsed together from this point of view signifying, as have most of the other theories we have discussed, that the fight against racism and capital are necessarily and inevitably intertwined.

In our view, the major stumbling block for the Marxist analyses discussed is that by starting with the economy or the mode of production as a way of understanding racism, only one form of relationship between the two can be established. Thus racism is seen as being reproduced, (if not initially produced), via the dictates of the social relations of production, and Blacks, in so far as they are wage labourers, become part of the working class. We are not arguing here that the context of capitalism in which we live our lives can be dismissed, nor are we denying that the subordination of ethnic groups in the workplace constitutes a most significant dimension to their experiences under capitalism. What we are questioning, however, is whether capitalism can explain *everything* about racial oppression and how far economic subordination can account for the other forms of racialized subordination that out-groups continually experience. For it seems to us that the economic relations of capitalism cannot totally explain racism and racial oppression in this way.

In particular, they cannot explain the xenophobia, the extreme hatred and violence, with which racism has historically been expressed. Nor can they deal with the strength of feeling frequently expressed in Black nationalist movements which usually transcend class lines. For Marxists, such struggles must either be identified as a form of false consciousness, or the significance of racial oppression is denied, through the assumption that the 'proper' class struggle will be waged at a later stage when national or racial liberation has been achieved. But in colonial situations, for example, such class divisions are buried under racial boundaries, so that freedom from racial oppression becomes a specifically *political* issue rather than an entirely economic one. Racial domination forms a basis for inter-class solidarity within the dominant groups and conversely a common oppression provides a basis for inter-class solidarity in the subordinate 'race'. Thus: 'Colonial oppression or racial domination is experienced as a totality, and stimulates a racial or national response, transcending class lines.' (Kuper, 1974, p.225). Similarly, in South Africa, the white workers' privileged position over black workers stems from their identification with the racially superordinate group. Along with Kuper we find it difficult to understand how primary emphasis can be given to class and class struggle in understanding the position of Blacks in South Africa, when the life chances of an individual there are specifically defined in racial terms and appreciably determined by racial identity. Moreover, we cannot argue for the importance of 'race' in understanding Black oppression in countries such as South Africa, without acknowledging that, to a significant extent, the Black populations of countries such as Britain and the United States also conceive their oppression in racial rather than class terms.

Yet another factor which raises problems for the Marxist analysis of 'race', is that it can by no means be demonstrated that racism itself is as functional for capitalism as is often suggested. Rather than racism being moulded to fit the requirements of capital, some authors have argued that in fact a pre-existing racial framework shapes the form and mode of development the economy takes (Blumer, 1965; Kuper, 1974). In South Africa, for example, where a racial hierarchy was already deeply entrenched, the growth of industrial capitalism has meant, essentially, a transfer of the framework of the established racial schema to the new economic setting. Additionally, the 'colour bar' in South Africa has continually placed social fetters on production from the very beginning. In this way capitalism can, and does, tolerate a wide latitude of inefficient operation and still achieves acceptable production and profit. Where there is deeply entrenched racial separation and exclusion, any attempt to change the racial code of employment to boost productivity is likely to provoke protest or the breakdown of employer-employee relations. In such a situation adherence to the existing racial code is more likely than pursuit of higher profit. Blumer sums this point up when he says: 'In a strongly organized racial society, the industrial apparatus is not a free agent but is subject to a network of strong social controls.' (Blumer, 1965, p.246). Furthermore, the viciousness of the apartheid laws and their strengthening, both legalistically and practically, over the last few decades is in no way tied to the needs of capital or the requirements of economic exploitation. Rather, these aspects of South African society can only be explained *politically* as the activities of a racially superordinate group increasing its domination and control over its supposedly black inferiors.

Of course, the situation in South Africa is not the same as that in Britain or the United States. Indeed, it can be argued that the system of apartheid makes it a special and distinct example of racial oppression. Also, most of the material we have discussed focuses either on migrant workers, or on the situation of Blacks whose position is essentially structured historically through slavery. Of course, we acknowledge these differences and the historical specificities in which particular forms of racial oppression must be understood. Our major point is that in no country can a class or economic argument explain the power of whiteness, the strength of feeling with which it is expressed and the extent to which populations are prepared to go in order for it to be upheld. It is the general racial oppression of Blacks by whites, and not the specific oppression of black workers by capital, which needs to be explored and explained. Finally, we must emphasize that for black women, who experience the triple oppression of 'race', sex and 'class', the existing Marxist explanations are particularly inadequate. Not only do most accounts of migrant labourers assume that the latter are men, the very focus on *labour* renders invisible those female immigrants who do not undertake paid employment. For black women, the effects of white oppression are necessarily compounded by male oppression as well.

Marxist and Marxist Feminist Approaches to Class and Gender

Although Marx and Engels have quite rightly been criticized for their sex-blindness, they have more to say concerning women than they do about 'race'. However, although Marx mentions women, in both their work and family roles, it is clear that he regards the typical wage labourer as male. In addition, by defining the bourgeois class with reference to the ownership of the means of production, and the working class in terms of their sale of labour power, he is unable to account for the structural position of women without paid employment, whether they are the wives of the bourgeoisie or the proletariat. His formulation is unsatisfactory since it assumes that class position is allocated to a whole family on the basis of the class position of its male breadwinner. Such an assumption denies status and independence to a substantial number of women on both an analytical and a political level.

Engels took the Marxist analysis of women a little further in his work on the family (Engels, 1972). However, despite his recognition of male dominance in the household, Engels still identifies woman's location and interests as synonymous with those of the working class. He is able to achieve this via the claim that a new form of family arises within that class with the development of modern industry, which draws women into economic production. As Rosalind Delmar has written:

> Engels . . . locates women's oppression at the level of participation in production, links the conflict between the sexes to the appearance of private ownership of wealth, and posits the reconciliation of the sexes as possible only when private property has been abolished. The fortunes of women and of oppressed classes are intimately connected: neither can be free until economic foundations based on private property have been abolished. (Delmar, 1976, p.275)

Thus Engels defines women's oppression in terms of their position in the productive process and sees their emancipation in terms of the absence of private property and the corresponding demise of capitalism. The connection between these kinds of arguments and those of Cox, and Castles and Kosack on 'race' are immediately apparent.

For example, the arguments concerning both women and Blacks emphasize the selling and exploitation of labour power as crucial. In both, women and out-groups are to be structurally located within the working class and their freedom attained with the abolition of the property relations of capitalism. In addition, both understand oppression as an integral part of the capitalist system of exploitation. In neither does the gender relationship between men and women or the relationship between ingroup and out-group, black and white, warrant specific comment or analysis.

Women's Position in the Working Class

More recent writers on the 'Left' have also argued that women are structurally part of the working class, with the explicit or implicit corollary that their future is therefore crucially determined by the fate of capitalism. Some seem to regard women's oppression as specific to capitalism and thereby as both created by, and in the interests of, capitalist relations of production. This is despite all the evidence indicating the differentiation of female from male work in pre-capitalist societies and woman's clear subordination to man. For example, central to the reasoning of Adamson *et al.* is a comparison between pre-industrial society, where women contributed to the production of the household, and the more recent position of women working under privatized conditions in the home, now outside of economic production (Adamson, Brown, Harrison, and Price, 1976). Because they regard this later situation as a consequence of, and a benefit to capitalism, due to the unpaid labour involved, they are able to claim that women's oppression in fact derives from capitalistic relations. The struggle against domestic work is therefore to be viewed as synonomous with the struggle against capitalism. Women's interests coincide with those of the working class due to their exploitation as houseworkers and their position in low-paid, insecure jobs. Their political involvement must be alongside that class in proletarian solidarity. The logical extension of such an argument is that feminism divides the working class, by diverting some of its members from the class struggle, and is, therefore, presumably a form of false consciousness. As we have already seen, a similar argument has been made about Black consciousness from within this kind of framework.

The problems with these 'orthodox' analyses of women's position under capitalism and her relationship to the class structure are very similar to those advanced with regard to 'race'. Firstly, they are frequently almost conspiratorial in their implications that women's domestic work in the family, and their poorly paid work in production, are deliberate contrivances on the part of the ruling class, enabling them to pay low wages to the working class as a whole. This is the case because women's household duties are performed free of charge so that male workers do not have to be paid an amount to cover such expenses. Also, keeping employed women's wages especially low tends to reduce the level of wages overall. Such an analysis reduces the two spheres of women's labour simply and mechanistically to the needs of capital and fails to deal with any contradictions which may exist between these two forms of work. In addition, the emphasis on the functions for capital of women's work is ahistorical. This is because the functions are treated as static and unchanging and the impression is given that they are continually being met in an uninterrupted and unproblematic way. Again, historical evidence would challenge such a view particularly through its accounts of womens' labour struggles in both the domestic and the economically productive arenas (Cockburn, 1981; Hartmann, 1979).

Secondly, we should look more closely at precisely what sort of problem is being addressed and subsequently explained here. In fact, the arguments concern the nature of the sexual division of labour and focus on those forms of work which are particular to females. But under this formulation gender divisions as such are taken for granted and are not the object of attention. That men and women perform different roles and carry out distinct tasks is not in itself a matter for analysis. Nor is the possibility that the two sexes develop different interests and access to power on the basis of their separate activities explored. Rather, the only point of interest is woman's supposed place in meeting the requirements of capital. The unequal relationships between men and women, which have been documénted both historically and contemporarily, are not, and could not be explained from within this framework.

Thirdly, the arguments are highly economistic in their assertion that everything can and should be explained in terms of its relation to the means of production in society. As we have just suggested, this severely limits both the questions that can be asked and the analyses proffered regarding women's oppression. Baldly it asserts from the start that if women are oppressed, they can only be so through the mechanisms of capital.

Finally, the assumption again, as in the comparable 'race' literature, is that the working class is a homogeneous group into which woman can be slotted unproblematically. But we would argue that on any number of occasions the interests of males and females have been obviously contradictory. Women's long struggle for equal pay in the context of strong male opposition is clearly an example here, as are the many historical and contemporary instances of men's strategies for keeping women out of skilled work. It is our contention that such conflicts cannot be explained simply by invoking the requirements of capital or the conspiracies of the bourgeoisie. For, in addition to necessitating an awareness that woman's position is much more complex that these assertions admit, we should also take into account the existence of gender relations between men and women and the material and ideological consequences of these for the two sexes.

A rather more sophisticated approach to some of these issues has been taken by those Marxist feminists who argue that an analysis of women's actual situation in the family is crucial to an understanding of their overall position within capitalism. Veronica Beechey, for example, argues that it is married women's dependent place in the family which makes them a particularly advantageous group for capital to employ, suggesting that single women are similarly effected by assumptions concerning their familial role (Beechey, 1977). Women comprise a useful group of workers to capitalism because of their flexibility and cheapness. But they can only be regarded as such in terms of a particular family structure and ideology which renders them supposedly dependent on a man. Married women are not considered to be materially dependent on their own wage, because it is assumed that their husband's higher wages contain an element to keep their wives. They can, therefore, be employed 'on the cheap'. Additionally, because women are supposedly able to fall back on their husband's financial support, they can be moved in and out of the labour force according to the economy's demands, thus forming a reserve army of labour for capital. Beechey therefore gives women a specific relationship to capitalistic production and implies that it is this relationship of labour exploitation which constitutes their oppression. However, it is clear that she regards women as part of the working class, although they are also an identifiable section of it. She argues that the position of married women is akin to that of semi-proletarian or migrant workers. Their positions are similar because the latter are dependent on the subsistence economy of their homelands to supplement their meagre wages, in the same way that married women are dependent on the family for financial and material protection.

Some of the problems with Beechey's analysis relate to her marginalization of the significance of women's employment to capitalism. For example, the existence of a high proportion of jobs defined as 'women's work', such as clerical work, nursing, and shop work, indicates that females are not such an easily dispensible reserve army of labour as seems to be suggested, otherwise offices, hospitals, and the retail trade business would collapse. But, more important are questions asking why it should be women as a group who are singled out by capital for some kind of 'super' exploitation. Barrett expresses this clearly when she asks why it should be in the interests of the capitalist class generally to pay women such low wages, that husbands are entitled to higher payment so that they can support wives? (Barrett, 1980). Additionally, Beechey's formulation, like the others, reduces women's oppression to just another aspect of the exploitation of labour in general, since it analyses their situation only in relation to capital and does not consider their relationship to men. Yet even within the narrow context of wage labour relations the power of males is apparent. Cynthia Cockburn expresses this extremely powerfully when she comments on the blind spot in Marxist theorizing which renders invisible 'male power . . . deployed in the interests of men — capital apart'. Cockburn goes on to ask:

> where is the man as male, the man who fills those spaces in capitalist production that he has defined as not ours, who designs the machines and thereby decides who will use them? Where is the man who decorates the walls of his workplace with pin-ups of naked women and whose presence on the street is a factor in a woman's decision whether to work the nightshift? (Cockburn, 1981, p.54)

Such men are absent in those analyses which see women as unambiguously part of the working class.

Women's Dual Relationship to the Class Structure

Some Marxist feminists have argued that although Marxists have
given tacit acknowledgement to women's dependence on the family,
the theoretical and political implications of this have been ignored.
They therefore suggest that rather than constituting unambiguous
members of the working class, women in fact have a dual relationship to it (Gardiner, 1977; Barrett, 1980). Most of them experience
direct involvement in wage labour throughout most of their adult
lives. But women also have a mediated relationship to class through
their unpaid domestic work, dependence on men, and general situation in the family. On this basis, Gardiner advocates an extension
of the definition of working class to include not only those who sell
their labour power for a wage, but also those who are dependent on
someone else's sale of labour power. As Barrett explains:

> the old, the sick, the unemployed, children and housewives are
> all 'of the working class', but their indirect relationship to the
> sale of labour power, and hence the wage, affects their position
> 'materially and ideologically'. (Barrett, 1980, p.135)

Although not stated in this way by its advocates, such an argument suggests that there are two possible class positions for women.
In one they have a dual relationship to the class system because of
their 'work' and domestic roles. In the other, where they perform
only domestic tasks, their class connections are indirect and received
via their husbands. Of course, a dual relationship to the class
structure is not the same as a mediated one, although the supporters
of this approach tend to treat them as synonymous. In either case
such arguments imply that there is an objective male class system, to
which women are attached in some kind of tangential way. Class is
still defined through the 'normal' male relation to work and the
wage. Women's failure to mirror this customary interconnection
relegates her to the periphery of class as 'properly' defined, with the
result that her position there must always be framed and analysed as
some kind of aberration from the male 'norm'. We have here, writ
large, the problems that 'women' continue to present for the Marxist
analysis of class. Despite the fact that they constitute half the population, no successful formula has yet been discovered for their analytic and political incorporation into class analysis on equal or complementary terms with men. Attempts at redefinition continually fall

foul of the fact that women's familial location and responsibilities signify a completely different material position in the structure of society to that of men. Thus, any efforts to incorporate the majority of the population into a class system perceived in male terms cannot expect to include women in anything other than a marginal way. We are not making a cheap academic point here but simply trying to underscore the seriousness of the problem. The term 'class' is an important conceptual tool for the description and analysis of contemporary society. Surely questions are raised about the legitimacy of such descriptions and analyses if part of their major conceptual framework is found wanting in this way?

Barrett, for example, admits that many of the difficulties in considering women's position in the class structure are the result of general confusions in contemporary Marxist analyses of class. Yet this does not lead her to abandon the corpus of a Marxist approach because:

> the general relations of production by which capitalism is defined in Marxism constitute the historical context in which gender relations are now played out. (Barrett, 1980, p.137)

Despite arguing that woman's relationship to the class structure cannot be reduced to an analysis of the wage form, and that crucial also are her familial role and the family structure in which it occurs, it seems that, in the long run, these latter can only be understood in terms of their relationship to the capitalist mode of production.

> Feudal households were not, in any class, egalitarian as between men and women, but the development of capitalism brought an exacerbation of these divisions, a far greater degree of dependence of women on men within the household, and constructed a wage-labour system in which the relationship of women to the class structure came to be partially mediated by an assumed or actual dependence on a male wage. These developments, however, are only partly attributable to forces internal to capitalist production and also reflect a struggle within the working class. (Barrett, 1980, p.253–4)

In addition, although Barrett admits that many aspects of the gender relations between men and women are not reducible to class, as conventionally defined, these seem to be designated as peripheral issues when compared to the overall aim of conceptualizing a class system of economic inequality and exploitation, and women's place within it. There also seems some confusion between Barrett's argument that women can be regarded as members of the working class, and her assertion that this class is divided by gender, with the implication that men and women therefore have different locations and interests. This confusion is further compounded by the suggestion that the relations between men and women vary between classes and that the character of women's oppression also differs between the major economic groups. All this serves to reinforce our view that, in the last instance, Barrett prioritizes class over gender oppression, ultimately reducing the latter to the demands of capital. We say this whilst at the same time acknowledging that she argues strongly against such reductionism and clearly intended that her own analysis should not fall into this particular trap.

Capitalism and Patriarchy

A number of Marxist feminists have attempted to get round the problem of relating gender, class, and capitalism by proposing that in addition to their exploitation through the wage labour system, women are also oppressed by male relations of patriarchy. However, there are differences in the kinds of patriarchal control to which writers suggest women are subjected, and the ways in which the relationship between patriarchy and capitalism are theorized. For example, Eisenstein invokes the term 'capitalist patriarchy' to make her point that the two systems are neither autonomous nor identical, but rather mutually dependent (Eisenstein, 1979). Hartmann, on the other hand, reverses the term to 'patriarchal capitalism' in order to emphasize that there are no such phenomena as 'pure capitalism' or 'pure patriarchy', since the two feed into each other, although they are not inextricably and totally bound to the extent that Eisenstein seems to suggest (Hartmann, 1979). Similarly, Lucy Bland and her co-writers argue that capitalism has 'taken over' or 'colonized' the patriarchal relations which existed prior to its emergence (Bland, Brundson, Hobson, and Winship, 1978). None of these three formulations are particularly satisfactory, since the two separate hierarchical systems not only identify two different sources of oppression for women, but assign them different locations in relation to each hierarchy. A major problem, therefore, is how two analytically distinct positions can be meaningfully brought together to make historical, empirical, and political sense.

Other writers have maintained that the particular form and mode of operation which patriarchy takes, as manifested in male control of female procreation and sexuality, are shaped by the dominant relations of production. Here, an unquestioning acceptance of the conventional Marxist definition and approach to class leads to the argument that patriarchal control of women takes different forms for different social classes. For example: 'Though women are placed simultaneously in two separate but linked structures, those of class and patriarchy, it is their class position which limits the conditions of the forms of patriarchy they will be objectively subjected to.' (McDonough and Harrison, 1978, p.36). Although this argument has the advantage of acknowledging a specific patriarchal dimension to women's oppression, the significance of this is diminished by the assertion that such control is shaped by conditions in the mode of production. However, it is not clear precisely how this shaping takes place, nor is it apparent how the different forms of control experienced by women in the two classes can both be constructed in the interests of capital. Not only is this exposition as functionalist as some of the other explanations we have discussed, since it is assumed that both bourgeois and proletarian patriarchal mechanisms are functional for capital, it also evades the entire question of the relationship between class and gender.

In our discussion of class and 'race' we suggested that a major difficulty stems from the analytic priority afforded to the economy or the mode of production. This leads Marxists to posit the existence of only one possible sort of relationship between capitalism, class and 'race'. A similar problem limits Marxist feminism. For example, most Marxist feminists focus on the sexual division of labour, whether they are analysing woman's position in paid employment or her role within the home. However, we would argue that it is not *a priori* evident either that the sexual division of labour is the most significant aspect of woman's oppression or that it can explain her subordination at work or in the family. For example, we have already considered Cockburn's arguments concerning the patriarchal control of where, when, and at what women are allowed to work. Similarly, Lown, in her study of a nineteenth-century silk mill, indicates the considerable light that can be shed on the experience and subordination of women workers when attention is given to the nature of social relationships between men and women, rather than to capitalist economic relations (Lown, 1983).

We are not arguing that the sexual division of labour between the sexes is unimportant. Clearly such a division constitutes a major way in which women's subordination is accomplished and legitimated. However, we do suggest that it is the *sexual division* which is to be explained. The concept does not constitute an explanation in itself. Moreover, we believe that a focus on the sexual division of *labour* reinforces a concern with women's work, and its possible relation to the economy, and detracts from other forms and explanations of women's subordination. Therefore, in that Marxist feminism is governed by a model which is premissed on the economic, it is scarcely surprising that it should concentrate on 'labour' as the major source for explaining woman's overall oppression, and concentrate on 'labour' as the foundation for her class position within the social hierarchy. The reason for this is clear, since from any Marxist perspective, if women's position in capitalism's relations of production can be clarified, then their place with regard to the class structure becomes automatically demonstrable and thus resolved. But there is a difference between arguing that a woman's life is affected by economic conditions, and the claim that these necessarily determine and structure her position in society, to the extent that it can be analysed and categorized only with reference to a form of conceptualization defined from a male point of view (i.e., class). This is especially the case, since most Marxist analyses of women's labour indicate quite clearly that capitalist relations of production have consequences for women which are very different to those for men. We might add here that Marxist feminists focus almost solely on 'working class' women and are virtually silent concerning the experience of those from the so-called middle classes. More importantly, just as Marxist analyses overlook the 'white' dimension in racial oppression, the focus here ignores the 'male' dimension in female oppression at work, as in all other spheres of life. The power of machismo is obliterated from within this framework, just as the power of white supremacy cannot be accounted for in the literature on 'race'. In our view, if Blacks are more exploited than whites, and women more exploited than men, this additional exploitation cannot be simply reduced to the operation of class relationships and capital. Similarly, just as the violence and hatred ethnic groups experience cannot be explained in these terms, neither can the sexual objectification, rape, harassment, and violence women experience *because they are women.*

Woman as a Separate Class

The idea that women themselves constitute a class has been advocated most forcibly by those feminists who deny that woman can be fitted into traditional forms of class analysis. They therefore see women's oppression as analytically independent of economic class divisions.

Following Firestone, it can be argued that although such economic class divisions clearly exist, they are of only secondary importance and are themselves conditioned by, and dependent on, the primary class division which exists between men and women. Thus, to understand women's oppression we need to explore their primary class relation *vis à vis* men, rather than their economic class relation with regard to capital (Firestone, 1972).

There are many variants of this general formulation but two specific models will be discussed here. The first of these focuses on reproduction and the second on the domestic mode of production to elucidate woman's class position. The reproduction argument is exemplified in the early work of Ti-Grace Atkinson. She opposes the biological class of females, which is characterized by its specific sexual *capacity*, reproduction, with the political class of women which is characterized by a seemingly 'necessary' and 'inevitable' *function,* that is reproduction (Atkinson, 1974). Atkinson argues that it is the blurring of this biological and political class status that is the fundamental dynamic of women's oppression. In opposition to the political class of women stands the counter class of men who, because they have been able to seize power through the manipulation and control of women's reproductive capacity, are the agents of their oppression. Thus, the relative class position of the two sexes is defined in terms of their differing relationships not to production, but to reproduction. Although women perform the reproductive labour, the organization of reproduction itself is mostly in male hands. This occurs, for example, through their medicalization and organization of childbirth and via male control of such technological developments as contraception and abortion. However, the manipulation of women's reproduction begins much earlier than childbirth itself and is mediated through a complex series of institutions and values. Thus, the social pressure on women to conform to the accepted conditions of reproduction through such institutions as heterosexuality, heterosexist marriage, and mother-hood, together with their associated values of love and romance, all help to compound women's position as an oppressed class. They are such a class because *all* women are subjected to control of their reproduction and sexuality in this way. Adrienne Rich, for example, has referred to this as compulsory heterosexuality to underline its enforced nature (Rich, 1981). Other feminists have described how actual force and threat of force are used by the male class to retain control over women's sexuality and reproduction when they emphasize the significance of rape, sexual harassment, and porn-ography.

The stress then is on the antagonism of the class relations between men and women, and on men as the main enemy for women. There are two important aspects to this. Firstly, even the supposedly non-sexist male cannot eschew the class privileges and power which he daily receives as a member of the oppressor class. All men participate in sex-class oppression. Secondly, since the male/female relationship is essentially intimate and private, the personal must be regarded as political and not simply as an individual experience. Thus, the class position of women is underscored by the fact that all women share similar experiences with regard to men. Indeed, it is through such activities as conciousness raising that women become aware of the similarities between them, identify themselves as having mutual class interests and can organize politically to fight oppression. The existence of an autonomous women's liberation movement is clearly important here.

The model which focuses on the domestic mode of production also sees men as the 'main enemy'. Christine Delphy, who is the origina-tor of this particular view of women's class position, argues that domestic work, which all women perform, is the material foundation for a system of patriarchy whereby men dominate and control women (Delphy, 1977). Whilst acknowledging the existence of an industrial mode of production and its related forms of capitalist exploitation, Delphy focuses on the significance of the domestic mode of production for woman because patriarchal exploitation in the family by men is the 'common, specific and main oppression of women.' (Delphy, 1977, p.18). It is common because it affects all married women, specific because only women are expected to provide free domestic services for others and main because even when women are in paid employment their economic class membership derived from that work is conditioned by their patriarchal oppression. The domination of women by men in the family is conceived in class terms by Delphy because in the domestic mode of production the man and woman are respectively owner and labourer, in a manner similar to the way in which the capitalist uses the worker to perform tasks for him. In addition, women together share a common class position within this mode of production by virtue of their primary relationship to men, through marriage.

These various positions are highly significant in that they focus on woman's oppression *as* woman and on the male role as oppressor. Moreover, their stress on the importance of marriage, child-bearing and sexuality points to the fact that women become objectified and controlled to the extent that they perform particular functions and services for *men*. What is problematic here, in our opinion, is the contention that women themselves constitute a class. We find this a difficulty for a number of reasons but the most significant is the implied homogeneity in the use of such a term. This can be illustrated by returning again to the example of the black domestic worker in South Africa. We have argued previously that she is triply oppressed by her gender, her 'race' and her economic position. Is it possible to give gender priority over the other two? And even if it was possible to argue for this in a way that would not render the oppression based on 'race' or economic situation insignificant, in what sense can the three aspects of oppression be brought together in an overall framework? Precisely what kind of relationship exists between them in this example? Of course, the issue of 'race' is significant not just in the South African context but in the British and American situations too. Do Afro-Caribbean, Afro-American and Asian women share a common sex-class position with white women? Can we give gender priority over racial oppression in this way? We think not, and indeed Black feminists have cogently argued that their oppression as women cannot be divorced from their oppression as Blacks. Their experience is as *black* women and we cannot pretend that this fundamental difference does not alter their overall experience as women in a way which, on one level, differentiates them from white women. For we must not forget that white women can be racist, and whether an individual woman is racist or not has no bearing on the privileges she gains over black women in the overall system of white privilege and power. Following on from these arguments there are four further points we would like to make.

Firstly, we think a formulation which takes black women seriously should be alive to the fact that they themselves cannot be treated as an entirely homogeneous group. There are, for example, differences in the histories, experiences, and labour market and family positions of South African, Afro-Caribbean, Afro-American, and Asian women. These differences cannot be ignored.

Secondly, the relationship that black women have to black men is not the same or necessarily analogous to that which white women have to white men. Whilst not denying that these relationships are patriarchal and oppressive, we do assert that their form can be very different. Most crucially, black women have to join black men in their fight against their common racial oppression as well as struggling with black men over patriarchal oppression.

This brings us on to our third point, for although we do not agree with those who argue that the term patriarchy has little or no value, (indeed we see it as crucial in denoting male power over women), the case for its use could be made even stronger if it was possible to point to its specificity in different contexts. We are not thinking here only about the situation of black women in Western countries but of Third World women who, whilst undoubtedly oppressed by their menfolk, as anthropologists have shown, experience an oppression which is qualitiatively different to that of Europeans or Americans.

Finally, although we have been asserting the significance of 'race', we must also remember the importance of differences in the material conditions of life for white women. We are not trying to re-introduce the concept of economic class by the back door here, for it is clear that all such existing formulations are incapable of adequately incorporating gender divisions. However, it does seem important to assert those things that can divide women, as well as those which unite them. In this context two examples must suffice. Firstly, we cannot ignore the material advantage that accrues to those women who, say through access to cars, are able to avoid the street harassment of men to which other women will fall prey. Secondly, it is important to remind ourselves that a woman's actual standard of living and the availability of various resources to her, are dictated not so much by her family's economic position, as by the way that finance is distributed within a particular household. Thus, given two families with the same level of income, it is possible for the woman in one to be living near poverty, while the second experiences relative affluence. The distribution of money plays a significant part in determining these women's material well-being.

The Black and Coloured Populations as a Separate Class

Just as gender is given priority in the above accounts of woman's class position, so some writers have argued that 'race' or ethnicity is a principal factor in constructing either a social hierarchy of racial or ethnic stratification, or constituting the Black population as a separate and distinct class. The British sociologist John Rex, together with his various collaborators, argues for the latter position. The American sociologist, David Wellman, argues the former.

The crux of Rex's argument seems to be as follows. Firstly, he sees class and class struggle as determined by, and expressed in, a number of different struggles over the allocation of resources, such as jobs, housing and educational opportunities. Secondly, he claims that as far as the indigenous working class are concerned, the struggle for resources has led to a period of truce, whereby the benefits won in the form of welfare rights stabilize capitalism as a social system and alter the orientation of the working class towards it. Thirdly, Rex suggests that because the problems of 'race relations' occur in different circumstances, at different times in history, it is important to take into account the current setting within urban areas. Even where persons from different ethnic backgrounds do collaborate together, as at work, they do not tend to mix in extra-industrial contexts. Rex regards immigrants' residential location in the 'twilight' zones of the inner city as an important aspect of their overall position in society. He argues that 'it is the existence within the city of a system of differential access to housing and a kind of status and class order that goes with it, which does much to explain urban politics and, within the pattern of urban politics, of race relations and immigrant-host relations.' (Rex, 1973, p.157).

He goes on to postulate a system of housing classes which result from an individual's particular command over housing resources and place in the housing market. Immigrants are to be found in the lower echelons of this housing class system which appears to effect all other aspects of their lives by operating 'to structure the social, cultural and political processes of urban life.' (Rex, 1973, p.158).

In his later work, and particularly in his research with Sally Tomlinson, Rex explores the relationship between housing and the job market and educational systems (Rex and Tomlinson, 1979). He concludes that there is sufficient evidence of the exclusion of immigrant groups from these three areas to make them not simply a disadvantaged housing class, but more generally an underclass. This underclass can be distinguished from the white working class because the latter are incorporated into the welfare state, while the former are not. The class differences are not simply quantitative, but qualitative and structural as well. In addition, the underclass has the potential to become an 'underclass-in-itself' and organize in its own political interests, in the same way that the white working class may also develop class consciousness and organize politically to its own particular advantage. Rex therefore sees immigrants as 'caught up in a complex and three-sided class struggle.' (Rex, 1983, p.xv).

Rex's analysis has come under much criticism during the last few years, most commonly from those of a Marxist persuasion who claim he ignores the centrality of the means of production in society as a defining feature of the class location of all groups, including immigrants. We have already distanced ourselves from these kinds of arguments. However, we do not feel that Rex's position is entirely satisfactory.

Firstly, within his reasoning, racism becomes merely a form of disadvantage and inequality manifested as a conflict between groups over access to resources. But this obscures the relations of power and domination which structure the overall organization of, in this case, British society. To take just one example, it is not simply that black children perform badly in school because they are denied certain resources, but rather the whole education system which is structured to prevent their success, as many commentators have argued. The significance of white supremacy and black subordination is overlooked in this analysis. Rex can account for neither the significance of 'whiteness', nor for the viciousness of racism within the white working class and the role of the latter generally in the maintenance of white privilege.

Secondly, Rex seems to conceptualize 'racial disadvantage' as the product of the racist practices of the individuals who allocate the resources in the separate institutional spheres of society. This implies that to remove the former it is necessary to tackle the latter. But, as we have previously suggested, racism and racial discrimination do not occur in a vacuum. Rather, they have their place in a certain sort of society, in certain sorts of circumstances. To deduce racial inequality from racism is to lapse into a form of idealism whereby racial prejudice exists in a void with a life of its own. This cannot explain how particular racist practices come to be organized in some kind of consistent way nor why they should take the particular form that they do.

Thirdly, there is a problem with the designation of immigrant groups as a coherent underclass. For do people from Asia, Africa or the West Indies necessarily have the same interests and experiences in the British context? (There is, of course, every reason to argue that they have histories and life styles which are related to their own particular cultures and which are mediated by what happens to them in the British situation). Unfortunately, even though coherence is the pivot of the underclass argument, there is substantial evidence that the interests and experiences of West Indians and Asians are different in the three areas of housing, education, and work, and some of this data is in fact provided by Rex himself in his own empirical research. In additon, although white society may define immigrants as a homogeneous group, the latter themselves clearly do not share such a view and are very aware of what divides as well as of what unites them. There is, for example, nothing to suggest that Asians and West Indians will organize collectively together as the underclass thesis suggests, since their political activities are most commonly articulated on a separate ethnic basis. Moreover, since Rex and Tomlinson refer themselves to 'some considerable overlap between the experiences of West Indians and Asians and their white working class neighbours.' (Rex and Tomlinson, 1979, p.275), we are forced to conclude that the underclass concept does not appear to retain the qualitative and structural properties which the authors acknowledge to be the foundation of this new and separate immigrant class. It is therefore difficult to support the claim that ethnic groups together constitute a particular class within the overall white class system.

The arguments of those Americans who favour the racial or ethnic stratification approach are also based on the distribution of and access to resources in society. 'Race' is regarded as an overwhelming determinant in this process. For example, Wellman, a contemporary

American advocate of this perspective, argues that within the current organization of society, there are only so many resources to go round. In his view, racism should be seen as a culturally sanctioned and rational response to the constant struggle over these scarce resources. The subordinate position of black people is a critical component in the organization of modern American society. Moreover, such subordination together with skin colour is 'a primary determinant of people's position in the social structure. Racism is a structural relationship based on the subordination of one racial group by another.' (Wellman, 1977, p.35). The issues that divide black and white people are therefore grounded in real and material conditions and differences. It then follows that racism systematically provides economic, political, psychological, and social advantages for whites at the expense of Blacks and other peoples of colour. From this point of view, what is important about the United States is the superior position of whites which is built into its structure and which cuts across all classes. Thus, we can see that for Wellman, as for others, racial categorization and not social class position is the basis for the stratification system in which black and white relate. This does not mean that stratification systems based on class are unimportant, but that 'race' and class constitute different and separate dimensions to the understanding of inequality. The two can, and should, be kept analytically distinct. When considering the position of Blacks in the hierarchical ordering of society it is 'race' and not class which structures their location.

These arguments exhibit similar problems to those previously outlined with regard to Rex's work. It is not clear *why* Blacks should constitute a particular target group. Slavery is mentioned but it is not integrated into the overall analysis. Moreover, it seems to us that one can hardly explain slavery, and its associated attitudes and prejudices, in terms of the allocation of scarce resources. Additionally, whilst Wellman talks about 'white racism', an emphasis that we have argued is sadly lacking in most literature, he seems to see this simply as produced by, and a legitimation of, the problem of distributing insufficient supplies. But can racism simply be reduced to a function of inequality in this way? Would racism disappear if there were sufficient resources for all? Through what sorts of mechanisms does racism become articulated in the very organization of American society and not simply in the minds and practices of individual whites? We do not think that Wellman's model can provide the answers to these sorts of questions. Furthermore, if the racial stratification system is one of a number of hierarchies, in what sorts of ways might it interrelate with these other systems? Wellman claims that racial stratification is part of the structure of the United States, 'much like class division', but neither elaborates this analogy nor studies the connectedness between the two. And of course, along with other writers, he completely fails to consider the position of black women within his stratification framework.

In this chapter we have focused on arguments relating to the relationship between 'race' and class, and gender and class, because traditionally the concepts of class and stratification have been used to analyse inequality, disadvantage, and subordination. However, in various ways we have found all the perspectives wanting, although some have been regarded as more problematic than others. Our disquiet regarding the various approaches can be summarized in the following terms. Firstly, it appears that in most cases the injection of 'race' and gender into a model is not considered to change the character of the model taken as a whole. Thus, whether incorporated into class analyses or posited as a separate class or stratification system, gender and 'race' are just 'added on' to what already exists — fitted into or beside the conventional class divi- sions. But apart from the fact that these class divisions are essen- tially male defined, as we have tried to argue, this 'additive' approach is simply unacceptable. It is untenable because of the implication that gender and 'race' simply *increase* the degree of oppression which is involved, with no understanding that they qual- itatively change the *nature* of that oppression. Black women are not simply subjected to more disadvantage than their white sisters, their oppression is of a qualitatively different kind. Similarly, the experience of black male workers is a different experience, founded on different factors, to that of their white counterparts. We would argue then that the arithmetic approach confounds the fact that it is not a question of degree but one of *kind* that is involved here.

Secondly, we think that the very ways in which class is defined make it difficult to use the term to link together the various forms of oppression in society. Class, however defined, takes its place in a bipolar model whether it be proletariat versus bourgeoisie, men versus women, black versus white. However, such a bipolarization can only properly deal with those forms of oppression which have their basis within a particular dichotomous formulation. Thus the

only way, for example, of explaining gender and racial divisions
from with the bourgeoisie/proletariat conceptualization is to reduce
them to aspects of that class relationship, thereby concealing their
own particular dynamic and dichotomous appearance. The tendency
to reduce everything to a particular class model means that different
forms of oppression are subsumed beneath one overarching schema.
In addition, dichotomization, because it can only properly take
account of one dimension, leads protagonists to argue that one form
of oppression can be given priority over the others. The economic,
gender and 'race' dimensions are all given primacy in this way by
their various supporters. However, and this is our third point, we
would argue that since all three clearly operate simultaneously and
in a fairly complicated way, it is necessary to move beyond 'class',
however defined, and away from a binary classification to an analysis based on the possible interrelationship and divergence of the
three hierarchical forms. In such an analysis, we argue, it is important to move beyond a mere concern with location or place in the
overall organization of society, which is the focus of much of the
class literature. For, if 'race' and gender signify relationships of
power and domination, it is not just the 'position' in society which is
of interest. Rather, the major emphasis must move from the allocation of 'place' to the analysis of oppression. Thus, our concern is
not with whether particular groups belong to this or that class. Nor
do we worry as to whether they are the lowest class or a section of it.
Instead, we focus on the mechanisms of oppression, on how people
are oppressed. We are concerned to understand the conditions
under which one group of people have control over another and the
ways in which they obtain access to the instruments of domination.
We stress the significance not of gender, not of 'race', not of economic position — but of all three.

3 Socialization and Resistance

In this chapter we intend to examine the connection between oppression and socialization. On the face of it there would not seem to be any obvious connection, because 'socialization' is supposedly a social process without any political and ideological implications, or at least this is how it is treated in most social psychological and sociological texts. In most instances it is given a very strong and pivotal role in accounting for the way in which men and women become locked into their respective genders. This 'strong' view of socialization is so pervasive that it appears to be tantamount to received truth. Socialization is given the status of a universal force which remorselessly shapes human personality and conduct. Gender from this viewpoint is moulded by the way in which certain people (parents, teachers, employers, etc.) continuously enforce the requirements of sex role behaviour. Children are exposed to incessant pressure to conform to the expectations of their parents or others. Somehow they *internalize* these expectations so that they become gendered beings. To be a man or a woman, therefore, implies a long process of indoctrination into appropriate forms of gender. Men and women are socially constructed, put together by other men and women, who themselves have been put together in the same way.

To a certain extent this picture of socialization seems to be very persuasive. Everywhere we look we discover society after society socializing children along various gender-specific lines. Moreover, in case after case, this is seen to be normal and natural, and strangely enough sociologists, social psychologists, and cultural anthropologists have reinforced these commonsensical views of socialization by their emphasis on the paramountcy of the parental role in determining a child's behaviour. All societies have specific child-rearing practices, and from this it is concluded that these practices are responsible for producing particular kinds of people. So, we have a view of socialization which centres on human passivity. Human beings are produced, moulded, shaped, and determined by totalitarian social forces which relentlessly grind them into acquiescence. Children are turned into men, women, workers, capitalists, Jews, Russians, Jamaicans, Afrikaners, etc. In addition, not only does socialization turn out passive conformists, it also gives these conformists a set of ready-made attitudes to other people and groups. Children are taught that the group, class, culture, gender they belong to are natural formations which stand in a natural relationship to other groups. For example, a white working-class boy brought up in Birmingham Alabama, will be expected to have attitudes towards white girls as well as attitudes toward Blacks. In other words, how a person relates to the world will depend entirely upon the way in which the child is brought up. If a child is brought up in a middle- or working-class home in a society like South Africa, or the southern United States, then the chances are that child will have internalized specific gender and racist attitudes.

The persuasiveness of this strong view of socialization is partially explained by its apparent allowance for variability. It does not assume a monolithic causality from society to the individual — rather it pays attention to the diversity of societies, cultures, groups, and classes. Nevertheless, in the end, the result is still the same. Wherever the child is socialized, he or she is in no position to resist or fight back. The child is passive — his/her racism or sexism is explained by socialization, by the unavoidable internalization of parental attitudes. And yet, when we look at the reality of the socialization process we do not necessarily find passivity. On the contrary, everywhere there is opposition, resistance, and counter-socialization. The evidence is that children do not automatically internalize their parents' expectations. If they did, if they completely conformed to parental demand, there would be no way in which we could account for the prevalence of conflict in personal and social life. Socialization cannot be conceived of as a process which absolutely flattens dissent in order to establish the realm of the social. In very naive and simple terms, we can say that people contribute to their own socialization. A child is not merely animal matter on which society imprints itself.

Proponents of the strong view readily admit to the fact of resistance and conflict, but they tend to encompass such anomalies under the rubric of deviance. If there is conflict, then this must be because socialization has not been successful. Children who show defiance to their parents or teachers have been improperly socialized, or under-socialized. Improper socialization leads to deviance; hence, deviance is a departure from ideal norms of what is appropriate and inappropriate in human behaviour. Hidden behind this image of socialization therefore, is a powerful normative and ideological commitment to a vision of the 'normal'. The normal is the status quo. Accordingly, if socialization practices reinforce the status quo, then it follows that the reproduction of racist and sexist attitudes must also be normal. Proper socialization involves an adherence to the norms of the sexual division of labour and traditional racist beliefs. Improper socialization leads to deviance, to the growth of oppositional attitudes and conflict; both feminism and anti-racism by this token would be deviant.

Certainly, the way we have stated the strong socialization case is perhaps a bit too cavalier. Nevertheless, if we explore the literature, we get the impression that once a child is born, then he or she is the focal point of a whole barrage of institutional pressures that operate to ensure her/his absorption into society. From the moment of birth the child confronts agents of socialization, in the first place the family, then the peer group, the school, the church, the office, the factory, etc. The inference is, that all these agents somehow collaborate to serve the purpose of society. It is this notion of purpose that is so problematic. It suggests that society has 'needs' and 'intentions'. Apart from the fact that this is to reify society, it also completely demotes human intentionality and agency.

We are maintaining here that the strong socialization argument seems to define society as a kind of prison whose jailers represent the interests of an absent but powerful board of governors. The inmates of this prison are portrayed as being so in tune with its requirements that they find it almost impossible to conceive of life outside, or any other alternative. People are locked into their roles, into their gender, into their ethnicity, into their class. At the same time, the board of governors are themselves trapped in the same prison. They too have been subject to socialization pressures which shape their destiny and personalities. However, the very idea of a prison presumes that it has been built by somebody — by human beings. What has been constructed can be pulled down. The notion that socialization is so inclusive and complete cannot be supported by the evidence.

The belief in the reality of this socialization model is an aspect of that kind of theory which divorces itself from the lived experience of people. We are being deliberately naive at this point. We cannot speak of socialization as a total process, as an explanatory theory of how people become social, unless we highlight the countless exceptions to the rule. And it is these exceptions which undermine the efficacy of the strong socialization case. Stanley and Wise put this point very strongly in the context of their critique of the abstract nature of some feminist and social theory:

> We believe that if theory can't be applied to people — some people somewhere — then it is of little use to feminism. Indeed, we feel that it runs counter to some of feminism's most fundamental beliefs and practices. We don't mean that theory should be capable of encompassing every aspect of someone's unique personality and experience. But we certainly do mean that feminism should attempt to dissolve the power differentials between 'experts' (who just happen to be male) and 'people', including the power differentials between those who produce 'grand' and abstract theory and the rest of us. (Stanley and Wise, 1983, p. 100)

It is certainly true that socialization theory does reflect its male origins. Its terminology is replete with words which express the power of overarching masculinity. In other words, socialization theory itself may be an aspect of male domination, of oppressive practice. Although we are not engaging in a polemic against socialization theory *per se,* we are suggesting that it can become an instrument of oppression by its insistence on treating all counter-instances and exceptions as being deviant. Of course, we still have to account for the way in which socialization often seems to take on the appearance of the strong theory. We have to ask ourselves why certain socialization practices seem to determine gender acquisition, and why other practices appear to foster racism?

In this respect we have to consider the following five dimensions:

1 the acquisiton of gender;
2 the acceptance or rejection of gender typifications;
3 the acquisition of racism;
4 the reaction to racism;
5 the acquisition of racism and sexism.

The Acquisition of Gender

The recent feminist critique of male dominated accounts of gender socialization has left us in no doubt about the prevalence of an orthodox view of the way in which men become masculine and women become feminine. This accepted orthodoxy is couched in the language of role theory. The separation of male and female roles is seen as being a logical consequence of the 'natural' sexual division of labour. The assumption was, and is, that men learn to become men and women learn to become women in terms of ready-made scripts which they automatically internalize. Of course, the word 'automatically' must be qualified. Men and women will internalize role scripts and expectations with a little help (force) from their parents, or parent substitutes. The claim that traditional role theory appeared to make was that this process was accomplished without too much difficulty and pain. In addition, it was also assumed that there was a natural progression through the life cycle that fitted both men and women. They would start off their biographical journeys as male or female infants, advance to childhood and learn the appropriate gender conduct associated with this stage, and then in adolescence, they would be inexorably locked into their sex-roles. After the completion of schooling, the life cycle would take on dramatically different emphases for men and women. For men, work and occupational roles; for women, the role of wife and mother. In the hands of somebody like Parsons this whole process took on a benign appearance. Men and women were differentiated in terms of instrumentality and expressivity respectively. (Parsons and Bales, 1956).

It is the benignity of this process which is suspect. From one point of view, it suggests that men and women are socialized without trauma. From another it implies that institutions are nicely harmonized without any friction between them, so that a person's location in the social structure is unproblematic. Yet, it is the lack of benignity which often defines the relationship between those who socialize, and those who are socialized. This is not to say that child-rearing practices, for example, are always exercises in force, but it is to say that there are power imbalances in a whole variety of socialization sites.

The question that we have to address ourselves to therefore, is why do men and women acquire specific gender roles, despite the fact that there is no necessary biological or other reason for them to do so? It is easy enough to answer that they are conditioned or brainwashed, but this is to beg the question. Why should being a man or a woman depend upon some kind of image of victimage in which they passively conform to the pressures and expectations of others? Is it simply that parents are powerful and children are not, and that consequently, children have to toe the line? If it was as simple as this then all we would need is a reward-punishment theory which emphasizes the method parents and others use to shape their children's behaviour.

On one level there is a lot going for such a theory. Boys acquire their masculinity, their gender role by a whole series of explicit and implicit negative and positive sanctions which ineluctably force them to shy away from anything that can be construed as girlish or feminine. Little Fred cannot take many liberties with his gender, especially in late childhood. He cannot, so the argument goes, cross over and join girls in their play and activity, because to do so, would expose him to ridicule from his peers and parents. On the other hand, girls cannot depart from their role slot without incurring the censure of everybody.

> Dolls, boyfriends, babies and grandchildren — the four ages of woman! All the studies undertaken in the West on child rearing patterns show that the qualities encouraged in girls are precisely those they will need in their adult role — dependence, obedience, nurturance and conformity while boys are encouraged to be self-reliant, active, dominant and outward-looking. Even the very youngest children, judging from the findings of researchers, are subjected to these controls. By the age of five, it has been found the great majority of children, in the psychological test situation, are spot-on in their choice of sex-typed toys, with the girls choosing toys which are wholly concerned with their domestic role and the boys choosing toys which are exclusive to the outside world. (Comer, 1974, p.11)

The mechanisms used to obtain this result are various, ranging from direct instruction to punishment and reward expressed in the giving or witholding of approval. In a sense, it could be argued that gender is acquired by the child via a constant exposure to the 'mustness' of roles. However, put this way, is to imply that there is something about roles which inevitably forces people to comply with their dictates. It must be remembered that roles are constructs we use to understand aspects of human conduct — they do not refer to real things out there. To say that the gender role 'requires', 'demands', 'forces' people to conform is to give life to an abstraction. When we talk about gender in terms of the determinacy of roles, we must be very careful to spell out exactly what we mean. In the final analysis it is what people do, and do to each other, that really matters. And what people really do is to believe and act, in terms of their commitment to the belief in the reality of gender. But it is not only men and women as participants who do so — it is also true of the experts who theorize on these matters. They too treat the gender role as if it had some sacrosanct quality, some kind of untouchable explanatory power. Still, when we look around us we can observe that the power of gender typifications seems to be extraordinary. Comer's cataloguing of the four ages of women is not simply descriptive shorthand — it represents in very real terms the expected biography of women growing up in capitalist and industrial societies. But is it also their experienced biography? Yes, if we look at the documentation of this experience provided by the weight of feminist testimony. Even so, this is not necessarily to accept the view that it is role expectations that determine the course of this or that biography. To do so would mean that we can point to a master gender stereotype which exists independently of the socialization process, and which somehow is available to parents as a prop to reinforce the shaping of their children. Put more simply, we are suggesting that the 'mustness' of roles depends on our acceptance of their 'mustness'. When a small girl is punished for playing with boys rather than girls (or vice versa), she is punished not because she is in danger of undermining her gender role — rather, she is punished because her behaviour is a possible threat to a taken-for-granted belief in gender. It is a threat to the power relations of gender, that is, to the ideology based upon the subordination of women. Hence it could be said that it is not the gender role which coerces the person. On the contrary, it is the coercion or oppression which is mediated through gender. To socialize a girl into gender therefore, entails more than her internalizing role scripts and expectations — it entails taking into account the power situation of the socializers and the socialized. And in our society, power and control are not usually in the hands of women.

There is a further problem which we have already noted, namely the assumption that gender is acquired with the minimum of psychic stress, and that the children are passive in the face of their exposure to role demands. If this is the case, then we could close this discussion here. Despite the apparent universality of heterosexual gender typifications, we know from all sorts of evidence that these typifications are tentative and variable. We also know that gender identifications are never as secure as the traditional stereotype implies. Indeed, for an unknown proportion of men and women, ambiguity is the rule. Why should this be so if traditional gender socialization is supposed to be so pervasive? Of course, the standard answer to this question is usually formulated in terms of deviance (something went wrong in early childhood, or the child was improperly socialized, etc.). But even in the case of those men and women who are presumed to be 'straight', it would seem highly unlikely that we can conceive of their gender in unambiguous terms.

The central discussion about ambiguity over the last decade has been focused on motherhood and fatherhood (although the latter has not received too much attention). Fifty years ago it would have been inconceivable to question the motherhood role. In this, social scientists were no different from anyone else. Granted, they pointed to the variance in parenting roles across cultures, but they never doubted for one moment that motherhood in particular represented the quintessence of what it is to be a woman. For a woman the whole socialization process was seen as a preparation for marriage and motherhood. Motherhood was given the status of being the prime reason for woman's existence. At least, it was given this status in religious, political and other forms of public discourse. Even though social scientists attacked commonsensical and biological views of motherhood, they too found it hard to give up their commitment to its importance. They may have emphasized its cultural variability, but they somehow inevitably described it as though it was the 'essential' female role.

But logically, if we push role arguments to their extreme, there can be no intrinsic roles — roles, by definition, are learned, they are historically specific, they are relative. Hence, to be consistent, role theory must assert the fragility of all social roles. It must assert that in this place and time women were biological mothers, but not necessarily social mothers. Accordingly, anybody should be able to learn a mothering role — men as well as women. Certainly today some men have made a conscious attempt to learn the skills of child-care. They have learned to change nappies, learned to cook, they do housework, and perhaps convince themselves that they have taken on the role of 'housewife', but this does not change the reality of motherhood. If men and women were able to flit from role to role without too much trauma there would be no talk about the oppression of women.

There are of course other arguments available which may account for the existence and reproduction of gender and mothering roles. Freudian explanations have been appropriated and modified by feminists and others in order to understand how gender is acquired. More accurately, they have used Freudian arguments to account for the power of gender roles. But Freudian discussions of infantile sexuality and motherhood are not confined to academic quarters — they have frequently filtered into popular versions of socialization:

> The ways in which girls are socialised toward notions of feminity and for motherhood, in our culture, are dominated by popularised psychoanalytic theory. It has contributed many pervasive and tenacious ideas about women and their sexuality. It supports the synonymity between female sexuality and reproduction suggested by earlier evolutionary theory. Freud's own theories of female sexuality have been adopted and modified (for better and worse) by later psychoanalysts. Erikson, . . . in characterising women as 'the bearer of the ova and maternal powers', represents a fairly reductive view, but most psychoanalytical writers agree in placing motherhood at the centre of woman's psycho-emotional development. (Antonis, 1981, p.62)

(Interestingly enough, psychoanalytical theory does not put fatherhood at the centre of a man's psycho-emotional development. Fatherhood is defined in terms of authority, not emotional involvement in the care-taking process, although admittedly, how a man displays his authority will to a large extent be traced to his own particular resolution of the Oedipus conflict.)

The popularization of Freud, and the acceptance by both experts and participants of the vision of a pre-determined gender, has had the effect of making the analysis of the actual mechanisms at work a daunting task. Gender seems to be implanted by overwhelming forces which break down the defences of boys and girls, ensuring their docility. But, as we observed in chapter one, from the psychoanalytical perspective such a result is obtained at a terrible emotional and psychic cost. If gender is acquired by repression, then in Freud's terms, this must be at the expense of something else. Hence, gender can never really be unambiguous — it must always be accompanied by anxiety and doubts about one's sexuality. It is precisely these doubts that are swept away in the popularized versions of Freudianism that dominate media and text-book discussions of Freud, especially in the United States (Holland, 1977; Jacoby, 1977). Our concern here is not to demystify Freud, but to take account of the way in which certain aspects of Freudian thinking have been used to naturalize the position of women in the contemporary world. It is also our intention to look at an alternative feminist reading of the Freudian construction of gender.

The psychoanalytical account of gender development assumes a sequence of developmental stages which turn men into 'men' and 'women' into women. For practical purposes, this sequence is completed by the age of five. All the pre-requisites of male and female gender are internalized by this age. However, the consequences of the resolution of the Oedipus situation reverberate throughout life. For men, it leads to the internalization of a strong superego and an imperious masculinity which rides roughshod over their intrinsic bisexuality. For women, it results in the repression of penis envy, and the emergence of a passive sexuality reflecting the demotion of clitoral sensitivity (Freud, 1977). The operative term is repression. In order for a woman to reach sexual and reproductive maturity, she must abandon her bisexuality and develop a truncated form of sexual identity which is supposedly admirably suited for motherhood (and marriage). Such a state of affairs is premised upon the successful completion of all the stages of psychosexual development, and given the obstacles encountered at each of these stages, it is most unlikely that anybody reaches adulthood without some kind of psychic damage. Repression in any guise must produce ambiguity, even though the subject is unable to recognize the source of this ambiguity.

In a nutshell, in the orthodox Freudian position, there is a tendency to see the acquisition of gender as having different consequences for men and women. In both genders the probability of personality imbalance is very high, but women appear to come off second best. Put another way, the psychoanalytic account of socialization ends up with the status quo, that is, with the subordination of women. The entire socialization process operates to encapsulate women in a gender prison. The pessimism and determinism in this view are paralleled by its postulation of a permanent crisis in the human psyche, a crisis which for both women and men is always tinged with an incessant battle to overcome neurosis and unhappiness.

Other readings of Freud have attempted to place gender in a far broader frame of reference. Gender, in these readings, is dependent on particular historical circumstances — on specific family constellations which themselves are tied into the mode of production, and other institutional networks. Chodorow, for instance, has attempted to relate the mode of production to the way in which gender is reproduced in family contexts. She writes:

> Family organization, child care and child-rearing practices, and the relations between women's child care and other responsibilities change in response particularly to changes in the organization of production. Women's role as we know it is an historical product. The development of industrial capitalism in the west entailed that women's role in the family become increasingly concerned with personal relations and psychological stability. Mothering is most eminently a psychologically based role. It consists in psychological and personal experience of self in relationship to child and children. (Chodorow, 1978, p.32)

The mothering role then is dependent upon the dictates of influences which are outside the family. Yet, at the same time, Chodorow points to the powerful unconscious factors at work in mothering:

> It is evident that the mothering that women do is not something that can be taught simply by giving a girl dolls or telling her that she ought to be a mother . . . nor can men's power over women explain mothering. Whether or not men in particular or society at large . . . enforces women's mothering, and expect or require a woman to care for her child, they cannot force or require her to provide adequate parenting unless she, *to some degree* and *on some unconscious or conscious level,* has the capacity and sense of self as maternal to do so. (Chodorow, 1978, p.33)

This means that Chodorow sees mothering as being the crucial dimension in the socialization process, and by implication, the mother as being the unconscious accomplice in her own future bondage. Motherhood is not a taught role — it is an effect of the lodging in the girl's unconscious of the historical forces which have made women responsible for child care and domesticity, and which therefore, inevitably reinforce the sexual division of labour. A mother is consequently seen as doing two things. Firstly, she reproduces in her daughters the unconscious acceptance of the mothering role, and secondly, she ensures that her sons reject femininity by denying or repressing their bisexuality. In both cases, it is the mother's influence that is determinative. She simultaneously is the unknowing instrument of her own daughters' subjection, and her sons' domination.

The way out of this gender trap, from Chodorow's point of view, is to break down the emphasis in our culture on the mother's singular child-caring role by the construction of collective forms of child-caring institutions, or at the very least, the transformation of the fathering role into one which is interchangeable with the mothering role. However, in the meantime, the reproduction of gender validates the inequality of the sexes. Moreover, there are a number of supposed terrible consequences deriving from the socialization of boys, namely their acquisition of a flawed identity which is expressed in feelings of resentment and hostility toward women.

> Masculinity becomes an issue as a direct result of the boy's experience of himself in his family — as a result of being parented by a woman . . . Dependence on his mother, attachment to her, and identification with her represent that which is not masculine: a boy must reject dependence and deny attachment and identification. Masculine gender role training becomes much more rigid than feminine. A boy represses those qualities he takes to be feminine inside himself, and rejects and devalues women and whatever he considers to be feminine in the social world. (Chodorow, 1978, p.181)

For Chodorow, the lodging of gender in the unconscious is a highly determinative process. Behind the family is the mode of production which demands that the sexual division of labour is always reproduced. This demand must be met if capitalism is to maximize its expropriating capacities, and this it can only do by maintaining the gender status quo. Given the forces ranged against them, it would seem highly unlikely that either men or women can transcend the limits of gender. In other words, despite the sophistication of her analysis, she too is advancing a strong socialization thesis which makes it difficult to envisage any viable kind of counter-strategy. Although she stresses ambivalence, it would seem that the internalized mother object is there for all time.

The notion that gender is fixed in the unconscious in early childhood is replicated in other psychoanalytic accounts, although these accounts have different starting points. Especially influential for a number of feminists is the work of Lacan. Indeed, the appropriation of Lacan has been a significant feature of certain aspects of feminist theory.

Any discussion of Lacan must be fraught with difficulty, because he does not address himself to simple issues in simple language. Like Freud and Marx, the readings of Lacan are many and contradictory. For feminists, Lacan provides a way of conceiving gender as a historically specific form of internalized ideological discourse, that is, as an unconscious symbolic representation of the sexual division of labour. A child becomes gendered in this view by its exposure and reaction to the symbolic order as mediated by its parents, but parents to whom the child does not relate as immediate objects of desire, but as signs or signifiers of a state of affairs which can never be satisfied. In resolving its Oedipal situation, the child, therefore, will not internalize and identify with this mother or that father, but will be enmeshed in the language of gender — a language already contaminated with the ideology of gender differences. The implication here is that, given an alternative set of social relationships with a different view of gender, it should be possible to undermine traditional gender relationships. In other words, feminists argue that instead of the universalistic claims of orthodox psychoanalysis, the Lacanian version allows for the possibility of a radical restructuring of gender and sexual realities (Lieven, 1981). But does it? Even a most superficial reading of Lacan does not suggest that he entertains any doubts about the determining powers of what he calls the symbolic. No matter the particular context, Lacan appears to document the timelessness of the Oedipal situation, even though he formulates it differently from Freud. It is language, a timeless language, which comes to play the key role in the Lacanian system. 'This passion of the signifier then becomes a new dimension of the human condition, in that it is not only man who speaks, but in man and through man that it (ça) speaks, that his nature is woven by effects in which we can find the structure of language'. (Lacan, 1982, p.78)

When Lacan talks about the constitution of man by language, he is not replicating the arguments of cultural theorists when they talk about the determining power of language. He is not talking about the acquisition of a self as the result of social interaction between language users. Nor is he suggesting that language is the medium through which the superego is internalized, as in the case of functionalist views of socialization. Rather, he is pointing to the way in which the unconscious is infiltrated by the symbolic order, so that the child's entire life span will always be shaped by its insatiable sense of loss about the irretrievability of the desired object. It is in the Oedipal situation that the child comes to know the irreversibility of its loss, and to accept the reality of its gender fate. Consequently, gender is pre-determined by the child's inevitable surrender to the symbolic order. Men and women are literally forced to become gendered beings by the shock of induction into a language of gender which is already sexist; or perhaps, it would be more appropriate to say they become gendered beings in a context in which the phallus has central priority and political significance, that is, in a patriarchal society.

Now the foregoing is a simplification of a very complicated process. It is not possible to be fair to Lacan in the space of a few paragraphs. Our intention is to sample the commitment he has to the power of the socialization process as manifest in the child's encounter and resolution of the Oedipal situation. In general, our object has been to pinpoint the remarkable consensus in various psychoanalytical accounts of the socialization process. This consensus, especially in relation to gender, emphasizes the way in which the child's experience and construction of its sexual reality (sexed subjectivity) is attributed to the transformation of its bisexuality into the straitjacket of male or female identity. In whatever manner the Oedipal situation is resolved, the implication is that something is always lost, given up, surrendered to a powerful enemy, an enemy who will always be resented unconsciously. The cost of the enemy's victory will be expressed in neurosis, unhappiness and sexual ambiguity, and in Lacan's case, by the gendered subject's inability to recapture the object of its desire. In any event, the results appear to be the same — gender is experienced as a thing, as a preordained reality. From the subject's point of view, any ambiguity he or she might experience is repressed, or given a respectable veneer.

It seems that what all these practitioners are doing is to describe the mechanisms whereby human beings are inexorably compelled to become their own jailers. They enter a world in which their parents provide them with all the necessary emotional and symbolic materials to build their own prisons. In contrast to role theory, psychoanalysis does not envisage this happening without trauma — the psychoanalytical jail is built on repression. Furthermore, it never can contain the rumblings of the id, nor can it ever deny the power of intra-psychic conflict. Role theory on the other hand, is far more concerned with describing the fit between the individual and society, and in more extreme cases, in defining personality as nothing more than internalized role scripts. Nevertheless, despite the marked differences between psychoanalytic and sociological views of the socialization process, the end result is very similar. In both cases, gender is a trap from which there is no escape.

The previous discussion has been premissed on primary socialization, on child-rearing practices. Yet, if we examine standard sociological and non-Freudian texts on socialization, we realize that socialization is not only associated with child-rearing. In the broadest sense, it is concerned with the sum total of social influences on the individual through his or her biographical journey. We do not have to instance the sites of socialization in great detail here. From the cradle to the grave there are social and personal forces which intermesh with the individual's development. Friends, the school, the factory or office, the media, class affiliations, language, all contribute to a person's life story. But in what way do they contribute? How is gender related to the various sites and contexts of socialization? From the strong socialization point of view, the argument is that all socialization sites are interrelated in a systematic way, so that what happens to a person in the family will be reinforced by what happens in the school and factory. But, of course, to assert that socialization sites are integrated into some master system is to beg the question. We have to uncover the reason for such systematization. And when we attempt to do this we come back to some notion of determining processes which force the individual through his/her life cycle. However, even if we question this assumed integration, we still are committed to the notion that each site, to a lesser or greater

degree, will reinforce male power. In other words, every socialization site is the scene for the confirmation of the subservient status of
women. If this is the case, it simply cannot be socialization which
makes it so. It would seem to us that socialization cannot be
considered as the source of oppression; nor for that matter, can it be
considered to be identical to oppression. In our view socialization
reproduces oppression, but it can only do this if oppression is seen as
something other than the process through which it is mediated.

The Acceptance or Rejection of Gender

Earlier, we made the point that the strong socialization thesis
implies a view of gender as being forced and moulded into shape by
determinate forces. We also suggested, by implication, that this
thesis appears to be the dominant orthodoxy among a large number
of social scientists. Other practitioners have objected to the pessimism and fatalism of this view. They argue that socialization should
not be conceived of as a stamping-in process whereby an individual
is gradually shaped to fit the needs of society. Gender, from this
perspective, is not a prison whose walls cannot be breached. The
imposition of a set of rules and norms on an infant does not imply a
pre-determined biographical journey. There are accidents, contin-
gencies, and more importantly, there is the fact that children often
resist the dictates of their parents and other authorities.

We can, of course go on to the other extreme. We can posit a
world in which there is no guarantee of continuity across time, no
integration of experience, and where each situation is paramount.
Put another way, we can see socialization as having no direction as
the child *drifts* into adulthood. Gender in these circumstances is not
a hard reality — it is rather a construction that a particular person
puts together out of a multiplicity of possibilities. Accordingly,
instead of the integrated and powerful universe of gender typifications so pervasive in the 'strong' socialization argument, we have
here an indeterminate world in which who and what you are can
never be encapsulated in past history. Your gender is what you
decide it is 'now' — it is a creature of circumstance, of this situation
and that episode.

So, instead of confronting a hard world of gender, the child is born
into a fragmented and episodic mosaic of conflicts and ambiguities.

However, behind this kind of thinking is a very specific view about the nature of society and social relationships. Fragmentation is not, in this view, something inherent in the nature of things — it is, on the contrary, an effect of the complexity of industrial and capitalist development. The subjective experience of the social division of labour is manifested therefore, in a lack of certainty and confusion about identity, especially gender identity. Because there are so many competing pressures on the child from birth onwards, there is no guarantee that she/he will accept the gender definitions of parents and others. Instead of gender being conceived of as monolithic, it is discovered to be fragile and tentative.

Goffman's notion of role distance may illustrate this argument. The strong socialization thesis places women in a particular role, namely that of mother and housewife. But the alternative claim is, that although there may be vague master gender scripts which inform a specific historical context (industrial capitalism), there is no way in which these scripts are accepted in a stereotypical way. In becoming a woman, an individual female does not have to become what others say she should be; she does not have to 'take the role of the other'. In spite of all the pressures directed at her, she can stand aloof from her gender role — she can distance herself from it, and in so doing, can sow the seeds of her opposition to her status. The point here is that gender socialization is partial, not total. Socialization cannot ensure a person's total absorption in society, because by definition she is a reflexive being capable of opposing those who want to make her toe the gender line. Thus, the givens of gender identity are subject to reinterpretation and reconstruction.

Obviously, such a point of view appears to be based on a highly speculative analysis of the contents of consciousness. It seems to suggest that reflexivity is the cornerstone of the opposition to gender ascription, and that in a fragmented society all women are potentially aware of the fragility of this ascription. If this is the case, then we could certainly be optimistic about the possibilities of changing the status quo. But awareness and reflexivity do not in themselves constitute the grounds for revolutionary action or social change. Indeed, they could conceivably be the grounds for inactivity and a debilitating pessimism. A heightened consciousness of the limits and bounds of one's oppression may result in a surrender to the awesome power of one's oppressors.

It is the last point which has created problems for the reflexive argument. The fact that a woman can reflexively distance herself from the conditions of status as a housewife and mother, does not guarantee her freedom. The fact that one knows one is in a prison does not mean that its walls will come tumbling down. But there is a more serious point, namely that only a few women may be in a position to indulge in the luxury of a liberated reflexive consciousness. It is usually only those who are privileged who can translate their reflexivity into action, albeit in a circumscribed way. When we look at the condition of the majority of the world's women, it does not seem likely that liberation through reflexivity is a viable possibility — although reflexivity is certainly not a white, middle-class prerogative.

To be sure, this is not what is at issue here — what is being claimed is that it is only the middle classes in industrial societies who presumably are able to take advantage of their greater access to linguistic and educational resources. In this respect, a white middle-class woman is more likely to distance herself from her gender than is a woman in a third world or slave context. Put differently, the argument is that in advanced capitalist societies, the fragmentation of social and personal life is reflected in the socialization practices of their populations, especially among those people whose economic position has purchased them the appropriate reflexive tools. Accordingly, the acquisition of a middle-class identity is, from this perspective, likely to be accompanied by identity confusion and anxiety, especially about the limits of gender. Middle-class children will be exposed to a wide range of emotional and cognitive inputs, often of a contradictory kind. For example, in the home they might conceivably be exposed to a rhetoric of gender equality. Their parents may speak about family democracy, there could even be the semblance of an equal division of labour in the household. But they will observe and know that things are not necessarily what they seem. The sight of a girl's mother's constant immersion in housework, and her father's long absence in the world of 'work', does not encourage her to accept the reality of this rhetoric. Moreover, because she is socialized in a middle-class home, she will be encouraged to be more reflexive and 'rational'. Even before she is anywhere near completing her secondary education, she will realize that she will be expected to achieve academic success:

> Social and educational aspirations are very much part of middle-class life. The continuing inequalities of the education

system mean that although all parents want 'the best' for their daughters, some 'bests' will be better and more accessible than others, and it is more likely to be the middle-class who can provide most for their children. They have often benefitted from education themselves, and give helpful interest and support, as well as better and quieter facilities for studying. (Sharpe, 1976, p.143)

Now we are not really concerned with the fact that middle-class children are better off than working-class children. Our interest is in the consequences of this for their view of themselves as gendered subjects. The implications of the fragmentation thesis is that middle-class socialization practices allow for a degree of reflexive questioning of gender. The exposure to education, to 'rational discourse', may enable both women and men to detach themselves from the conditions of their existence, thus enabling them to formulate possible alternatives to this existence. But this is altogether a far too optimistic thesis. It seems to suggest that gender can be negotiated away, provided you have the reflexive resources to do so. It is based on the assumption that gender is simply a problem for the individual. Once a woman can recognize what constitutes her oppression, she will be in a position to overcome that oppression, and to redefine her gender identity.

But what is meant by identity in this context? In relation to gender it may be given two meanings. Firstly, it is often seen in essentialist terms. Gender is described in terms of a quality which exists independently of social definition. Obviously, in many cases, an essentialist definition will tend to be biological. However, there is an alternative meaning which refers to the sense of sameness over time. Gender in this view is a person's image of herself/himself as a distinct sexed subject with a recognizable history. In existentialist literature it is this sense of identity which is seen as being problematic and threatened by the impingement of the 'other'. For a woman, the other is 'man'. It is men who define and limit her sexuality and autonomy. This limit is experienced as an attack on the integrity of her own subjectivity. Because men control both the public and private spheres, there are few opportunities for her to display her true reality, her true sense of self. Implicit in this notion is the belief in an essential femininity, which is overlaid by the inauthenticity of male culture. For a man, a woman is the other whom he reduces to an object in order to define himself. In so far as he is able to control her, he is comfortable in his masculinity — he knows who he is — his identity depends upon the continuous assertion of his power. In imposing their masculinity men ensure that women come to accept their secondary status (de Beauvoir, 1972). It is only through recognizing the inauthenticity of her own passive appropriation of male values that a woman can recover her own identity. However, in de Beauvoir's view, such a recognition is inevitably limited by her involvement in reproduction and motherhood. In order to transcend her passivity, she must somehow become like a man, although she can never, in the final analysis, escape from the nature of her body as an object for men. But where does one find authenticity if the body's reproductive capacities imprison one in a never-ending round of child-bearing and catering for men's needs? Where do we discover authentic gender identity, if it is always hidden away and trampled upon by others? One answer is that instead of emulating men, women should assert their femininity in the strongest possible manner. But this is to presume that in principle human beings are autonomous, and that a woman will somehow choose to become a woman, because she intuitively knows what the quintessence of womanhood is. Yet such a choice is not simply available to most women, because of the restricting demands of their everyday lives. The quest for true identity is, like the quest for human nature, a will-o'-the-wisp — we are never sure that we can ever really know what it is that is supposed to be real. Presumably this is not too important, as long as we know what it is that prevents us from attempting to go on such a quest. And, for most women, this is the power represented in their other — men.

Secondly, instead of an essentialist meaning, gender identity may be seen as being highly flexible and negotiable. One's gender is defined contextually — it depends upon the particular others with whom one is associating. It depends on the site of interaction. In a pub, a man is masculine and aggressive. In his office, he may be passive and conformist. At home, he may be intolerant and authoritarian. Each situation, each site, demands an appropriate response which may not have anything to do with his true identity. And indeed, the notion of a true gender identity is problematic given the fact that each situation seems to evoke a different self.

Obviously, it does not make sense to speak of gender identity simply as a function of this or that situation. We are not talking about a form of sociological schizophrenia in which a person does not know who she/he is from moment to moment, but we are stressing the reflexive nature of social life and the way in which people negotiate their identities in particular situations. The strong socialization thesis maintains that there is a minimum space for identity negotiation. It claims that identity is determined by key learning or traumatic experiences, and that gender, for instance, is essentially laid down in early childhood. In this formulation, socialization is asymmetrical — it is the socializers who socialize, and the socialized who are socialized. The negotiation or reflexive model on the other hand defines socialization as a two-way process in which all parties to the interaction actively contribute to the construction of an identity. In the case of a girl, despite the strong forces lined up against her, it is suggested that she does not merely model herself on an appropriate gender model in a mechanical way, but that she may actively either reject or accept the model. Given her reflexive capacities, she may choose not to be who others say she must be. And even if it appears that she conforms in the home situation, it is open to her not to conform in another context.

One might just as well say there is no gender identity. There is only a schedule for the portrayal of gender. There is no relationship between the sexes that can so far be characterised in any satisfactory fashion. There is only evidence of the practice between the sexes of choreographing behaviourally a portrait of relationship. And what these portraits most directly tell us about is not gender, or the overall relationship between the sexes, but about the special character and functioning of portraiture. (Goffman, 1979, p.8)

If there is no essential gender identity, only 'a schedule for the portrayal of gender', then it follows that this schedule is highly volatile, depending on the way in which the situation is interpreted. Accordingly, gender is presented as an aspect of a social relationship, that is, it is displayed as a ploy, because the situation is defined as one in which such a display is appropriate. When a girl is told by her parents that she must behave with a degree of modesty at a party at which boys are to be present, and if she complies, then this is not because she has necessarily internalized her parents' prohibitions —

rather, she may take her cues from other girls who cooperate to project an acceptable gender identity for the situation at hand. Gender, in this sense, is a negotiation, a tacit agreement between participants that a certain portrayal of identity is relevant.

Of course, the notion of relevance is critical here. How do men and women negotiate gender in this or that context? In terms of the reflexive model, it would appear that the negotiation process is open and flexible — hence, what is perceived as relevant or appropriate depends upon the agreement of both genders. So in principle, any situation could be the occasion for role reversal if that is what the participants want. However, this is to suggest that gender is simply a matter of whim in which men and women can swap identities. If this was the case, then there would be no need to talk about male dominance, because each situation would be the site of a different pattern of power relationships in which either men or women assume the dominant role.

And indeed, it is the question of power which limits the negotiation model. Or perhaps more accurately, it is the access to negotiating power which is important. When we talk about socialization, although we might point to instances of resistance on the part of the child in which she/he manages to secure for her/himself a strong negotiating position *vis à vis* parents, this is not equivalent to saying that children control and dominate their parents. Similarly, an individual victory in a gender situation does not mean that a woman has changed the terms of male domination. In the final analysis, negotiating power depends upon who is in the position to secure the maximum benefit from the negotiation, that is, it depends upon the extent to which men do or do not control and manipulate women, not only in sites like the family, but also in other spheres. Accordingly, in granting the possibility of negotiation, and allowing for reflexive resistance, gender identity cannot be talked away — it cannot be discarded like old clothes. In order to change the terms of gender power, we have to accept that such a change does not only involve individual commitment and consciousness, but must also involve collective action.

The questions we have to ask are: Why is gender identity experienced as a given? Why do women appear to accept the male version of their identity? Why do women appear to exist only as objects of men's needs and desires? One possible answer to these questions is formulated in terms of sexuality.

What defines woman as such is what turns men on. Good girls are 'attractive', bad girls 'provocative'. Gender socialization is the process through which women come to identify themselves as sexual beings, as beings that exist for men. It is that process through which women internalise (make their own) a male image of their sexuality *as* their identity as women. It is not just an illusion. Feminist inquiry into women's own experience of sexuality revises prior comprehensions of sexual issues and transforms the concept of sexuality itself — its determinants and its role in society and politics. According to this revision, one 'becomes a woman' — acquires and identifies with the status of the female — not so much through physical maturation or inculcation into apropriate role behaviour as through the experience of sexuality: a complex unity of physicality, emotionality, identity, and status affirmation. Sex as gender and sex as sexuality are thus defined in terms of each other, but it is sexuality which determines gender, not the other way around. This, the central but never stated insight of Kate Millett's *Sexual Politics*, resolves the duality in the term 'sex' itself: what women learn in order to 'have sex' in order to 'become women' — woman as gender — comes through the experience of, and is a condition for, 'having sex' — woman as sexual object for man, the use of women's sexuality by men. Indeed, to the extent sexuality is social, women's sexuality *is* its use, just as our femaleness *is* its alterity. (Mackinnon, 1982, p.17)

Hence, it is 'sexuality which defines gender'. It follows (if this argument is correct) that gender cannot be considered to be a matter of negotiation between men and women, the outcome of which is problematic — gender is 'determined' by the power resident in male sexuality. Male sexuality is political and manipulative — it uses the female body to establish the primacy of male gender. In a sense, the ascendancy of male sexuality is demonstrated in sexual practice — in the manner in which men typically express their 'rights' over women's bodies. Rape, sexual harassment, the 'wolf-whistle', pornography, emphasize the generalized sexual power of men in society at large. Thus, rape is not a deviant phenomenon, it is rather one dramatic example of the way in which men use women sexually. Sexuality is the terrain, the domain in which both men and women come to define themselves in terms of a taken-for-granted gender identity. For a girl, this definition begins from the moment she is made aware of the coercive nature of men's sexuality. Her father, her brothers, the boys she plays with at school, the media, the books she reads, her own mother, other women and girls, all somehow appear to assent to the passivity of women. Given the evidence of her own eyes, she too comes to give credence to male potency, and accepts heterosexuality.

One implication of this argument is that male sexual behaviour is seen in political terms. The subjection of women is accomplished sexually. Accordingly, women can only challenge male domination if they come to know that the personal is not a self-contained privatized universe, but one in which men act as sexual transgressors and oppressors. This occurs through understanding and recognizing that the 'normalcy' of sexual relations in the family is a normalcy defined by a male dominated culture. But does such an understanding denote the possibility of freedom? In making women conscious of the way in which men have treated and defined them as objects, can we see the first glimmerings of reflexive self-knowledge which will create the conditions for political transformation of the personal, and by extension, of society itself?

If the answer to this is in the affirmative, then it means that male supremacy could be subverted by those women who understand the nature of their oppression. And certainly, there seems to be evidence that the revival of feminism in the sixties has had a significant effect on the way in which some men have tried to confront their own sexuality. This is not to say that feminism has undermined the collective self-assurance of men in general, but it is to recognize that 'some' men find it difficult to define their gender identity in unambiguous terms. When we say 'some men', we are, of course, not saying very much (Tolson, 1977). Now it may well be true that these men have consciously attempted to read the lesson of feminism as being important to their own experience of sexuality and gender, but to suggest that men in general have taken aboard the feminist critique of their sexual imperialism is wishful thinking. What in fact has happened is that marginal and peripheral concessions have been made in the field of employment, and in other public spheres, but the reality of male power is still all around us.

So far then, we have suggested, in a rather broad way, that the strong socialization model is premised on a view of determinate social and psychological forces which ineluctably turn men into men and women into women. We contrasted the strong socialization model with those views which emphasize reflexivity as a key element in gender acquisition. The problem with the reflexive model is that it assumes that men and women are free to negotiate their identity without taking into account the restrictions imposed by social structure and history. Reflexivity cannot be outside history. While it may be true that some men and women are fortunate enough to experiment with their gender, the chances are that most people are not presented with the opportunity, or believe there is an option to do so. The optimism of the negotiation model is tempered when we consider sexuality in political terms. If sexuality is the terrain in which men secure the subjection of women, then it makes no sense to consider the possibility of gender negotiation.

In maintaining that the root of women's oppression lies in the manner in 'which women come to identify themselves as sexual beings, as beings that exist for men', we may seem to be implying something about male sexuality in essentialist terms. However, we do not believe that there is anything essential or natural about male sexual domination. Men treat women as sexual objects in a social context — it is in the social matrix that we have to explain the oppression of women, not in male psychological and biological predispositions. In other words, we have to come to grips with the way in which the ideology of male sexual power is produced and reproduced, that is, we must understand how both men and women continue to give allegiance to their respective genders. (This is a problem we hope to elucidate in chapter 6). For the remainder of this chapter our task is to inquire whether or not the acquisition of racism can be described in the same way as the acquisition of gender.

The Acquisition of Racism

When commentators talk about racism and socialization, there is a tendency to use prejudice as the critical explanatory tool. Put simply, the prejudice argument states that children will become prejudiced against out-groups if they are brought up in a climate in which prejudice is sanctioned. So, taking South Africa as an example, white children growing up in a society which systematically discriminates against the black majority will learn automatically, the prejudices of their white parents. In a country like Britain the acquisition of prejudiced attitudes is not so straightforward. Here, we have to ask, Do all white children learn to be prejudiced against minorities and migrants? If the answer to this is that only *some* children acquire prejudiced attitudes, then we have to ask a further question. Is there any way in which we can distinguish between those who become prejudiced and those who do not? The answers tend to be many. One of these has had an enormous literature devoted to it over the last forty years, namely, the argument that prejudice (racism?) is directly related to the kind of disciplinary experiences to which the child is exposed. Another answer is based upon the presumed differences between working-class and middle-class child-rearing practices. The inference here is that children brought up in working-class homes are more likely to be prejudiced against migrants than middle-class children, because they are more directly involved with them in the struggle for scarce resources.

In general prejudice is usually regarded as an attitude, an attitude acquired in early childhood, which is directly related to parental views and feelings about out-groups and other social issues. Although it is extremely difficult to claim that parental attitudes 'determine' children's prejudices, the evidence from the social psychological literature would seem to suggest that:

> Parents have a unique control over the information that is available to the child, and that is the raw material from which meaning is constructed. It is not surprising, then, to discover that children do become aware of their parents' attitudes and values from quite an early age, and frequently seem to swallow them wholesale, reproducing them as their own. (Milner, 1983, p.55)

How children come to accept, internalize, and reproduce their parental attitudes is, of course, the problem. Whether we suggest as Milner does (Milner, 1983, pp.55–62) that prejudice acquisition is a function of the intermeshing of direct tuition, identification, modelling, and role learning, we are still talking about prejudice in terms of its individual effects, that is, as something of consequence only to prejudiced people. The danger in concentrating on prejudice as a phenomenon is that we may conceive it as being the cause of racism. Now it is certainly true that racism does not exist independently of human actors — it has to be mediated by people, but this is not the same thing as locating it exclusively in socialization processes. If children acquire racism in early childhood, then we have to ask, why is it that parents and significant others somehow act as a conduit for this acquisition?

Perhaps we can understand this question if we revert to the South African case. White children acquire their racism from their parents who already are part of a system in which 'racism' is legalized, and generally supported by the white population. To be white in South Africa therefore, is to have a sense of oneself as belonging to a particular group with particular enemies. While it may be true that this sense of belonging is mediated through the socialization process, this is not equivalent to saying that socialization is responsible for apartheid and racism.

At this point it might be objected that we are contradicting some of our earlier criticisms of the strong socialization thesis, by our apparent insistence on the role of parents as mediators of racism. As we have stated it, white children are faced with predefined racist typifications which they reproduce as their own — the implication being that they passively become what their parents say they must be. And because their parents belong to a dominant minority, they too acquire membership of that minority. Hence racism is seen as a crucial aspect of a white child's identity — it is a means whereby she/he can claim this membership.

But what about the child who does not fit in with the requirements of group membership? Do we have to invoke personality explanations in order to understand why she/he is different? Or alternatively, given a liberal democratic society in which racism is not legally sanctioned, in which white children are supposedly brought up to respect the rights and integrity of out-groups, what are we to make of the child who turns out to be racist? Has she/he a personality problem? In either case the temptation is to construe the response of the child as though she/he has some deficiency, some kind of character disorder which explains her/his deviance. Consequently, if we say that all those people who are not racist are deviant or have personality problems, we are certainly engaging in a dubious exercise. We may have accepted at face value the way in which members of a particular group stigmatize non-conformists. The point we are making is that you cannot explain the white anti-racist in South Africa simply in terms of inadequate socialization or personality problems.

What we are suggesting is that non-conformism may be seen as a consequence of a counter-socialization process in which some people manage to construct an alternative identity. Certainly, the chances are that most white South Africans will be racist, but there is no inevitability in this, only a relatively strong probability. Yet having argued that anti-racists are conceivable even in the most rigidly stratified racist societies, we might say 'so what?' Are we not falling into the trap we attempted to avoid earlier, namely, of defining racism as prejudice? Because if we engage in the numbers game by pointing to the proportion of non-racists to racists, we are thereby implying that racism is merely a function of the aggregation of prejudiced people. By inference, this would mean that if we could somehow reduce the number of prejudiced people, we would reduce and eventually eliminate racism.

In this connection, Wellman makes a traditional sociological point (Wellman, 1977). He argues that social scientists, including sociologists, have frequently started their analysis of racism from the premise that the elimination of prejudice will lead to the elimination of racism. It is as though racism is a form of belief open to rational argument. If people can be persuaded that their prejudices are misconceived, and have no basis in fact, they will readily be prepared to change their behaviour and give up their prejudices. But, as Wellman argues, if prejudice was all that was at stake there would really be no problem at all. All we have to do is to devise the appropriate socialization and educational strategies to ensure that children grow up with favourable attitudes to West Indians, Jews, and others. But prejudice is not an autonomous, psychological phenomenon.

> Sociologically it makes much more sense to anchor attitudes in social contexts and organization. Without an understanding of the structural context within which attitudes occur, we cannot grasp their meaning. Their importance is also exaggerated; it seems as though the attitudes 'cause' the structures. (Wellman, 1977, p.15)

In other words, racism is not discoverable in the feelings and attitudes of people, but in social structure. When Wellman asserts that 'prejudiced people are not the only racists in America' he means that racism is institutionalized and embedded in American society and culture. Hence, white children grow up as racists, not because of some mistaken beliefs and misplaced feelings, but because they discover the presence of racism.

Wellman's view of racism and prejudice contrasts sharply with that of Milner who sees the socialization process as being the crucial element in the acquisition of racist beliefs.

> When racism has taken root in the majority culture, has pervaded its institutions, language, its social intercourse and its cultural productions, has entered the very fabric of the culture, then the simple process by which a culture is transmitted from generation to generation — the socialization process — becomes the most important 'determinant' of prejudice. For then it reaches all sections of the population, including those who are neither objectively or subjectively threatened by black people, nor stand to gain anything by discrimination against them — in other words, those who have neither 'social structural' nor 'personality' reasons for prejudice. (Milner, 1983, p. 75)

The trouble with this argument is that racism is defined in cultural terms, and moreover, culture is seen as central to the socialization process. Yet a person who acquires racist beliefs and practices in South Africa does not do so only because white South African culture is racist; she/he does so because South African society is structured in such a way that it allows a minority to oppress and exploit a majority. To participate in white South African culture is to benefit simultaneously from the fact that one belongs to a dominant group. To be sure, not all white South Africans benefit equally from their privileged situation — there is obviously a great difference between the benefits accruing to the affluent middle-class and the working-class, but nevertheless, their collective position *vis à vis* the black majority is one in which they collectively enjoy the fruits of power.

So, when we say that racism is transmitted through socialization, we have to assume that racism is not simply a set of beliefs which people reproduce and internalize — but rather that the reproduction of these beliefs is tied into the reproduction of power relations. In Britain, for example, people learn they are black or white, not only in terms of stereotypes, but also in terms of their relative power and status. A black child in Brixton does not have to go very far to learn that she/he is not regarded and treated in the same way as a white child. Children are socialized into a set of social relationships, not only a culture; hence racism is not merely a cultural phenomenon — it is also an expression of the way in which certain groups are located in a society.

The Reaction to Racism

In our earlier discussion of reflexivity and gender negotiation, we examined the argument that gender is not constituted in a simple determinate manner, but is subject to tentativeness and counter-socialization. We took Goffman's notion of role distance as a benchmark in order to understand how both men and women could conceivably resist the demands made on them to conform to gender typifications. Can we use the same formulation to come to grips with racist typifications?

At one level we might want to refer to the way in which slaves were supposed to behave in the *ante bellum* South. The typical image we have of the slave's behaviour is that of a person who smilingly accepts the inevitability of her/his situation. The implication from the white person's point of view is that slaves were contented. Now from the perspective of a slave-owner, this perception of the slave as a smiling acceptor of her/his lot was obviously an added justification of slavery. It assumed that millions of men and women actually enjoyed being docile and passive. Historically, of course, the truth is completely different. There is a great deal of evidence that not only did slaves resist at the plantation level, but that they frequently rebelled on a larger scale (Genovese, 1975, pp.587–612)

Our concern here is more limited. Within the active expressions of resistance by slaves, we can also discern a further form of resistance which counters the assumption of passivity. The smiling face of acceptance is, from this viewpoint, merely the way in which the slave survives in a society in which her/his entire life is dominated by the whims of the slave-owner. Conformity therefore, is signalled by passivity and docility. It is a mask behind which the slave hides her/his feelings and reflexive resistance. Put differently, we can define the slave as a person who, even under extreme duress, did not always allow herself/himself to become the object that others believed her/him to be.

Slavery, a particularly savage system of oppression and exploitation, made its slaves victims. But the human beings it made victims did not consent to be just that: they struggled to make life bearable and to find as much joy in it as they could. Up to a point, even the harshest of masters had to help them to do so. The logic of slavery pushed the masters to try to break their slave's spirit and to reconstruct it as an unthinking and unfeeling extension of their own will, but the slaves own resistance to dehumanization compelled the masters to compromise in order to get an adequate level of work out of them. (Genovese, 1975, p.317)

It is in the tacit mocking of their oppressors, in their songs, in their religious practices, and in the subtle way in which they 'sassed' their masters that we can discover opposition and resistance. Indeed, it was only by resisting in this way that they managed to live through the slave experience. This is similar to something Goffman talks about when he discusses the manner in which inmates of institutions endeavour to handle institutional requirements. In appearing to conform, patients and inmates hide behind rules and regulations in order to retain an area of private space in which to hold on to an element of self-respect. In performing a role, in managing the self, people can (to a degree) resist complete absorption into an institution (Goffman, 1968). Granted that a slave plantation is not equivalent to a mental hospital, we can still discern resistance in the slaves' refusal to accept the white slave-owners view of her/his commodity status.

What is at issue here is the current preoccupation with identity. In various formulations, the claim is that racism has certain negative consequences for the way in which members of out-groups see and define themselves. It is believed that discrimination and oppression lead to low self-esteem, to a negative identity. The strong socialization thesis would postulate that those people who are reared as slaves, or are subjected to racial discrimination are likely to suffer from a sense of inadequacy as well as low self-esteem. The implication here is that discrimination has personality consequences. The discriminated come to believe that they are inferior and deserving of second-class status. This kind of thinking assumes that a person needs to have a reasonable degree of self-respect in order to function effectively as a social being. Those who are denied the opportunity to do so will be disadvantaged.

Negative identity, from this point of view, is dependent upon the evaluations and behaviour of others. The oppressed define themselves from the perspective of their oppressors. They come to believe that what their oppressor's say about them is, in fact, true. From early childhood, children pick up cues from their parents and others which shape their view of themselves, as being deficient in certain qualities and resources in comparison with other groups. For example, a black child growing up in an 'inner city' slum is not likely to be unaffected by the signs of poverty she/he observes in the neighbourhood. From the moment she/he can differentiate between black and white, the connection will be made between power and powerlessness. The poverty and the political powerlessness of the group that the child belongs to will register as a 'reality', as a condition of her/his existence in a society in which 'others' control scarce resources. Further experience will reinforce this negativity. The child will read books in which black and third world people are depicted in derogatory and condescending terms — she/he will watch biased television programmes and at school will be subjected to abuse from white children, and perhaps, from some of their teachers. Obviously, such a picture may be overdrawn, but it does highlight the experiences of Asian and West Indian children in British cities. But do these experiences entitle us to make any comments about their self-esteem? The kind of evidence used to support the low self-esteem hypothesis is derived from American experience, although it has received some kind of corroboration in the United Kingdon (Milner, 1975 and 1983).

This evidence is based on studies which purport to demonstrate that immigrant and minority children tend to show a marked preference for the values and culture of the dominant group (Clark and Clark, 1939).

The process starts from early chilhood, and evidence of its existence comes from many countries and many cultures . . . In the late thirties, the Clarks . . . published the first of a long series of studies demonstating that black children in the United States could be directly and objectively shown to have serious identity, identification and group preference problems already at the age of six or seven, or even earlier. The methods used by Clark and Clark, and in many subsequent studies consisted of presenting each child 'with a variety of dolls or pictures representing the various racial groups in the child's environment', and then asking the children a number of questions about which of the dolls they looked like, which one they would prefer to have for a friend, to play with, to be at school together, etc. It was found that the minority children (for example, the blacks in America, the Maoris in New Zealand, children of the various 'coloured' minorities in Britain) sometimes misidentified themselves in the tests (i.e. they said they were more like the white than the black doll) and that most of them 'preferred' in various tests the white to the other dolls. (Tajfel, 1978, p.10)

While there have been doubts about the validity of conclusions drawn about the child's mistaken identification with the majority group, it appears that subsequent studies have supported the notion that oppressed minority children prefer the phenotypical characteristics and way of life of the majority or dominant culture. In an extreme form, this would lead us to suppose that members of disadvantaged and oppressed groups will not only denigrate themselves, but they will also positively hate themselves. Jewish self-hatred, for example, has been a common enough theme in literature and philosophy. When Sartre wrote 'Anti-Semite and Jew', he argued that anti-Semitism defines the Jew. Sartre, of course, was writing in the context of the aftermath of Auschwitz. In concentration camps, victims accepted their victimage — they often accepted the stigma of inferiority and unworthiness. But most people do not live in concentration camps. To say that South Africa is a vast concentration camp, and that its black population are its inmates is to presume that millions of people define themselves negatively. Furthermore, it is not true that all concentration camp inmates passively allowed themselves to be led to the gas chambers. Some resisted, others maintained an element of self-respect.

To summarize the above: we have examined the argument and evidence that discrimination and racism have marked consequences for the way in which oppressed groups define themselves *vis à vis* the dominant group. The more vicious the oppression, the greater the likelihood that the oppressed will develop low self-esteem. Conversely, we would also have to assume that the dominant groups (the oppressors) are likely to exhibit high self-esteem. When stated like this, the whole exercise seems to become futile. Take for example, the case of a single child reared in a family in which she is continuously exposed to the derision and the ambiguity of her parents. Theoretically, we would expect that her experiences would indeed leave their mark — she would, so the theory predicts, define herself in negative terms. This is certainly what the strong socialization thesis would imply; but as we have repeatedly argued, this is to see socialization as a process which pre-defines a person's biography.

Accordingly, when we talk about the self-esteem of groups, it becomes very difficult to know what this means. Certainly, if a group is subjected to constant deprivation and discrimination, then it is probable that it may develop a collective view of itself as being powerless and inferior. Yet, if we look at the history of national liberation movements in South America, Asia, and Africa, and at recent Black American history, we discover an alternative version of identity which asserts the values of the oppressed group, minority or nation. The Black Power and Black Consciousness movements in the United States and South Africa have revamped the negative connotations of being black in a racist society. In other words, black identity is given a positive evaluation. Furthermore, this assertion of identity is not merely a rediscovery of a cultural past and present — it is also a political statement about the way in which black people should act in relation to white power structures. Hence, if we want to retain the concept of self-esteem, then we have to locate it in a collective framework in which oppressed groups struggle with their oppressors to secure reasonable access to scarce resources. This involves seeing identity in terms of group awareness, as an extension of the 'I' to include the 'We'. In general, the socialization argument is premised on the assumption that we only become social if we take on the characteristics of the group into which we are born. The question we have to ask in this connection is this: Does the mere fact of belonging to an oppressed group enter into the way in which a person will regard her/himself?

In the case of 'race' and ethnicity, the evidence of practitioners like Milner, Clark and others, that out-groups tend to devalue themselves and give esteem to dominant group values, is certainly not to be ignored. But if we take this evidence to its logical ending point, it leaves us with the image of passivity and docility; the implication being that when Jews, West Indians, Pakistanis define themselves, they always do so in reaction to others who impose their own definitions on the minority. Or alternatively, instead of a passive reaction, they may adapt a defensive posture in an attempt to bolster low morale. They may redefine their identity.

Ethnic redefinition is a reassertion of the values of a stigma-
tized group . . . . It contains not only a new identity but an
explanation of the original stigmatization; it thus deals explicitly with the attitude of the dominant group and offers an
explanation for it . . . . Because black ethnic redefinition is a
redefinition against the assumptions of white society, it is in
large measure still defined by these stereotypes. Rather than
deny the stereotype validity, redefinition accepts it and gives it
a positive value or plays rather uneasily with it, challenging
white society with a mirror of its own prejudices. (Littlewood
and Lipsedge, 1982, pp. 142–3)

In adapting a defensive posture by redefining identity, or in
re-emphasizing the history of its particular culture, an ethnic group
is reacting to the pressures of the dominant group. The implication
is that Pakistanis, West Indians, Jews, and others assert their dis-
tinctiveness, their history, because it is the only means to survive in
a hostile environment. But in seeing ethnic identity simply as a
response to racism, we may inadvertently deny the group its own
reality. And indeed, some race relations literature often appears to
foster the impression that migrant communities from the Caribbean,
for example, arrived in Britain without a distinctive culture of their
own. What culture they possessed was supposed to be derivative,
acquired from their exposure to slavery and British colonialism.
This experience was so traumatic that it completely robbed slaves of
their African past. Hence, Caribbean identity is conceived of as
being a production of slavery, as being a distorted image of English
or British culture. It is only after arriving in Britain that West
Indians find themselves having to invent an alternative identity,
after their experience of British racism.

The trouble with this formulation is that it replicates the strong
socialization thesis in an almost doctrinaire fashion. It assumes that
entire societies can be de-cultured; it also assumes that the oppressed group automatically internalizes the culture of its oppressor.
Furthermore, there is the additional implication of there being
something pathological and deviant in the kind of adaptation that the
migrant community is forced to make. (This last point is elaborated in
chapter 4).

Thus, while we believe that it is evident that racism and
discrimination do have profound consequences for minority and
out-groups, we do not subscribe to the view that racism is

responsible for the creation of their culture. We do not, in other words, accept the argument that Asians, West Indians, and others respond to racism in a hyper-passive way. Certainly racism wounds — it can often mutilate individual self-respect, but this is not the same thing as saying that it conditions an entire community's perception of itself. Moreover, what is left out of this image is the group's actual history. This history is not one in which passivity was the name of the game. Colonialism was not accompanied by the quiescent acceptance of the colonized — they were conquered, yes, but this did not mean they gave up resistance. Even slavery did not entail complete dehumanization. On the contrary, the evidence is that slave women and men resisted in all sorts of ways! In short, what we are maintaining here is that, although there appear to be strong forces at work in metropolitan societies which attempt to devalue the migrant group's past and present, we cannot assume that these forces do in effect achieve what they are assumed to achieve. We badly underestimate a group's potential for resistance, if we measure this potential in terms of factors like self-esteem.

The Simultaneous Acquisition of Racism and Sexism?

So far we have not discussed the possibility that racism and sexism are jointly mediated through the socialization process. Intuitively, it is very tempting to argue that children acquire their racism in more or less the same way as they acquire sexism. Certainly there is evidence that gender and 'race' stereotypes appear very early, but this is not equivalent to claiming that there is a necessary connection between them. After all, children acquire a whole set of categories and stereotypes at an early age.

In general, the claim that racism and sexism are intimately connected is made in the context of discussion about the nature of specific child-rearing practices. This discussion usually centres on the relationship between authoritarianism and personality. Crudely, this relationship can be stated like this: In a family in which a child is exposed to rigid and strict disciplinary practices, the child will tend to grow up with a personality structure that will directly reflect these practices. This proposition is frequently accompanied by a second proposition, namely that the authoritarian personality is produced in particular kinds of families, that is, they are located structurally. An early candidate for this role was the petit-bourgeois family (Fromm, 1942), especially the German petit-bourgeois family after the First World War. Later, the notion of the authoritarian family was exported to other settings, including the United States. The literature and controversy which this formulation produced has been enormous. Our concern here is to see whether or not the concept of authoritarianism can give us some kind of linkage between racism and sexism.

One of the problems we encounter is the fact that the authoritarian personality is regarded as a sick personality. In expressing hostility to Jews or Blacks, the authoritarian attempts to cope with her/his unresolved anxieties and ambiguities. In particular, the authoritarian is described (by Adorno *et al*, 1969) as a person who is incapable of coming to terms with uncertainty and ambiguity. The authoritarian, therefore, operates in a world in which everything is categorized in rigid dichotomies, them and us, etc.

> The theory was that in early childhood the potential fascist idealized his or her parents, which in later life gave rise to a need to idealize other figures of authority. No hostile feelings against parents, or any other legitimate authority, could be tolerated, and the negative feelings, which accompanied the outward idealization, had to be projected on to other targets, as did the desires of the id. Thus, ambivalence had to be repressed with the negative aspects directed outwards. In consequence, the authoritarian needed to experience the world in rigid categories — people or social groups were to be classed as wholly 'good' or wholly 'bad', and each had their alloted place in a strictly hierarchical perception of the world. The authoritarian's own repressed 'bad' feelings would then be projected on to inferior outgroups, such that it was always the Jews, or the blacks, or any other convenient scapegoat, who were sex-obsessed, violent, anti-social and so on. The authoritarian would be the last person to admit that such feelings may have arisen from the self. (Billig, 1982, p.105–6)

So, in becoming an authoritarian, the argument is, the child represses her/his feelings of ambivalence towards parents whom she/he is supposed to idealize and respect. But repression does not prevent this ambivalence towards parents from somehow being directed or projected outwards to an appropriate target or object.

All the authoritarian's rage and pent up hostility is focused on those groups, who are perceived as being threatening and dangerous. The male authoritarian (and it is usually the male in the literature) tends to be violently anti-homosexual, and decidedly rigid in his attitudes towards women.

As we indicated, the class position of a family is sometimes taken to be a measure of authoritarian tendencies. (Lower socio-economic status is supposedly correlated with authoritarianism) (Grabb, 1979). But does this correlation relate to the kind of child-rearing practices in working-class families? Are working-class families more authoritarian than middle-class families because of the way they socialize children? For example, if we observe the behaviour of young male working-class members of the National Front, and conclude that they are both sexist and racist (not unwarranted), do we immediately explain their behaviour in terms of their particular experience of socialization? What about the thousands of other young males who belong to left-wing groups? Are we to absolve them from racism and sexism? Highly unlikely. The fact that a large number of National Front supporters appear to be working-class does not entitle us to infer that they joined the National Front because of personality needs, or because they were brought up as authoritarians in working-class families. This is similar to claiming that National Socialism was simply an expression of the irrationality of the petit-bourgeoisie.

> Nazism cannot be explained by saying that its rise in the 1930's was due to the existence of large numbers of people who were unable to resolve their intra-psychic conflicts without projecting hostility onto convenient scapegoats. Similarly, the decline of Nazism as a social movement canot be attributed to the resolution of these . . . conflicts . . . Nazism did not just affect the Germans who had highly authoritarian personalities; non-authoritarians who were not even members of the Nazi party also fought for the Third Reich and failed to register any protest against the persecution of Jews. (Billig, 1976, in Milner, 1983, pp.33–34)

Undoubtedly, if we examined the membership of the National Front or the Nazi Party we would discover racism and sexism as the norm. But is it the norm because members all share the same personality and have been exposed to similar socialization? Or is it the norm because the membership is predominantly male? Earlier we looked at various accounts (Chodorow, 1978) of the way in which the socialization process not only damages women, but simultaneously, creates the conditions for the emergence of a male identity which resents women. Against this we argued that we cannot explain male power in terms of male psychology — to do so would reduce the whole problem of sexism to faulty socialization. It would seem to us that attempts to theorize authoritarianism in terms of pathological socialization is equally deficient, especially the argument that it is men who always seem to become pathological authoritarians. What is left out of these formulations is any consideration of the sociology of masculinity. While white men may be both racist and sexist, this does not enable us to understand the historicity of this fact; if racism and sexism are seen to be endemic to white male identity, then we can only account for this by examining the way in which this identity is constructed and reproduced in Western societies. Moreover, there may be other societies in which men are sexist, but not racist. For example, is it possible to talk of racism in African societies before the advent of European colonialism? This is a fundamental difficulty. We do not usually speak of racism outside the European context, and yet we know that before the period of European expansion Asian, American, and African societies engaged in warfare. They often embarked upon genocide, as well as enslaving rival groups.

> One recalls the more horrifying genocidal massacres, such as the terror of Assyrian warfare in the eighth and seventh centuries B.C., when many cities were razed to the ground and whole populations carried off or brutally exterminated; . . . or the destruction of Troy and its defenders and the carrying off into slavery of the women (as described in legendary accounts and the Greek tragedies which have come down to us); . . . But the razing of cities and the slaughter of peoples were not isolated episodes in ancient times. One has only to refer to accounts of the many genocidal conflicts in the Bible, and in the chronicles of Greek and Roman historians. (Kuper, 1981, p.11)

We use the Kuper quotation to remind us that ethnocentrism and genocide are not contemporary phenomena. Men have been engaged in the business of massacre and warfare for a very long time. And it is not only European men, but men everywhere. Certainly there is a great deal of evidence to document the fact that men waged war, enslaved others, raped and sexually abused entire communities of women, but this still does not make the case that they did all these things because of pathology. Nor does it make the associated case that this identity is the product of socialization practices which are continuously repeated across generations.

Accordingly, while we know that both racism and sexism are often acquired in early childhood, we cannot *a priori* demonstrate their apparent affinity. To say that the answer lies in the specific way men are socialized does not tell us why they are socialized in this way. Furthermore, there is enough evidence from anthropological sources to suggest that men are not invariably aggressive. The answer presumably cannot lie in the socialization process *per se*. If the family is the site in which men first begin to resent women, and if the family is also the site in which they acquire racism, this still does not entitle us to claim that racism and sexism are inevitably connected through socialization. There is also an additional difficulty. It is not only men who become racists — women are just as likely to acquire their racism in the family. Hence, when we talk about racism, we are not only pointing to men — we are talking about whites as racists, not a particular gender.

It may be objected that women acquire their racism in a setting which is dominated by men — they become racists because the ruling ideology (masculinity) is also racist. Women learn to be racists in a society in which racism is naturalised as a component of masculinity. In Nazi Germany, for example, the State's emphasis on the family and motherhood, on the role of women as producers and breeders of pure Aryan types was premissed on the assumption that women are instruments of the nation's will. But it is not only Nazism and Fascism which emphasise motherhood and the family as central to the health of the nation — we can find the same ideas expressed in the practice of liberal, social democratic, and conservative politics in Britain, Europe, and the United States. The family is regarded as a natural site for the inculcation of 'national' values. In staying at home, a woman as a mother contributes to the strengthening of the nation — she becomes a part of the great struggle against 'aliens', 'strangers', and 'foreigners' whose very presence in our society constitutes a threat to our survival. Indeed, the family is seen as the nation in microcosm — its cohesion and its well-being constitute the bedrock on which politicians construct their appeal to the electorate (Barker, 1981, p.44).

It may be, therefore, that the connection between racism and sexism is made in the family, because of the way in which the family is identified with the state or nation. The family mediates the ideologies and values of the state — it reproduces the ideology of the naturalness of the distinction between 'them' and 'us', and it reaffirms the primacy of masculinity.

Hence, it could be suggested that the relationship between racism and sexism should not be treated as if it were something internal to family dynamics. Socialization therefore is not just the concern of those immediately involved — it is also a collective relationship in which the state, class, and ideology profoundly influence the socializers and the socialized. In Britain today, the fact that most white children acquire their racism early, is not simply due to the family *per se* — it is also related to the fact that the family is a collective form whose members are enmeshed in collective relationships. Racism and sexism, accordingly, enter the child's world not simply because the child has a racist and sexist for a father, but because both her/his parents are themselves part and parcel of a network of reciprocities which influence their particular constructions of the world. When we talk about British or American society as being both racist and sexist, we are not thereby claiming that this is so because everybody has been socialized in the same way — racism and sexism exist not because of socialization — on the contrary, socialization reproduces what is already there.

In this chapter we have provided an overview of socialization in so far as it effects racism and sexism. In so doing, we objected to the way in which the strong socialization thesis implies that both gender and ethnic identity are determined by uncontrollable external forces. It is our contention that, despite the strong forces lined up against out-groups and women in our society, this does not mean that these forces cannot be resisted or overcome.

We also looked very peripherally at some of the evidence purporting to establish the relevance of child-rearing practices for the joint acquisition of racism and sexism. Although we rejected the argument that they were correlated with the reproduction of authoritarian personality syndromes from generation to generation, we did not reject out of hand the notion that families may reproduce the ideology of an authoritarian social structure. In other words, we would want to claim that socialization is simultaneously a collective and interpersonal process in which both individuals and collectivities mutually reproduce and construct what is already there. And what is already there are families and other institutions which reproduce both racism and sexism. Accordingly, it is in this respect that we would suggest that oppression and socialization are closely related. Some of these issues will be discussed in the next chapter.

4 The Family as a Site of Oppression

We have suggested several times in the previous chapters the significance of the family for understanding socialization processes. The family is the place where psychic structure is formed and experience characterized, named and moulded. Within the family parents, but primarily mothers, prepare their children psychologically and emotionally for the world outside. Not only are gender and ethnic identity acquired within the family but the major figure to be found there is woman, in her role of wife and mother. It is hardly surprising, therefore, that those who are interested in analysing woman's position in society, and accounting for her inferiority and subordination, have focused primarily on the family to provide them with answers. For many feminists the family constitutes the site of women's oppression. It is by looking in the first instance to the family, that we can understand woman's exclusion from other areas of social life.

Similarly, those who are concerned with the position of minority groups in society have also turned to the family for explanations. However, the emphasis here has been rather different. Instead of focusing on the coercive aspects of the family, as do feminists, the literature mainly concentrates on the supposedly problematic aspects of minority group households. In claiming to locate deficiencies in these, it is suggested that they can be used to account for 'problems' in minority group behaviour. Thus, 'identity problems', 'vandalism', and 'educational failure' have all been described as being caused by pathological family structures.

In this chapter we will examine the thesis that the family constitutes the foundation of woman's oppression. More specifically, we will address the question as to what it is about the family which might be considered oppressive and whether existing approaches to its analysis adequately comprehend the consequences of this for women. We will challenge the static and ethnocentric picture of the family which is often presented, and argue that it is partly through this idealized portrayal that sexism and racism are reproduced.

The Politics of the Family

Most of those who have analysed women's oppression within the family, as a specific structure, have done so from some kind of Marxist perspective. In saying this, we mean that the writers have consciously utilized a materialist rather than an idealist framework and have attempted to develop their theories by adopting the concepts of Marx's political economy. The vast majority have also begun their work by critiquing Engels' account of the privatized family (Engels, 1972). This sees the family as a product of private property, which will cease to exist once the relations of production which brought it into being have been abolished with the demise of capitalism.

Engels' view is rightly regarded as being functionalist, and having little empirical foundation, since there is no evidence of a breakdown of the nuclear family form in any of those societies which have made the transition to 'socialism'. Most Marxist feminist accounts attempt to explore the relationship between the family and the relations of production in society, in the hope of reformulating Engels' very mechanistic approach. In addition, it is claimed that Engels insufficiently explored the significance of woman's activities in the home, and that he failed to question the sexual division of labour and the consequences of such a division for women. These criticisms provide the major springboard for subsequent Marxist and Marxist feminist developments in the analysis of the family. However, to say this is not to imply a necessary consensus among the various protagonists, since the resulting accounts differ substantially in both emphasis and political implication. From the vast amount of literature that has been generated, there seem to us to be five major ways in which the question of women's oppression and the family has been tackled.

The first of these approaches takes the family as *an identifiable and distinct sphere of activity* and considers its relationship to the mode of production in contemporary capitalist society. It argues that the whole relationship of the family to the productive enterprise has changed radically with the rise of capitalism. Prior to capitalism, and in its early stages, the family household as a whole was the basic economic unit for the production of goods and services. All family members, including women and children, contributed to the maintenance of the household. By the nineteenth century, however, the family had been stripped of its many productive functions and the development of the factory system, together with increasing industrialization, had established the economy and the family as separate spheres. As Zaretsky says, the logic of capitalist development removed labour and the basic processes of commodity production from the private efforts of individual families to centralized large-scale units (Zaretsky, 1976). Thus, production was transferred from the family to separate economic institutions of work. The significance of this bifurcation for women is to be found in the synonymous creation of two separate spheres: the public and the private. According to Dorothy Smith, domestic activity becomes relegated to the private familial sphere and women have a place only in this private domestic arena (Smith, 1975-6). Men, on the other hand, enter the public sphere of work as the breadwinner, and are able to move between this area of activity and that of the private. It is argued, therefore, that these two spheres of activity and the designation of one as female and the other as male, is a creation of capitalism. For Smith, the 'externalization of the productive process in the capitalist enterprise . . . which alienates the worker alienates also the women, although in a different way'. (Smith, 1975-6, p.57), and Zaretsky corroborates: 'The housewife emerged, alongside the proletarian — the two characteristic labourers of developed capitalist society.' (Zaretsky, 1976, p.64). Woman's particular oppression is to be understood in terms of her exclusion from waged work, which is a consequence of changes in the family structure brought about by capitalism. Her location in the private female sphere is oppressive, because it keeps her out of the economy and production. It is being placed in the one arena rather that the other which is oppressive and not anything particular to the operation of the privatized family itself. The implication of both Zaretsky's and Smith's arguments is that what is required politically is a reorganization of production, including women's activities in the home, which will negate the destructive separation between public and private as distinctive areas.

The second appproach to women's oppression regards the family as *relatively autonomous from the mode of production and focuses on the ways in which female consciousness is generated within it.* A structuralist interpretation of Marx is used, which sees the social totality as an internally complex structure of various layers and levels, in all sorts of relations of determination and independency. These various layers, (of which the family is one expression), have their own autonomous development but only within limits, since the economy is determinant in the last instance. Psychoanalytic accounts of female psychology are used to explore the genesis of female consciousness since, it is claimed, these are theoretically consistent with the writers' versions of structuralism. Juliet Mitchell, for example, uses the work of Freud, while Annette Kuhn borrows from that of the more contemporary theorist, Jacques Lacan (Mitchell, 1974; Kuhn, 1978). They attempt to demonstrate how male domination becomes psychically represented in woman's thoughts and feelings and thus part of her gendered sexual identity — how women are mentally as well as physically controlled. The focus is on those structures of female consciousness which can account for her readiness to succumb to male power, particularly the mother-father-child triad within the patriarchal nuclear family. Female, (and male), psychology, within such a structure, are determined by the significance attributed to the penis and the ways in which this is symbolically internalized and given meaning. For Kuhn, the family is defined in terms of property relations between husbands and wives and the consequences of these relations for everyday activity. It is also defined as a set of psychic relations which reproduce subordination and domination in individual consciousnesses. Thus, it is particularly through an analysis of the psychic aspects of patriarchy that the continued reproduction, and apparent intransigence, of women's oppression is to be understood.

Thirdly, there are those analyses which focus on *one particular aspect* of women's familial position, (housework, mothering, child-bearing), to argue that these form the major foundation of her oppressed condition. For example, Shulamith Firestone focuses on woman's child-bearing function as the material basis of her oppression (Firestone, 1972). Now it might seem strange to be including Firestone's work here, when the other approaches have some, if rather differing, associations with Marxism. However, commentators have continually overlooked the fact that Firestone herself explicitly acknowledges the use of a Marxist historical materialism, whilst substituting the dynamic of sex class for that of economic class.

Firestone claims, not just that 'procreative reproduction' forms the basis upon which other aspects of woman's oppression have been built, but that it is the foundation upon which economic class and 'race' divisions have also been moulded. She argues that procreation is the source of the historical, and continuing, conflict between the sexes and that the differing forms of the biological family unit have been structured in the interests of men, to ensure the continued reproduction of the species. Thus, male and female constitute two antagonistic sex classes. For Firestone, it is only when women can control childbirth for themselves, (through artifical reproduction, contraception, abortion, etc.), that the basis for male exploitation and oppression disappears. The family unit, constructed to facilitate male control of female biology, would also be rendered redundant.

On the other hand, the various contributors to the Domestic Labour Debate see housework, as it is constituted under the socio-economic relations of capitalism, as the cornerstone of women's oppression (Malos, 1980). In attempting to elucidate this, they site the household within the capitalist economic system and address themselves to the complicated problem of the nature of the relationship between capitalism and housework. The question which occupies them is, what sort of value, if any, is produced by the housewife during housework? This conundrum has led to much protracted argument which it is not necessary to summarize here. The point is that, despite disagreements on the exact meaning of the work of the housewife relative to capital, there *is* agreement that the housewife works for the maintenance of capital, rather than simply for her individual family. It is this job of doing unpaid domestic service to the benefit of capital which constitutes her oppression. For example, it is argued that unpaid domestic labour helps to keep wages down since, if workers had to pay someone to do it for them, a massive redistribution of wealth would be required. For women then, it is their status of unpaid houseworker under capitalism which forms the basis of their subjugation.

The fourth approach, that of *Christine Delphy*, also focuses on *housework*, although from a completely different theoretical perspective (Delphy, 1977). Delphy designates her work materialist, rather than Marxist, since she claims that the latter cannot account for the oppression common to all women and focuses, not on the oppression of women as such, but on the consequences of this for the proletariat.

Delphy postulates the existence of two modes of production, the industrial and the domestic. The first gives rise to capitalist exploitation. The second gives rise to patriarchal exploitation. She refers to women's position in the family as comparable to serfdom. Marriage is a labour contract. The husband appropriates the labour power of his wife in a similar manner of the capitalist to the worker. In return for being kept, she provides unpaid domestic services. The conditions of work are not under her control but his and depend on his wealth and good will.

> For the same work (for example, the rearing of three children) the wife of a business executive receives as much as ten times the benefits received by the wife of a worker. Conversely, for the same benefits a wife may furnish very different quantities and kinds of services, depending on the needs of her husband. (Delphy, 1977, p.14)

Moreover, women who are in paid employment are able to finance their own keep and perform domestic work for husbands for no return at all. Therefore, according to Delphy, unpaid housework in the family is the material basis of women's oppression. However, we should note that this formulation is different from that of the Domestic Labour Debate. Whereas the latter approach analyses housework and woman's position in relationship to capital, Delphy regards housework as the material foundation of the system of patriarchy, whereby men dominate and control women. It can, therefore, be analysed completely separately from the capitalist economic structure.

Finally, there are those who in looking at women's position in the family uncover *contradictory* rather than unproblematic relationships. Heidi Hartmann, for example, sees female oppression as originating from man's control over her labour power (Hartmann, 1979). This control is maintained, she claims, through woman's exclusion from access to essential productive resources, (for example, jobs that pay reasonable wages), and via the restriction of their sexuality. Both these things are achieved through monogamous heterosexual marriage. However, Hartmann suggests that conflicting interests often arise between men *qua* men and men *qua* capitalists. For instance, although most men might want their women at home in the family to personally service them, some, in their role as capitalists, might want most women (though probably not their own) to work in the wage labour market. On this basis, Hartmann believes that the partnership between patriarchy and capitalism is not as harmonious as it might sometimes appear. Antagonisms and conflicts can arise. Similarly, Irene Bruegel has described contradictions between the family and capitalism, concluding that the latter tends to both destroy the family and maintain it. Its relationship to the family is therefore contradictory (Bruegel, 1978).

Our purpose in outlining these five approaches to women's oppression in the family has not been to score subsequently academic points by subjecting each to detailed criticism. Indeed, we feel that all have pushed the parameters of debate way beyond that to be found in the sociology of family literature of the 1950s and 1960s. However, we are concerned that certain assumptions in the material discussed prevent particular questions regarding women's position in the family from being addressed. For example, all the writers take the nuclear family, two adult parents and their children, as their model and most assume that such a form is a product of industrial capitalism. But it is by no means certain that this is the case. Some historians argue that the nuclear family was the pre-dominant family form in the West long before capitalism, while others maintain that there has never been one predominant struc-ture but rather a diversity of forms. While the fact that capitalism gradually took the most obvious aspects of production away from the home does not appear to be in dispute, it has not been estab-lished that capitalism altered the family form as such.

Although the significance of women's familial activities changed with industrialization, since it no longer directly contributed to production, the fact that it was women who performed domestic work did not alter. Quite clearly, the nature of domestic tasks does change over time. We can only properly talk about housework and child-rearing, for example, when people are living in reasonable accommodation and have the money and resources to make such things as cleaning and childhood worthwhile and meaningful. However, the point we are making is that, whatever the specific requirements families have had historically for the servicing, maintenance and emotional care of houshold members, it is women who have been given overall responsibility for them. It seems quite clear to us therefore, that the explanation as to why women are given these tasks must lie somewhere other than in the capitalist economic system, although we can happily concur that this system may make use of, and gain benefits from, woman's particular family position. In saying this we are, by implication, rejecting all arguments which wish to explain woman's position in the family and her general oppression solely in terms of some specific relationship to the mode of production. Part of our reason for asserting this, is a concern that such accounts are not able to focus on the male-female elements in a relationship and the possibility that this might generate structures of power.

A further consideration is that, in our view, society has been able to accommodate a range of household and living arrangements. That it still does so, is illustrated by such examples as the peasant household system of rural France, gypsy families and that much reviled Western phenomenon of the single-parent family. More importantly, there are the family systems of so-called ethnic groups. In the United States we find the close-knit ties of Italians and the supposedly matriarchal form of the Afro-Americans. In Britain there is the self-contained kinship structure of the Asian population and, so many have claimed, its opposite form in the loosely framed Afro-Caribbean household. In South Africa, a familial identity is retained by the black population, although the individual members are likely to be physically separated by pass laws and by adult wage earners working in areas away from 'home', which is in the specially designated reservations.

Not only do all these family forms differ in organization, but it cannot be assumed that women's involvement in them is everywhere the same. Our concern is that in taking the white nuclear family structure only, the ideal form of which applies to just a minority of the population in Britain and the United States, we ignore the differing circumstances in which women, particularly minority group women, may find themselves. And, of course, this means glossing over their different experiences of oppression too. To return to the South African example, the major employers of black female labour in that country are white women who buy in domestic servants (Cock, 1980). Black women perform a majority of the domestic tasks, especially the most menial, thus freeing their female employers for other more social activities. It is clear therefore that one of the major beneficiaries of black domestic work in South Africa is white woman. This situation is further compounded since, due to time spent travelling and the fact that servicing the white woman's family involves working long hours, the black woman is forced to neglect her own children and family members.

The paradox is that in South African society the mother has a pivotal role — for whites. This role is made possible by the work of black women who, in doing it, are forced to jeopardize their own maternal status. The experiences of the white and black woman in South African are therefore very different. We are not arguing that the latter is oppressed and the former free, since there are many ways in which the white female is excluded, on grounds of sex, from equal participation in South African society. In fact, in this society she has a relationship of structured dependency with her husband, on whom she is reliant for material and financial resources and from whom she derives any social status. Not only is she dependent on her husband but she is expected to be deferential to him also. However, it is obviously difficult to discuss the situations of white and black women in the same terms and it is essential that we become aware of the potentially racist implications of doing so.

Finally, in much of the literature women are seen as so synonymous with family life that they virtually become the family. However, men live in these families also and their relationships with their wife (and children), and to her domestic activities should also be explored. The Domestic Labour Debate, for example, assumes that the houseworker is female, but fails to specify the nature of the tasks she performs. Although all the evidence unequivocally demonstrates that women are responsible for the running of the household and most of its day-to-day tasks, it is apparent that men do undertake some activities and are prepared to do some child care. We must not overestimate these contributions, since it is clear that most men merely 'help' and avoid the dirtiest, most menial and repetitive tasks. In addition, the amount of time they actually spend helping is relatively small. Still, they are there and this is something which a lot of the material neglects to mention, let alone analyse. Similarly, the position of women who do not have families, in the senses discussed here, is ignored. The literature overwhelmingly focuses on heterosexual women who are, or have been, married, and who therefore are likely to have children, if not always husbands, to care for. But what about women who are not married? What about young and adolescent girls, single women, women living on their own or with others? If woman's oppression is structured by her position in the family, as wife, mother and houseworker, does this mean that those women not in this position are not oppressed? We will be returning to this question at a later stage in the chapter.

The Politics of Public and Private

We have already seen how the separation of production from the home has been described, by some writers, as creating a split between public and private spheres. However, Smith and Zaretsky are not the only theorists to make use of this distinction. The division between public and private has been used by many feminists, as a metaphor to express the limitations placed on women by having to operate within the restrictions of domestic life. The implication is not just that there are distinctive zones for male and female activities but that man has the whole of the public world, outside of the family, at his behest, whereas woman is confined to a very limited sphere of influence. Women are excluded from decision-making processes and from the formal, political sphere. This exclusion is itself regarded as political, since its consequence is to prevent women from exercising control in matters significant to them. Men, it is said, command the arenas of power.

There are three major ways in which the politics of public and private have been approached. The first of these concentrates on a division between activities, particularly between those which occur within the family and those associated with the operation of the economy (Zaretsky, 1976; Smith, 1975-6). Such a distinction assumes that the family does not itself have a clearly defined productive role. Thus, it is described in terms of a variety of dichotomies: production/reproduction; production/non-production; non-work (home)/work. The production/reproduction distinction has raised problems, since the literature often fails to spell out precisely what reproduction involves. It is possible to distinguish between reproduction that contributes to: the generational replenishment of society's members through child-bearing; the daily maintenance of family members through feeding, clothing and generally keeping them in good working order, together with the sexual servicing of men; the continuation and legitimation of the social relations of patriarchy and/or capitalist production, through the socializing of children and maintenance of the family structure.

The production/non-production distinction assumes that the

family operates only as a unit of consumption. The housewife's relation to the wider economy is merely that of consumer. Consumption of commodities produced elsewhere is one of her defining roles. However, such an account is not unproblematic. For example, although research suggests that women are the major consumers in Western society, this does not necessarily mean that decisions about consumption are solely under their control. The production/consumption distinction, by focusing on the household as the unit of analysis, ignores relationships within the household. Like traditional economics, it does not invade the privacy of the family to ask how decisions are made. Because relationships within the home are disregarded, the household in fact acts as a disguise for male authority since women normally have the power to implement decisions but not to make them. It would be wrong, therefore, to see consumption as subject to female direction only, and as a source of female autonomy.

Other writers have suggested that woman's domestic work *is* in fact productive. For example, Christine Delphy has indicated that unpaid work performed by women in the home, where the home is part of a farm, small retail business or small craft workshop, can make a significant, though hidden, contribution to the unit's productivity (Delphy, 1977). She also points out the absurdity of treating the manufacture of something like flour as productive, when the final act of making it into something edible might not be so regarded. Yet we cannot consume flour and the baking of a cake, for instance, is the final culmination of a series of processes. Delphy suggests that it is absurd to introduce a break in this process, making some activities productive and some not.

Others have maintained that the family is really a small factory combining capital goods, raw materials and labour to clean, feed and otherwise produce useful commodities (Berk, 1980). This framework acknowledges the existence and importance of production in the home where, it is argued, time and market goods are combined to produce commodities that are immediate sources of utility. Such commodities can take various forms from a made bed, a cooked meal, to a disciplined child. The major point is that the family is not just a unit of consumption, it is productive too.

It is important to note that this does not mean binding the family to the capitalist mode of production in some kind of mechanistic fashion. Rather, it is to indicate that it is impossible to make a sharp distinction between family and economy and, by analogy, home and work. Feminists have been pointing out for some time that, if numbers of hours occupied and arduous nature of tasks were taken into account, housework would quite clearly be seen to be work. However, its invisibility and supposedly unproductive status have prevented it from being seen as such. Before industrialization, activities such as keeping animals, making clothes, preparing food, and growing vegetables had economic value since they were performed to satisfy household needs. This kind of work was indistinguishable from women's other household and productive chores (Tilly and Scott, 1978). Thus, during the seventeenth and eighteenth centuries, the term 'work' encompassed all of these activities. To use subsequently the term 'work' to refer only to wage-earning occupations ignores the implicitly economic nature of women's domestic and reproductive tasks. Activities previously regarded as work are now excluded, by a somewhat arbitrary definition of work as concerned only with waged labour. The absurdity of this is underlined by the example that a housewife making a meal is not performing an economic activity, whereas she would be if hired to cook a similar meal in a restaurant. Similarly, whereas the housework performed by a housewife is considered a labour of love, the same chores carried out by a domestic servant are regarded as an example of work. This obscures the fact that the domestic tasks women perform, and have always performed for their families, constitute useful and valuable, if unpaid, work.

   A second way of conceptualizing the private/public distinction has been to focus on the intimate personal and affective dimension of the former compared to the impersonal, rational, and unemotional characteristics of the latter. The family has supposedly become, to coin Lasch's phrase, a haven in a heartless world, a retreat for men enabling them to escape from the ruthless alienation of the industrial world outside (Lasch, 1977). The family exists as a separate sphere of personal fulfilment, where women have particular responsibility for ensuring love, happiness, security, and emotional well-being for other family members. The very privatized nature of the modern household adds an intensity and significance to its patterns of relationships. However, in scrutinizing the details of woman's privatized state, feminists have opened up its political dimension. It is shown that the personal is political and hence just as significant for social and political analysis as any other sphere of life. It is not just about the state and parliament, parties and elections (Coleman, 1982). If politics is about the exercise of influence and power, and the mechanisms through which these are transmitted, then it exists in all groups and organizations — even the family. Although it is usual to regard relationships between individuals as purely personal, this overlooks the fact that they are social as well, that is structured in part by factors that exist outside the immediate relationship. As the Redstockings Manifesto explains:

> Because we have lived so intimately with our oppressors, in isolation from each other, we have been kept from seeing our personal suffering as a political condition. This creates the illusion that a woman's relationship with her man is a matter of interplay between two unique personalities, and can be worked out individually. In reality, every such relationship is a *class* relationship, and the conflicts between individual men and women are political conflicts that can only be solved collectively. (quoted in Coleman, 1982, p.22)

Thus, there are relations of power and influence between men and women and hence within the family, sexual and personal relations. No part of the private sphere can escape. This is the area known as sexual politics. The two sexes confront each other, and one is able to control the other through various acts of power, influence, and authority. It is possible to analyse the construction of femininity in terms of sexual politics. Foreman sees femininity, with its emphasis on living through personal relations, as a product of the public/private split (Foreman, 1977). She argues that such meaning is constructed by men so that women can provide them with relief from the industrial world. Men may struggle to succeed in the public world of business and the factory but they unequivocally rule in the home. This is achieved by relegating women to the sphere of emotionality, where they 'cannot escape the intimate oppression of being foils for men' (Barrett, 1980, p.192).

A third focus has been on the geographical or spatial dimension of the public/private dichotomy. This implies that whereas women are physically confined to home life, men are much more free to explore the public parameters outside. We can see this in a number of ways. For example, parents are more prepared to let sons roam away from home, while fear of sexual molestation means daughters' activities are limited to those that can be performed in or near the domestic environment. Similarly, research on housework suggests that men are more likely to perform sporadic outside jobs such as putting out the rubbish, cleaning the outside of windows, mowing the lawn, while women do the everyday inside chores.

One of the most powerful arguments concerning the inside/outside dimension is to be found in Dominique Poggi and Monique Coormaert's analysis of the city being off-limits to women (Poggi and Coormaert, 1974). They point out that the streets, parks, and riversides of cities are accessible to women only if they exercise discretion. This is because the public area of the city is controlled by men and it is dangerous for women to stray from certain areas or refuse to make the expected detours. The area outside the family is dangerous to women. They can be followed, hustled, and raped, so that only a woman who is immoral, looking for trouble or mad would want to leave the protection of her family at night. As the authors say: 'Isn't her place beside her husband and children, in a good home, proof that she is sexually and morally balanced?' (Poggi and Coormaert, 1974, p.11). However, the daytime also has its risks: 'What woman, whatever social category she belongs to, hasn't felt uneasy about walking along certain streets, about crossing bridges at certain hours of the day or night?' (Poggi and Coormaert, 1974, p.11). Even during the day, certain streets, certain parks, certain areas have to be avoided for moral, physical, and other safety reasons. The only way that a woman can gain access to some parts of urban areas is if she is accompanied by, and therefore protected by, a man. The irony of this has not been lost on feminists who point out that it takes a man in the role of husband, father or boyfriend to protect women from harassment by other men. There is, though, another way in which women can take advantages of city facilities. This is when they are accompanied by children or performing one of the other domestic tasks assigned to them. Then they are not in the city for themselves, but for others. They are sitting with the children in the park, picking them up from school or shopping, often for other family members. Thus, even though women without paid employment might appear more mobile and ambulatory than their employed counterparts, male or female, their access to areas is limited by their domestic role. For Poggi and Coormaert, the fact that all women have restricted use of the city creates a common denominator between them. Women of all social categories are affected. Their only guaranteed space is inside, in the home. Their private life is devised so as to compensate for their exclusion from equal participation with men in the city life outside.

We have seen how the public/private distinction has exposed the political basis of women's lives in the family. It draws attention to their predominantly domestic role, its privatized nature and the consequences of these for women in personal and physical terms. However, it is also clear that the use of public and private as a sharp dichotomy is somewhat problematic. The discussion of production and consumption, for example, indicates the economic significance of domestic labour and the fact that it should be regarded as work.

In our view, part of the confusion here lies in the need to make a distinction between public and private as an empirical description of women's place in society, and its use in analysis. More specifically, whilst it is clear that women experience the world in terms of such a split (hence its significance in feminist thinking), it is not so apparent that such a clean-cut separation aids understanding of women's familial position. There is a difference between acknowledging the conditions under which women work in the home as privatized and the judgement that this means they must be analysed in isolation from, and as if unaffected by, other social relations. The analysis of the private realm has itself to be 'de-privatized' before we can begin to understand its real nature.

It seems obvious to us, for example, that what goes on in the family is to a significant extent publically defined. Thus, it is definitionally a heterosexual institution and the fact that women are materially (also socially and emotionally), dependent on their men is enshrined in social policy. Moreover, we only have to turn to advertising and popular entertainment to find that women should wash clothes whiter than white, and feed their children a certain brand of baked beans, while for men to attempt any domestic activity is a winning recipe for farce. However, the present construction of the family form ensures that such public definitions are easily incorporated into its everyday operations. Part of the reason for this is that, although men control the public sphere, they control the private as well, and it is clearly in their interest to ensure that the family continues to operate to their advantage. Although woman's place is in the home, it is the man of the house who exercises overall control and responsibility. Imray and Middleton have documented how husbands control what food is bought, when it is served, how furniture is arranged, how much leisure a wife has, what sort of family holiday is taken, etc. (Imray and Middleton, 1982). Despite changes in the content of the relationship between husband and wife, any egalitarianism in the home, let alone female autonomy, is more apparent than real. In some circumstances an individual woman can gain power *vis à vis* a particular husband — but more power is not the same as equal power. The really vital decisions about the nature of a woman's place (its location, whether to sell it) are taken by husbands, not wives. Bell and Newby have referred to this as the deferential dialectic.

> The home represents, so to speak, the spatial framework within which the deference of wife to husband operates. The encouragement of ideologies of the home and home-centredness enables the identification of the wife with her husband's superordinate position to increase by emphasizing a common adherence to territory, a solidarity of place. A woman's 'place' is therefore in the home, partly because to seek fulfilment outside the home could threaten to break down the ideological control which confinement within it promotes. (Bell and Newby, 1976, p.160)

Thus, we are not just talking about a complementary sexual division of labour here, but the exercise of authority and power. Although women inhabit the private sphere it is men who control it and of course they may resort to violence or rape to do so. As Goode remarks:

> Because people have been socialised to accept the family structure in which they live, and because they take that social structure for granted, they do not test whether force would be applied if they challenged it. They know in advance that they would fail. In most families the structure is not overthrown, because it is viewed as unalterable or, at best, the only real alternative. The rebellious child or wife knows that the father or husband is stronger, and can call upon outsiders who will support that force with more force. (Goode, 1971)

The husband then, has power vested in him by the public sphere to control the behaviour of his wife and children — or not — in whichever way he wishes.

Under these circumstances, it seems to us that the term private, with its connotations of seclusion and privacy, is something of a misnomer. For what is being described here is a location where people with different interests and activities often, though not inevitably, come into conflict with each other. Thus, rather than being privatized, women are more likely to be living in situations of isolation, tension, and conflict. Such solitariness is underlined by the state's, and its various agencies', refusal to intervene in domestic matters to prevent women being abused by their men. It is small wonder then that terms such as 'house arrest' and 'prison' have been used by feminists to describe women's familial location.

However, we once again come up against the problem that this emphasis on public/private is ethnocentric and more appropriate to some, particularly white, sections of North American and European society. Anthropological material, on the other hand, indicates that there is no absolute distinction between these two spheres. Instead, cross-cultural evidence suggests that privacy should be viewed as a continuum, with something regarded as private to an individual or family until it gradually turns into its opposite, public designation. Moreover, the parameters shift depending on its cultural context and meaning (Sciama, 1981). Thus, the definitions of public and private, and what they mean in terms of the lives and experiences of women themselves, cannot be regarded as absolute. There is a tendency in feminist literature to assume some kind of universal distinction, implying that women from cultures which are more obviously sex-segregated than our own are somehow more deprived and oppressed than their European and North American counterparts. But, as Rosaldo says, whereas it is relatively easy to identify the domestic sphere of the white suburban housewife and oppose it to the public and social world of industry, business and prestige, this is much more difficult for other cultures (Rosaldo, 1974). She discusses, for example, the Mbuti lean-tos, which are hardly separated at all from the life of the community, and the Iroquis long-houses which hold several families and are themselves a kind of public and social arena.

The structure of the domestic group and the degree of privacy associated with it are, therefore, highly varied. Although purdah in Hindu culture restricts women's activities and contact *vis à vis* men, the traditional emphasis on living with husband's parents, his brothers and their wives, means the presence of a female community which provides help and support in child care and other domestic chores. Certainly such situations are not without tension, but the public/private boundary in this instance clearly does not render women privatized and isolated with their children, as is the tendency in the Western world. Additionally, as Rosaldo has said, the very symbolic and social conceptions that appear to set women apart from men and circumscribe their activities, can be used by them as a basis for female solidarity and worth. Such arrangements are to be found among the Iroquis, and in the prestigious female political and religious societies of western Africa. After all, when men live apart from women they cannot completely control them, and may unwittingly provide them with the symbols and social resources on which to build a society of their own (Rosaldo, 1974). Such cultures only give women control within a specified autonomy, since men still exercise overall power. However, it is illuminating to contrast the situation of the woman restricted by purdah to an all-female environment, with that of the privatized white woman whose family position separates her from female friends, neighbours, and even relatives. It seems impossible to simply state that the former is more oppressed than the latter.

We would argue then, that the public/private distinction is more usefully regarded as a culturally constructed continuum which gives rise to different patterns of male power and control. We are not disagreeing that this power and control appear to be widespread, but suggest that it is expressed in different ways which have differing consequences for women's everyday existence. Although seeing women's oppression by men as largely defined through their domestic and familial location, we are also aware that there are contexts, particularly where groups are subjected to racist attack, in which the family can provide protection. The black family can provide space and security away from racial harassment and supply emotional and material support for regeneration and resistance. Thus, the black family of the American slave system has been seen as the source of such support as has the black family of South African society. There, home is elevated to a place of refuge, where dignity can be maintained against the humiliations of slavery and apartheid. Similarly in the United States and Britain, black writers have spoken of Afro-Caribbean and Asian families as havens from the heartless world of a white racist society. It is clear, therefore, that as black women have said, the family is not the unequivocal site of oppression that some feminists assume. Although undoubtedly incorporating their own patriarchal structures, black families under white supremacy can be a retreat from racism, whilst at the same time, exhibiting their own particular versions of sexist practices.

The Politics of Location

We have seen how woman's significance in the family has almost made her synonymous with this sphere of life. Woman's most 'natural' place, the location which is pre-eminently hers, is in the domestic realm. The term 'natural' is particularly important here. Common sense regards the family as a naturally given, inevitable, and immutable unit. It is regarded as socially and morally desirable, and as basic to society's well-being. Motherhood, particularly, is endowed with notions of the natural maternal instinct which impels women to self-sacrifice for the good of their children and/or the species in general. Since nature has ordained all this and present social arrangements allow for it, it would, so the argument goes, be going against nature to alter things in any way. To do so is to invite social disaster. And, of course, on a number of occasions such social disaster is said to have occurred, as when politicians, sociologists, psychologists, social workers, etc. on both sides of the Atlantic blame riots, hooliganism, educational failure, and a host of other 'social problems', on the breakdown of the family and particularly woman's failure to perform her natural mothering role.

If woman's natural place is in the home, then that of 'ethnic' groups is also supposedly away from the public areas of social life. For they too are regarded as being marginal, and are given a particular location of their own. They are associated with the non-commercial area of the inner city, with all its accompanying negative connotations of bad housing, unhygienic conditions, crime, etc. Here, as numerous commentators have suggested, are the 'twilight zones' of inadequate schools, insufficient medical facilities, and few jobs (Rex and Tomlinson, 1979; Phizacklea and Miles, 1980). These are identified by sociology and common sense alike as 'racial' ghetto areas, even though, unlike South Africa, there are few such regions in either America or Britain which are not culturally mixed.

In South Africa, of course, the location of Blacks is even more heavily circumscribed by their place in the Bantustans and the operation of the pass laws, which control the areas of the country and parts of towns where they can live and work. In Britain, however, the designation of areas such as Brixton and Bradford respectively as West Indian and Asian locations, ignores the very real differences which exist within Caribbean, Indian, and Pakistani cultures. It has been argued that the description of West Indians and Asians as culturally identifiable groups is a white racist construction, which facilitates the stereotyping and marginalization of different out-groups (Centre for Contemporary Cultural Studies, 1982). Most West Indians regard their island identity as paramount and for most Asians their religious and regional background provides the basis for community association. These migrants have only come to regard themselves as pre-eminently West Indian or Asian in the context of a society which denies them a more specific cultural identity. Moreover, through the designation of particular areas as West Indian or Asian, the inner city becomes racialized (Phizacklea and Miles, 1980). It is regarded as synonymous with the presence of migrant, or in the case of America non-white, groups.

The association of migrant groups with the characteristics of inner cities then becomes transposed into a causal dimension which works in two contradictory ways. Either migrants are accused of *causing* inner city decline (that the presence of migrant groups is the urban problem) or it is argued that their presence in an area will lead to such decline as whites move out. However, as Phizacklea and Miles persuasively argue, 'race' is not, nor has it ever been, in itself a causal factor in the inner city problem, for economic and social decline is not only to be found in urban centres. They demonstrate that urban decay was present before immigration, and its origins do not reside in the specific characteristics of the migrant populations. As Sivanandan has cogently expressed: 'the forced concentration of immigrants in the deprived and decaying areas of the big cities highlighted (and reinforced) existing social deprivation; racism defined them as its cause.' (Sivanandan, 1976, p.350).

The point to be emphasized here is that ethnic groups are now equated with urban problems and decline. The inner city, shanty town and ghetto are regarded as the 'right place' for them. It is 'natural' that they should live in inferior environments to whites, since it is assumed they are inevitably incapable of meeting white standards. Witness the outcry about cooking habits, cleanliness, lowering the tone of the neighbourhood, and house prices when Blacks started moving into so-called respectable neighbourhoods on both sides of the Atlantic. As in the case of women's place in the house, ethnic-groups' marginal place in the city is supported by the supposed naturalness of it all. Ethnic-groups are racistly defined as naturally inferior to whites, inevitably culturally different, biologically incapable of fitting into the mainstream of white society. Thus, just as women are given a place in society, a location supposedly justified by nature, so Blacks are also given a particular space which is also supported by reference to 'natural' differences. These locations have three additionally similar characteristics.

Firstly, they can be said to locate two subordinate groups, women and ethnic groups, outside of the mainstream of society. They are both placed on the margins of society politically and on the margins of the city physically. The realm of the public is left to white men. This, of course, is also reflected in mainstream social science where both women and out-groups are still seen as separate areas for study, peripheral to the main academic task of dissecting the public sphere. Secondly, one of the consequences of this marginal positioning of women and Blacks is the way it designates and legitimates their secondary position in the labour market. We are not arguing here that women and ethnic-groups have some kind of similar position in the employment structure — what would that mean for black women? But we are suggesting that it is in part their segregation from the principal public arena that permits the structuring of the labour force against each of their interests. For women, it is their familial position which legitimates this, for ethnic-groups it is their stigmatization as inner city problems. Thirdly, although women and Blacks are given a place, they are not given any space to go with it. Thus, the overcrowding and poor material conditions of the inner city militate against privacy for either the individual or the family, and the heavy policing characteristic of these areas ensures that any Black can be stopped and searched, since being Black seems to be suffcent reason to the police. Women in the home have no space of their own either, since they are supposedly part of a couple. There is no room to develop as an individual, for it is impossible to disentangle when domestic tasks finish and leisure begins. Women frequently watch the television, for example, while ironing or making the family's clothes. Whilst men have space outside of the family in which to affirm themselves, women seem to fade away as individuals, through their identification with the home and the giving of themselves to their families.

The Politics of Pathology

We have already suggested that it is expected that everyone will live in a family and that, in the West, this will take the nuclear form of two parents, one of each sex, and two or three children. The rest of life is constructed on the assumption that this is the kind of social organization in which most people will spend the major part of their lives, even though presently only about one third of the population in America and Britain are in fact living in this way. Indeed, most aspects of society are constructed with the nuclear family in mind. We have family homes, family holidays, family entertainment, and the presumption, for and on the part of the young, that they will eventually move from their family of origin to matrimony and a family of marriage (Barrett and McIntosh, 1982). Living on one's own, with friends or foregoing marriage altogether are hardly countenanced, except as some kind of defiant fling before the eventual nuptials take place. For such arrangements to become a permanent *modus vivendi* or to set up house with a member of the same sex is to invite ridicule, scathing remarks and challenges to the nature of one's sexuality. Other forms of household organization, such as single parents, cohabiting couples and multi-generational units are treated as aberrations and discussed in terms of the problems they create, both for the individuals involved and for society as a whole. Any alternative way of living that does not match up to the norm of the nuclear family is, therefore, regarded as pathological.

If these are the parameters which set the terms for debate on the white family, they are even more important for migrant and black families. The focus on black families has frequently taken the form of dissecting the 'culturally bizarre'. Not only are black families regarded as different, but their differences are seen as indicative of other underlying ethnic 'aberrations', such as sexual behaviour and religion, music styles, and eating habits. The point implied in much of the literature is that a lot of the culturally 'abnormal' behaviour of minority groups can be traced back to supposed family deficiencies. Additionally, the problematic black family background is often implicated in explanations for unrest, decay, and violence in the inner cities. For example, the by now notorious Moynihan Report, published in the United States in 1965, provoked great controversy by arguing that the problems of the black ghettos, swollen over the previous decades by large-scale rural-urban migration, were mainly due to weaknesses in the black family.

Similarly, the 1977 report of the Select Committee on Race Relations and Immigration saw a connection between the problems of Blacks in Britain and their Caribbean family traditions. The argument in both cases rests on the assumption that the black family was destroyed during slavery. Forced transportation to the United States and the West Indies totally destroyed the African family structure, since such ties were not allowed to exist by the white slave-owners. Nor were there the wider kinship bonds to support and sustain it. According to this view, it is the mother-centred family, with an absent or ineffectual father, which has survived the slave experience and which is now the most prevalent black family type. This mother-centred structure is regarded as problematic for a number of reasons.

Firstly, it is supposed to be unstable, because it lacks the system of mutual expectations and obligations which characterize the white nuclear family, and is without a clearly defined hierarchical structure. Secondly, the black family is seen as being 'weak' because the mother rather than the father is at its centre. It is defined as matriarchal. Thus, the Moynihan Report, for example, castigated black women for emasculating the black male by destroying his sense of worth and masculine identity. Black women supposedly achieve this by being the dominant family figure and the main family provider. They thus prevent the black male from asserting his 'normal' masculinity in the home, forcing him to find other ways (street crime, promiscuity) of venting his manhood. There is no reason for the male to value living in the family and keeping it intact, when black woman has appropriated his major reasons for doing so. This means, thirdly, that the black family is disorganized, as evidenced by high rates of illegitimacy and low rates of legal marriage — both regarded in the literature as signs of social pathology. Black parents are viewed as lacking the ability to socialize their children into conformity with their own ideal norms which, of course, are seen as being identical to those of wider society. Black children grow up confused, and with negative self-identities, because they have not been subjected to the stability, authority, and discipline of their white counterparts.

It is small wonder then, so the argument goes, that such children do poorly at school, see nothing of value in the immediate or wider community and ultimately create urban and racial unrest. The black family is, therefore, seen as being at the basis of the black problem. It presents problems for both blacks themselves and for white society, since it makes assimilation into the wider culture difficult, if not impossible. The family is given such importance because not only is it recognized as the site where an 'alien' culture is reproduced, but as Lawrence has noted, it is also the principle place where it has to be acknowledged that black people have a degree of autonomy (Lawrence, 1982). This makes it possible for some to argue that the cultural obstructions to fuller participation in white society are reproduced within black families, by black people themselves. As Lawrence suggests, the 'problems' created within black families are seen as being handed on from generation to generation, rather like original sin. Nothing changes, unless of course Blacks can be taught to put their house in order, take on the image of white society, and assimilate the white nuclear family structure, the proper and natural form upon which social order is founded.

This stereotyped, if not racist picture of the black family, can be challenged on a number of levels. It is historically inaccurate, as several recent works on slavery in the United States demonstrate, since it exaggerates the extent of disruption within slave families (Genovese, 1975; Gutman, 1976). Not only was it in the slave owner's interest to keep some kind of black family intact since among other reasons, it ensured a ready supply of slave labour, but the slaves themselves had an active commitment to stable nuclear units. For example, Gutman has emphasized that the slave family was an important survival mechanism, which provided a buffer and a refuge from the harsh and humiliating routine the slaves had to endure. Gutman shows how the slaves engaged in a determined struggle to protect their families, and he persuasively documents the sorrow evinced when they were broken up, together with the distances travelled in order to maintain contact with loved ones. Moreover, slave families were supported and sustained by an extended network of family ties. Gutman's point is that all this grew out of African values regarding kinship and family, that were adapted to meet the harsh realities of slavery. But this does not mean that black culture should be understood as a poor compromise between African and white styles of life. Rather, it represents the living creation of an active Afro-American ethnic culture which persists to the present. In Gutman's view, the culture of Blacks in the United States is not pathological but adaptive. Black family life is not disorganized and disintegrated but flexible and creative.

Similar views have been expressed by writers on the Afro-Caribbean family which has also been seen as an unhappy compromise between African and European cultures — neither one thing nor the other. This literature has also been plagued by the ethnocentric condemnation of apparently matriarchal families and lack of commitment to them on the part of black males. Such approaches must be challenged for the sexism and racism on which they are based. They are sexist because it is assumed that there is something *prima facie* wrong with women acting as head of the household. The problems with this are never clearly stated nor their effects on children demonstrably proved. Rather, it is just taken for granted that, since letting women play a dominant role is not in the natural order of things, it must therefore represent something abnormal. Apart from the fact that there is no conclusive evidence for either the Afro-American or the Afro-Caribbean population that their families are more likely to have absent fathers or problem children than working-class whites, the very supportive role that maternal kin have provided in child-rearing is ignored.

The point we are making here is that just because families might appear to organize themselves differently from some expected norm is no reason to berate or blame them without sound evidence. In our view such evidence is not forthcoming, from either British or American sources. Instead, we are presented with the image of a matriarchal household juxtaposed against a whole set of problems which Blacks contemporarily face in society. We are unconvincingly asked to conclude that the former causes the latter. But, in addition to being sexist, this way of looking at things is racist as well. It completely ignores the historical complicity of white society in the slave trade and the ways in which white interference in black culture provides the backdrop to how the black family is organized now. As Amos and Parmar say in their discussion of Afro-Caribbean migration to Britain, 'We are here, because you were there' (Amos and Parmar, 1981, p.134). In Britain, for example, disavowal of history has led to what has been termed 'collective amnesia' on the part of the British people (Centre for Contemporary Cultural

Studies, 1982). Such historical forgetfulness makes it easier to assert
that the 'black problem' is a relatively recent phenomenon, coinciding
with the large-scale migration of the 1950s and 1960s and supports
the notion that the problems have been imported by Blacks themselves. Such approaches to black families also fail to confront the
nature of the white supremacist societies in which Blacks are forced
to exist. To put it bluntly, they ignore racism itself. By focusing on
the inadequacies of particular family forms, they absolve white
society completely. There is little acknowledgement of the institutional racism which structures decent jobs, education, and housing
out of the reach of most of the black population. Nor is there
discussion of the racism and hostility that Blacks are likely to
experience as individuals, every day of their lives, thereby
influencing their reactions and responses to living in a society which,
for them, is structured by white power. Contemporary accounts of
the black family, therefore, in treating it as a pathological form, are
able to push much of the blame for the difficulties created for Blacks
in a racist society back on to that community itself. It is the black
family which is seen as responsible for perpetually reproducing the
problems that Blacks face. The issue is one of individual inadequacies produced by a deviant home life.

The significance of this can be more fully understood if we com-
pare the above accounts of Afro-American and Afro-Caribbean
families with those of Asian households. Again, the focus tends to be
on the culturally strange and abnormal, although the Asian family is
presented as having characteristics which are almost diametrically
opposite to those of the black family form. For example, instead of
being disorganized, unstructured and individualistic, the Asian
family is supposedly highly structured and cohesive, due to its
elaborate rules concerning kinship rights and obligations. Whereas
in the black family the father figure is replaced by the dominant
mother, Asian life is seen as controlled by an authoritarian and
powerful father who directs the lives of all those in his family. The
Asian woman is pictured as passive, docile, and completely under
male control, as evidenced by such practices as purdah and
arranged marriages. The Asian family form is viewed as creating
problems both for individual members and for white society. It
reproduces a set of cultural norms and values emphasizing mutual
interdependence and duty in a society where individuality, initia-
tive, and drive are valued. Thus it is claimed that Asian children

experience cultural problems at school and have difficulties in combining the different values of home and school life. They live in some kind of continual culture shock.

In addition, the authoritarian family structure is regarded as creating inter-generational conflict, since purdah and arranged marriages, together with other cultural practices, appear increasingly alien to second-generation Asians brought up in the 'freedom' of white society. Whereas the black family creates individual and societal problems because of its lack of mechanisms for imposing constraint, the Asian family creates such difficulties for opposite reasons. It is too structured, too inward looking, and too conforming. This also, so it is said, makes it difficult for cultural assimilation to take place, since Asians can retreat into their own communities and their own cultural practices.

Such an approach is, of course, highly stereotyped. It ignores the impact that differing religions, caste, and regional background can make on the Asian way of life. These, for example, can affect the operation of and emphasis given to purdah. In certain areas of Bradford and London, for instance, a significant number of Asian women are engaged in paid employment. Moreover, black feminists have recently challenged the prevailing impression that purdah and arranged marriages constitute particularly harsh processes of oppression (Amos and Parmar, 1981). They point out that white women do not have unlimited access to the public areas of life, as we have already seen, and are likely to enter marriage constrained by similarities of class, educational, and family background. They do not have a free choice in marriage either.

Other writers have suggested that the inter-generational conflict, much vaunted as youth's challenge to traditional and outdated customs and values, should be seen in the context of all young people's general tendency to oppose parents and authority. This is not specific to the Asian or black communities, since all youth have rebellious periods after which they mellow and eventually settle down. The literature on Asian familes also shares the 'collective amnesia' of work on black families, since it is silent on the significance and impact of foreign imperialism on this and other cultural forms (Centre for Contemporary Cultural Studies, 1982). The approach is also remarkably ahistorical, giving the impression of a static and unchanging way of life that simply reproduces itself generation after generation after generation. But this of course is perceived as part of the problem. In the context of an emphasis on assimilation, the absorption of one cultural system by another, the fact that Asian culture appears so enduring can only be regarded as leading to difficulties for Asians and for whites. And this is the crux of the matter. In American and British society where a particular nuclear family form is heralded as the norm, the natural and moral basis of social order, any other sort of household is almost definitionally pathological. Because the family plays such an important part in the daily and generational reproduction of society, any abnormal variations are viewed as a threat to that continual process.

Thus, in the context of white society Afro-American, Afro-Caribbean, Asian, and other 'ethnic' group families appear aberrant, and their aberrations are then used to explain the various difficulties they face in the wider community. We maintain that such an approach is racist, and that it helps to perpetuate and legitimate the common-sense assumption that Blacks are responsible for their subordination and oppression by failing to conform. It is racist because it ignores the differences in living arrangements apparent among, not just minority groups but whites as well. It is racist because it assumes that anything that doesn't approximate to the idealized white norm is deviant. It is racist because it perpetuates a most insidious form of victim-blaming. And, finally, it is racist because, in focusing only on the cultural strangeness of minority groups, it fails to acknowledge the problems for Blacks created by and within white society.

The Politics of Heterosexuality

Up until now we have been focusing on the various ways in which the concepts of location and of family can be used to explore the operation of sexism and racism in society. However, we have been continually stressing the existence of families, black and white, which do not reflect the idealized nuclear form to the extent that we must now ask the question — does it make sense to talk about *the* family? Is there a readily identifiable entity called the family which forms a common object for analysis and discussion, and to what extent is woman's oppression to be located there? In common with a number of recent writers, we would argue that such a term is not in itself useful as a vehicle for understanding woman's position in society. This is because it implies a fairly rigid institution, separated off from the larger world, and tends to lead to emphasis upon *one* aspect of woman's familial position (domestic work, child care) as *the* cause of her oppression, to the neglect of other possible familial sources.

Additionally, there is the tendency to see the family structure itself as oppressive and to obscure the active part played by individual actors, particularly men *qua* men, in circumscribing female activities. It seems to us that it is necessary to deconstruct the family. By this we mean going behind the phenomenal appearance that the family has as a united and coherent form, to look at the various activities and relationships which constitute the backdrop and the basis on which that appearance is accomplished. More specifically, if the family *is* the site of women's oppression, then we need to know what it is about this site that is oppressive and how this is articulated. We do not wish to imply here that the family can somehow be deconstructed away, that it doesn't 'really' exist. Obviously, the family is experienced by us all as a concrete entity, with a major role in the creation of our immediate environment. However, it is important from women's point of view to analyse the particulars of that environment, so that the features of its construction can be displayed.

At once a caveat must be made here. The kind of deconstruction we are talking about can only be achieved by looking at each particular family form individually. It is, initially at least, a synchronic rather than a diachronic approach. In adopting this strategy, we are adding support to Poster's claim that we need to understand how a particular family form is structured, before we can understand anything else about it (Poster, 1978). We need to understand what sorts of activities and forms of consciousness constitute a family, as a basis for discussing the implications for individual members, mechanisms of family change, etc. We also agree with Poster that it is more profitable to view the history of the family as discontinuous rather than linear, continuous, and evolutionary. All the evidence suggests that the family should not be conceptualized as evolving towards small, conjugal units or as an increasing form of patriarchy tied to the mode of production. Rather, there have been numerous distinct family structures and it is only when these have been perused that it will become possible to understand more fully the history of the family and the kinds of mechanisms that lead to family change.

Any deconstruction of the contemporary nuclear family is made easier by the vast amount of material, in the form of description, analysis, empirical research, and diaries, which has been produced during the last decade, due to the impetus of the Women's Liberation Movement. This rich material, based on women's first-hand experience of family life, provides a ready starting point for deconstruction. On the basis of such work, it is possible to delineate four areas for analysis. The first of these focuses on the particular types of *activity* which women undertake within the family and which constitute the various material underpinnings to their position there. The second is concerned with the ways in which women themselves develop a *consciousness* about the centrality of these activities and the influence this has on their identity. Thirdly, on the basis of these activities and women's consciousness of them, it is possible to look at the *relationships* that are thereby generated between men and women. These relate both to the asymmetrical relations of everyday life and to their more institutionalized forms. Fourthly, hidden within these day-to-day and institutionalized relationships are the particular forms of *male power and social control of women*, which are rooted in the family.

If we turn initially to the major sites of women's activity in the family, it is possible to distinguish four areas. The first refers to the bearing and rearing of children and includes, not just the physical process of giving birth but the whole area of socializing, playing with and generally bringing up children. These are usually brought together under the social label of 'mother'. The second focuses on the domestic services that women perform — the 'shit work' of cooking, cleaning, washing, etc. that is carried out for children and husbands. These jobs are usually those performed by a woman with the social label 'housewife'. Thirdly, women have a familial duty to sexually service their man which they do under the social designation 'wife'. Lastly, women engage in emotional servicing for all family members. This is partly accounted for in the three previous activities since they are all carried out under the rubric of love and affection. However, they do have a particular scope of their own as evidenced in such things as remembering birthdays and anniversaries, buying gifts, etc.

On the basis of these four sites of female activity in the home we can identify four related forms of female consciousness. Women see themselves as pre-eminently *carers*, foreseeing and catering for other family members' material and emotional needs. Secondly, they see themselves as *coping*. This means grappling silently and successfully with all the day-to-day problems of family life. It involves balancing the demands of one family member against those of the others. It entails contending quietly and obediently with the possibly contradictory needs of children and husband. In the context of women's daily lives, coping has two dimensions, as Graham has indicated (Graham, 1982). It implies responsibility: taking on the obligations and duties which go with your role. It also concedes culpability. Thus, a woman can be blamed for any faults and failings in herself and her family. Women, thirdly, acknowledge themselves as *sexual beings,* but in the heterosexist context of the family their existence as such is largely directed to the pleasure and fulfilment of men. Finally, women recognize their role in *succour,* in the provision of a sympathetic ear or an unflinching shoulder for any emotional problem brought their way.

The various activites women perform for their families, and the forms of female consciousness associated with them, are not simply about what women do or think but define for them an asymmetrical power relationship with men. There is an asymmetry of caring — women care for individuals in the family but there is no-one in the family to care similarly for them. There is an asymmetry of coping, whereby women put the needs of family members and the good of the family as a whole before themselves. As a sexual being, a woman is supposed to be sensitive to, and understanding about, the fluctuating needs of her man but is rarely given the opportunity to make demands premissed on her own sexuality. As a source of succour, women are people on to whom all troubles can be poured but who are not expected to have troubles of their own. Such asymmetries do no more than indicate on a day-to-day level the inequality generated for women in the family. They are the everyday expressions of more general tenets that structure the family relationships between men and women. Important here are the expectations built into the activity of marriage (we include cohabitation here), which involve women in an unwritten servicing contract, whereby they are obliged to perform the unpaid domestic activities, outlined above, in return for being kept by their husbands. But marriage involves other aspects too. It assumes monogamy on the part of both partners, but especially the wife. It entails deference by the woman to the man's authority inside the home. Perhaps most

importantly, marriage places the woman in a dependent relationship to the man. She is dependent on him materially, since it is
assumed by everyone, including the couple themselves, that the man
provides for his family. This is the case even when it bears little
relation to reality. She is dependent on him socially, since there are
few spheres of leisure activity where it is accepted that women can
go unaccompanied by an individual man or uncensored by men as a
group. The woman is also emotionally dependent on her husband
inasmuch as she is expected to relate expressively only to him and
their children.

All this is made possible by the norm of heterosexuality. This is
not to argue that women's position can be reduced to heterosexuality, as some kind of absolute explanation. Rather, it is to indicate
that, for example, the activities of mothering and domestic, sexual,
and emotional servicing are the material expressions of heterosexuality at this point in time. In our society the preferred unit is the
heterosexual couple who are presumed to have children. Moreover,
heterosexuality is the precondition of a division of labour based on
sex, whereby the various tasks performed by men and women are
supposed to complement each other. The family, therefore, appears
as a relationship of reciprocal dependence between the two sexes.
However, we would argue that such a division of labour as occurs
within the family is not mutually beneficial and in fact works to the
absolute disadvantage of women. The various tasks that women do
in the family mean that they can never be regarded as individuals in
their own right. They are John Smith's wife or his mother, never
themselves. Moreover, the work they do in the home is largely
invisible and only becomes apparent when not completed or managed properly. It is only when there is something wrong with what
has been done that the task itself can be seen. Because of their actual
or supposed dependence on their man, women are not entitled to
welfare benefits in their own right, but only as dependents of men or
as women who have lost the support of a man (Coward, 1983).

Additionally, women are constantly relegated, and confine themselves, to low-paid, predominantly female employment, because of
their material location in the family and the presumption that this
will affect their ability to be satisfactory employees. We regard
woman's subordination in the family as a major source of her
oppression. However, it is not the family *per se* which is oppressive
but the particular servicing activities, previously described, which

together form the material bases for her position in this heterosexual unit. Mothering, and domestic, sexual and emotional servicing constitute the family for women. We regard such activities as oppressive for them because they are expected of women, but not of males, and are supposed to take place in splendid isolation from the world outside. They are oppressive because women are directly and indirectly coerced into taking on these tasks and acquiring the identities of mother, housewife, and wife that go with them. We regard this coercion as taking place via the very real material difficulties posed for women living without a man. These range from financial and social pressures to those of physical and ideological harassment. Most women simply cannot afford to set up home on their own because their wages are set on the assumption they will be dependent on a man. Additionally, it is still not generally socially acceptable for women to frequent public houses, restaurants, theatres, and other social spaces on their own. If they are not treated as being sexually available, it will be inferred that they are childless spinsters who were never able to catch a man. It is small wonder then that the vast majority of women do get married. No real alternative is ever presented to them.

We would argue that woman's various activities in the family either preclude or severely limit the interest that she can take in other things. For example, she is either excluded from the workplace or must take a job which fits in with other family members. She either has few leisure pursuits or makes complicated arrangements for combining them with domestic responsibilities. She either has only a small number of friends or makes acquaintance with the mothers of her children's friends or wives of her husband's workmates. To the extent that women are limited in this way, men are able to gain power and relative freedom.

The power that men have over women is exercised primarily through their work as mothers, houseworkers, sexual satisfiers, and emotional supporters. It operates by circumscribing woman's location and how she should see herself, ensuring that basic family needs are met and freeing men for alternative things. Such power resides, not just in the social expectation that women should be mothers and do domestic work, but in the everyday reality that individual men benefit from the fact that women do such chores. We are not persuaded by the argument that such a situation oppresses men as well as women. This is because men do have the opportunity in the evenings, weekends, and during holidays to take over domestic chores, (but there is also little evidence to suggest that they do so), whereas our arguments concerning women suggest that their family position impinges on absolutely every aspect of their lives and cannot be escaped. Whereas man's occupational role, alienating and arduous though it might be, provides the material justification for him to have other interests outside of work, woman's familial position is the material justification for the home to be her sole sphere of interest. Such an arrangement confers power on men, whether or not they are individually powerful. By this we mean that men receive the benefits of such work, whether or not they engage in physical acts of intimidation and violence to control women in the home. In addition, the ideological expectation that all women will marry, produce children and perform the ensuing domestic activities means that you do not actually have to live in a heterosexual nuclear family unit to be affected by it.

Thus, to the extent that every woman's job chances are structured by real and imaginary ideas about the limited availability and competence of women, because of their domestic work, they are oppressed. Women are also expected to provide similar services for their bosses to those performed for their husband. The point we are making is that no woman, adolescent, unmarried, lesbian or whatever her status can escape the oppressions built into her real or imputed family position. This is because all social relations are organized around the assumption that women are responsible for child-care, housework, and the sexual and emotional servicing of others.

A number of issues are raised by the above attempt at deconstructing the contemporary nuclear family. Firstly, we are aware that it does not in any way account for the origins of women's oppression: how or why did it first occur? Apart from the fact that we doubt whether there is the historical or empirical material available to form the basis for an answer, we question whether such an answer would be useful. For example, even if we could demonstrate that woman's oppression originated in her biological capacity to reproduce the species, that would not really help us to understand anything about the ways in which her contemporary life is structured now. In our view, the search for origins detracts from the very pressing task of trying to dissect the structures of women's position today and tracing the implications of these.

Secondly, we are concerned, but at the moment unable to rectify, the tendency exhibited here and elsewhere in the literature to discuss the family predominantly in terms of the oppressed. It can sometimes smack of victim-blaming, suggesting that if only women would stop doing the housework and child-rearing all would be well, although we hope that such a naive and simplistic line of reasoning has not been presented here. Our worry is that women's position is explained in terms of characteristics peculiar to her, while those of males remain largely unexplicated. In the same way as we argued previously that accounts of racial oppression should give consideration to the structures and operation of white society, we similarly maintain that the parameters of male society should be more fully explored. It seems to us, for example, that the social nature and construction of fatherhood needs to be investigated. We would argue that, although men undoubtedly control women through the various domestic activities expected of them, there may be other sources of male power deriving not from what women, but what men themselves do. Although women's position in the family has increasingly been the focus of analysis, we are still largely ignorant of what, if anything, men do there.

Thirdly, we wish to emphasize that our concern here has been with the white nuclear family in Western society and not with any other family form. We are not claiming that our arguments can be generalized, nor do we maintain that the various components displayed will form the basis of all families across culture and through history. We suggest that this is an empirical question which requires empirical investigation. We will not be pushed into the trap of taking the modern family form and projecting it backwards. Nor do we wish to be associated with those arguments that identify the white family, whatever its problems, as more progressive and enlightened, and thereby providing more freedom for women, than those of the black or Asian communities. We find ourselves in something of a dilemma here. Although we are sensitive to criticisms by black feminists that the Women's Liberation Movement, with its various analyses, has ignored black women and is therefore unable to confront its own racism, we do not see it as our business to deconstruct the family systems of other ethnic groups in order to tell black women how they are specifically and particularly oppressed. In any case, the material available to us, as a basis for such a task, has already been displayed as racist and sexist in its treatment of black families as pathological. However, a number of problems have been raised by black feminists with regard to black woman's position in the family and it seems pertinent to summarize these here.

Firstly, it has been suggested that a number of concepts routinely used by white femininists present problems. For example, Carby argues that dependency and domestic labour both have different implications when approached from the point of view of a black female's experience. Thus, she asks of the concept dependency: 'How then can we account for situations in which black women may be heads of households, or where, because of an economic system which structures high black male unemployment, they are not financially dependent upon a black man?' (Carby, 1982b, p.215). Similarly, the significance given in white feminist accounts, to the benefits derived by men from woman's domestic labour, ignores the fact that black women have frequently done housework and taken on a surrogate mother role in relation to white families, rather that in relation to their own. It can also be argued that the term 'reproduction' has differing connotations for black women, in the context of their battle not just to control their fertility, as for white women, but in their struggle against the racist experimentation with Depo-Provera, other contraceptives and enforced sterilizations. Even motherhood can be experienced as a source of power and autonomy, and much of the white literature fails to acknowledge the support mothers can receive from their extended, especially female, kin. In general, then, it cannot be assumed that the same concepts are applicable to white and black experience, nor that they will have the same meaning when they are used.

Secondly, as Carby again points out, the way the gender of black women is constructed differs from constructions of white femininity, because it is also subject to racism. Thus, sexist notions of Afro-American and Afro-Caribbean women as sexually promiscuous, with Asian women as more passively and sensuously erotic also serve to support racism. The overwhelming impact of such racism leads black femininsts to argue that white and black women can never be regarded as similarly oppressed or as some kind of equals. Racism always ensures that the oppression of black women is magnified.

The third issue relates to the black female's relationship to the black male. Whilst acknowledging that the family can be a source of oppression for them and that black males are implicated in this, black feminists point out that this does not put black males on a par with white men (Hooks, 1982; Carby, 1982b). Thus, racism ensures that black men have not held the same patriarchal positions of power in wider society that whites have been able to establish. Although united by sexism, racism always ultimately divides black and white men.

Finally, although the black family can be viewed as a source of sexist oppression for women, it must again be emphasized that it has also operated as a prime source of resistance to *racist* oppression. Thus, during slavery, colonialism and in present-day American and British society, the black family has been a site of political and cultural resistance. The family therefore comprises a contradictory set of relationships for black women. At the same time as providing a power base for the black patriarch, it also represents a basis for survival and physical and spiritual struggle against the daily indignities, humiliations, and acts of violence imposed by white society upon both black men and women.

The Family in the Politics of the New Right

During the late 1970s and early 1980s a new source of defence and support for the family has been generated in the politics of, what has come to be known as, the New Right or New Conservatism. Whereas the politics of conservatism is usually regarded as the embodiment of individualism, with its emphasis on self-help and self-support, this new political philosophy is more concerned with the family than with the individual. Such 'familyism' regards the family as the basis of social cohesion and order in society, the transmitter and reproducer of accepted values and traditions, and the instigator of basic loyalties (Barker, 1981). The family is regarded as representing the most natural and fundamental unit, and therefore must be protected and be allowed to protect itself from outside interference and intrusion at all costs. Margaret Thatcher recently blamed the decline in the moral standards of British society on 'our having stripped the family, the fundamental unit of society, of so many of its rights and duties' (Barker, 1981, p.44). Similarly, in the United States, George Gilder, in a book supposedly distributed by Ronald Reagan to all the members of his cabinet, blames the decline in family life on the cushioning it has received from the welfare state (Eisenstein, 1982).

Support for the family, and attempts to prevent its purportedly imminent demise, have been far more articulate and cogent in America than in Britain. In the latter, although Thatcherism takes a clearly pro-family stance, no consistent line of family policy is being pursued. On the other hand in the States, it is obvious that the welfare state is under direct attack because it is charged with taking over responsibilities, such as health, education, and welfare, which should properly be the family's concern. It is claimed that the cost of the welfare state is the major cause of high taxation and inflation, which are a drain on family resources. Thus more wives are forced to go out to work, and the authority of their husbands is thereby undermined. Gilder argues that such disruption of family life causes havoc in the economy since men need the sense of responsibility, to be found in marriage, in order to direct their sexual energies to work. They only do this when they are bound by familial obligations (Eisenstein, 1982).

However, although the public emphases in the United States and Britain might be rather different, the overall political consequences of this pro-family stance are not. In both countries the family form that is being supported is the white nuclear patriarchal family where, ideally, the man is the head of the household and women perform their 'natural' loving and caring role. The sexist and racist implications of such a model must be spelt out.

Firstly, it denies the reality of the black family form and the fact that married women, in both black and white families, constitute a significant proportion of the wage-earning population, thereby making important financial contributions to their families' well-being. Secondly, in both Britain and the United States, welfare cuts have been rationalized and legitimated via the argument that families should properly be responsible for the day-to-day care of groups such as the young, the elderly, the sick, and the disabled. But of course, it is not families themselves that take on these tasks but the women in the family. Cuts in welfare services, on both sides of the Atlantic, have considerably increased the domestic burdens that women are expected to bear. Additionally, in the States, the New Right has actively campaigned against married women taking paid employment, on the grounds that it leads to family breakdown by facilitating divorce or challenging the authority of the husband, which is necessary for a productive economy. Finally, the New Right's concern for the family has been harnessed into the elaboration of a 'new' racist ideology. We use the term 'new' here since this racism does not depend on the old style formula, that Blacks are inferior or innately different, but concentrates rather on the common sense notion of difference. This difference is found in culture rather than biology (Barker, 1981).

Thus, to the extent that the basic unit in white society is seen by the New Right to be the white nuclear family, the black family is regarded by them as obviously different. Moreover, if the white family is seen as important because it transmits society's values and generates loyalty to those values, then the black family clearly constitutes a problem because it will be reproducing different values, different loyalties and hence a different culture. For the New Right then, Blacks are different because they have different family structures which signify a different way of life. Following on from this, as Lawrence has pointed out, the assumption is made that Blacks, because of their particular way of life, will be loyal to and defensive of their own kind (Lawrence, 1982). But of course if this applies to Blacks it will apply to whites as well. It is natural and inevitable then, that different groups will adhere to their own way of doing things. As one British MP put it: 'I believe that a preference for one's own race is as *natural* as a preference for one's own family.' (Ivor Stanbrook, quoted in Lawrence, 1982, p.82).

It is therefore 'understandable' that distrust of, and hostility towards, other groups is a feature of a multicultural society. Moreover, as Lawrence indicates, it is a small jump from here to the idea that preference for one's own group is synonymous with national culture, national consciousness, and national character. This is seen as reflected, not just in a particular way of life, but in particular and different political cultures and political institutions as well. Thus, ethnic-groups are regarded as 'alien'. They have a different way of life and hence a different national character. Their national character produces a particular national consciousness and a loyalty to a whole set of different political and cultural institutions. From the point of view of the New Right, they are therefore a threat because they can never be expected to give their full commitment to the British or American way of life.

Our intention in discussing the New Right's interest in the family is to emphasize that recent political concern about the family is not benign, neutral or humanitarian. The use of 'familyism' to defend the attacks on welfare services in Britain and America will clearly have consequences for the whole population. However, for women and Blacks, the effects have been, and will continue to be especially acute. For women, the New Right's political philosophy signals the undermining of many of the equal rights gains and freedoms won over the last decade. For Blacks, it provides the basis for an insidious form of racism, dressed up this time as common sense rather than science, which will undoubtedly be increasingly used against them.

5 Sexism, Racism, and Opposition in Education

In the previous chapter we examined the relationship between the family and the oppression of women and ethnic groups. Our concern in this chapter is with the production and reproduction of sexism and racism within the education system, but particularly in schools. Education is often treated as an extension of primary socialization, in that it provides both formal and informal training outside the private confines of family life. In addition, it is also proclaimed as a potential 'leveller' in its supposed promotion of equality of opportunity and disregard of social differences. However, just as we have argued that the socialization processes in the family are not neutral or devoid of ideological implication, so too the activities of teaching and learning are socially constructed in ways which have political consequences. It is our contention that these consequences are of particular significance for women and members of ethnic groups, both as participants in the education system and as the targets for sexual and racial abuse. This is because women and ethnic minorities experience the school not only as a sexist and racist institution, but also as a major vehicle through which the language and practices of sexism and racism are communicated and learnt.

The State of the Literature

There are several difficulties in embarking on an analysis of education with the above concerns in mind. To begin with, compared to the material which has formed the basis for other chapters in this book, the literature is empirical and descriptive. For example much of it focuses, in various ways, on underachievement or the underrepresentation of particular groups in critical areas of the school curriculum. This is demonstrated in the concern over women's poor science and mathematical qualifications, and Blacks' position in the lower and remedial classes in schools. Of course, these are extremely important matters for consideration. However, the descriptive, rather than the analytic approach, often goes on to imply that 'solutions' may be found via the implementation of various ameliorative policies. Thus, for instance, the provision of special classes and compensatory techniques can lure young women away from the delights of English literature and office skills, to physics and computer science, and coax young Blacks out of the lower streams to compete equally with whites for educational qualifications. But this is to use the language of inequality, and not of oppression. It is not just *disadvantage* which is at work in schools in these sorts of instances but prejudice and *discrimination* as well. To simply describe particular aspects of disadvantage is to ignore the systematic and cumulative forces of oppression, which may render educational reforms, if undertaken in isolation, potentially insignificant and ineffective. It suggests that if policies can be devised to ameliorate disadvantage and restore equality, then all would be well. This, of course, is to completely misunderstand the complex nature of sexist and racist practices. Some of the feminist literature seems more ready to come to grips with this problem. It describes the inherent sexism of many of the attitudes, and pedagogical and management strategies, held by the personnel of schools, which become enshrined in their very organizational principles. This work has also emphasized how socialization into a culture of femininity, both inside and outside school, affects girls' educational experience. However, writers appear extremely loath to acknowledge that racism may have similar sorts of consequences for the schooling of children from ethnic groups. The literature concerned with their education is overwhelmingly empirical and piecemeal in orientation.

Even literature which has adopted a more theoretical approach poses problems. The authors usually write from some kind of Marxist perspective in their analyses of the school as the purveyor of things other than just learning and qualifications. The education system is regarded as reproducing the class structure of society by teaching pupils those skills, thought processes and attitudes required for the working of existing productive relations. Some writers have attempted to incorporate the dimensions of gender and 'race' within such a framework (Castles and Kosack, 1973; Deem, 1978; MacDonald, 1980; Rex and Tomlinson, 1979). Nevertheless, they still tend to conceptualize the end product of such educational reproduction in class terms. Thus women's education is said to support their position as a reserve army of labour, and the schooling experienced by ethnic groups plays a significant role in their reproduction as the most disadvantaged section of the working class. Both of these are considered to be beneficial to capitalist economic relations. But much of the evidence used as a basis for these arguments indicates that it is not in fact class which is being reproduced, but the systematic subordination of women and ethnic groups. For example most women are subjected, both overtly and covertly, to ideologies concerning the importance of male power and authority and their future roles in marriage as wives and mothers. Ethnic groups are also exposed to definitions of inferiority and cultural incompetence and, as we shall see, are the recipients of all sorts of attitudes and practices not apportioned to their white peers. One of our major criticisms of theories of educational reproduction, therefore, is that they do not consider the specific reproduction of male domination of woman and white domination of black. It is one of our intentions in this chapter to explore the processes of the reproduction of such oppression more fully.

A final difficulty with the extant literature on gender, 'race' and education is its location outside of the mainstream of research. Most educational studies still focus on white males, on the assumption that females can be subsumed under their general rubric while ethnic or out-groups constitute a specifically deviant case. In addition, most of the educational material on Blacks focuses primarily on males and thus replicates the male bias of educational research in general. (The work of Driver, 1980; and Fuller, 1980 and 1982, are exceptions here). On the other hand, much of the work on gender concerns itself only with women, perpetuating the notion that gender issues are of importance only to them. This implies that questions to do with relations between the sexes are satisfactorily resolved when research on women is undertaken. Against this, we would argue that gender should inform the analysis of both male and female circumstances. Moreover, in certain settings, for example the mixed classrooom, it is important that both should be taken into account in our understanding of the interaction and power dimensions that are involved.

There is also a second way in which work on gender, 'race' and education is marginal. In fact, it is doubly marginal. For, in addition to its peripheral position in relation to the mainstream of education literature, it is also outside the mainstream feminist and anti-racist material. We have already argued, for example, that much of the analysis of women's education focuses on their underachievement and subject choices in comparison to men. 'Success', it seems, means taking an interest in subjects conventionally typified as male and adopting the male characteristics of rationality and competitiveness as definitional of, and the major vehicle towards, academic success. But such a focus is completely at odds with all the feminist literature which identifies these characteristics as central to masculinity and an important instrument in man's oppression of woman. It is an express denial of all that is essential to the sort of femininity which many feminists would like to see extended to the population as a whole, because of its emphasis on such qualities as caring and expressiveness. From this perspective, science and sexual oppression are intimately related and man's appropriation of science serves as an effective means of affirming his masculinity (Easlea, 1981). Such an analysis rests uneasily with the call for increased training and participation of women in scientific activities. For Blacks, something of a similar contradiction exists between exhortations for their intellectual training and schooling, and the knowledge that, to their black peers, such education can be construed as creating token whites, 'Uncle Toms' or middle-class leaders who may be out of touch with the needs of their communities and the culture and language through which these are expressed. We are not arguing here that ethnic groups and women should be denied instruction where evidence indicates they are severely 'handicapped'. Our intention is to suggest that many of the approaches to such matters contradict other work on women and 'race' which is concerned with non-educational aspects of the social world.

This brief review of the existing literature is an important backdrop to the discussion of education which follows. It goes some way to explaining why we do not merely wish to consider the traditional areas of concern or afford them the usual emphases. The aim of this chapter is three-fold. Firstly, it will pay attention to the ways in which schooling not only reproduces disadvantages but also provides a context for the legitimation of racist and sexist ideologies and practices. Secondly, it will examine some of the social processes within the day-to-day practice of education through which such sexism and racism is reproduced. Thirdly, as the previous discussion has illustrated, it will be necessary to point to some of the inadequacies of present approaches to the schooling of women and ethnic groups and, in particular, to those which lapse into arguments and conceptualizations which are sexist and racist in character. Our main areas of consideration are the content of education, language as the vehicle for the transmission of knowledge, and certain aspects of the informal curriculum. Finally, we will explore ways in which it is possible for pupils to withstand some of the effects which, at first glance, schooling might appear to have on them. This means we must examine patterns of resistance, together with the implications of such strategies for those who use them.

The Content of Education and the Ideology of Superiorities

The most obvious area in schools where racism and sexism are continually displayed and reproduced is via the construction of and representations in the knowledge which is taught. For example, many courses, but particularly home economics, homecraft, and science subjects use language and examples which clearly demonstrate that they are directed to pupils of one sex. Thus, tasks in home economics may involve 'wives' performing domestic duties for husbands, homecraft lessons focus on the importance of mothering, and scientific experiments feature boys performing activities of particular relevance to interests related to a male cultural background (Kelly, 1981; Wolpe, 1977). Such stereotyping aids the division of the curriculum into 'boys' and 'girls' subjects and perpetuates the acceptance that such a division is a natural and satisfactory state of affairs. Moreover, the differentiation is frequently so entrenched that it is difficult for pupils to make unconventional subject choices without attracting derision from their peers. This seems to be a particular problem in mixed sex schools. For the children of ethnic groups, of course, most of the curriculum takes 'whiteness' as the norm, and it is only when special multicultural lessons are set up that phenomena such as black history and literature are likely to be considered. Their experience of education, therefore, is most likely to be governed by the assumed superiority of white Western forms of knowledge.

Most of the analyses concerned with the content of the education received by women and ethnic groups have concentrated on displaying the sexist and racist nature of school text books. There are two major elements here, each of which can be further subdivided. Firstly, both groups are invisible in the literature generally used in schools. They are absent actors in the annals of subjects as diverse as history, geography, politics, literature, and art, gaining attention only when it would be impossible to leave them out. For example, it would be difficult to discuss slavery without acknowledging the presence of Blacks, or domestic life omitting the role of women. On the other hand, commentators have found it possible to write about most areas of life where ethnic groups and women are not regarded as playing a special and specific part, as if they do not exist. This invisibility has two aspects to it. It is assumed that the experience of white men is generalizable to other sectors of the population. Since it is not expected that the situation of other groups will diverge in any significant way from the white male norm, there is no need, under this formulation, to make specific reference to them. A stronger, and second version of this invisibility, involves not simply disregarding women and ethnic groups but the production of interpretations and explanations from a white male viewpoint, as if this is the only objective and legitimate stance. For example, instead of showing colonialism as a process supporting economic exploitation and white supremacy, it is portrayed as a system of white benevolence for the salvation of uncivilized heathens (Proctor, 1977). Similarly, most accounts of the development of industrialization stress the destructive impact of married women's work on home life, with some even suggesting that women did not love their children. More women-focused alternatives challenge the assumptions and lack of sensitivity displayed in such interpretations (Lewis, 1981). These two examples, together with many more which could be cited, illustrate the one-sided and distorted picture of reality which can pass as objective knowledge. The point we are making is that the sexism and racism involved in such interpretations become the received truth because, of course, they are transmitted in the context of authority, that is the classroom.

The second way in which curriculum materials may be held to be sexist and racist concerns the stereotyped images of ethnic groups and women which are portrayed. These stereotypes relate to the activities performed and characteristics possessed by the two groups. Women, for instance, are invariably portrayed within the home, performing domestic tasks. Even when females do appear in paid employment, they are generally shown only in a very narrow range of low status jobs with limited prospects (MacDonald, 1980). The world depicted for women is thus not only stereotyped but more so than reality itself and is, in many ways, foreign to the majority of pupils reading the material in which such typifications are embedded. Members of ethnic groups are also inevitably pictured carrying out manual work. However, they are more likely to be doing this in some Third World country in the context of overpopulation, starvation, and general conditions of poverty (Gill, 1983). Of course, this is the situation of most of the world's people. However, these books fail to consider why such circumstances exist and how they are perpetuated. Also, they seldom admit to the multicultural nature of most Western societies. These sorts of absences contribute to the lack of understanding about the so-called 'developing' world and help to perpetuate the stereotyping of ethnic groups. Other stereotypes are employed to display the 'natural' characteristics associated with both gender and 'race'. Women are presented as passive and nurturant against males' active, aggressive and courageous qualities. For Blacks, entire continents are presented in a similar manner and treated as possessing the same supposedly lazy, childish, and uncivilized characteristics. All the evidence suggests, therefore, that school texts use a very narrow and limiting range of typifications through which to portray women and ethnic groups.

One way of compensating for and rectifying the curriculum problems previously described has been to set up black studies and women's studies courses. In both Britain and America programmes, variously designated as black studies, multicultural or multiracial education, have been devised. These range from the incorporation of black history and geography into existing lessons, optional or extra-curricular classes mainly attended by black pupils only, through to fully-fledged black studies courses which have occasionally gained examination status. It is argued that such courses help to reverse the discriminatory practices in schools, present black pupils with knowledge and positive images of their own cultures and counter the racism of whites. Women's studies courses are similarly designed to alleviate sexism and male bias. However, even though these kinds of developments clearly constitute a challenge to the stereotypes found within the content of education, any progress made must not be over-estimated. In Britain, for example, black studies are taught in only a few schools and only those where a significant proportion of the pupils are non-white. This seems to assume that white pupils, in all-white schools, are immune from the racist content of the curricula described earlier. Women's studies, on the other hand, are mainly confined to higher education and reach the school curriculum only for those who take sociology and social studies courses. In addition, both black and women's studies are victims of the 'ghetto effect'. This means that they are added to the curriculum in a marginal and circumscribed way. It indicates that women and Blacks are separated from the mainstream of debate and regarded as having no implications for it, so that education in general remains unaffected and unchanged. Thus, interests are controlled because they are catered for, but only in a peripheral fashion. In this context it has been argued that the so-called multicultural curriculum is nothing more than subtle form of social control, giving Blacks trendy, liberal things to do instead of teaching them basic knowledge and skills (Dhondy, 1982; Stone, 1981). Moreover there is something to be said for the claim that educationalists only began to countenance this sort of education when they recognized its potential for defusing the rising level of politicized black consciousness in schools (Carby, 1982a). Similarly, academics have responded to women's studies with benign tolerance rather than much enthusiasm (Evans, 1982).

It is our contention, therefore, that the development of black and women's studies programmes has had little overall effect on the education that children receive. This is because they have, as yet, exerted little influence on the content of most of the 'knowledge' taught in schools. Instead we have argued that the construction of, and representations in, the curriculum are stereotyped along sexist and racist lines. This is important in two ways. Firstly, it can be argued that because school literature provides ethnic groups and women with few significant role models and concerns itself with issues in which they are only marginally featured, the curriculum actively fosters disenchantment with education. We are not arguing that stereotyping *causes* educational indifference. Rather, an irrelevant curriculum fails to entice interest in those who are already alienated from, or culturally antagonistic towards, the learning process. Secondly, the ideological nature of schooling must be acknowledged. It is possible to make a distinction here between the more implicit messages and signals which are transmitted and the knowledge that is formally taught, learnt and repeated in school essays and examinations. It is suggested that the implicit themes, with their positive evaluation of everything white and devaluation of anything black, at best fail to challenge racist attitudes in children and at worst actually encourage the development of racial prejudice. Similarly, for women, it can be argued that the curriculum supports and legitimates attitudes and behaviour associated with male domination. In the more formal context, pupils appear to be taught a distorted view of womanhood, which not only misrepresents female activities in social life, but does little to challenge or correct patterns of sexual discrimination. Alongside this, the knowledge and facts that are taught in a number of subjects also give a false or incorrect impression of the lives of different ethnic groups. In fact they are quite often nothing more than blatant statements of white supremacy.

Language, the Acquisition of Knowledge, and Educational 'Success'

Language is obviously an important aspect of any child's schooling, since it is the major instrument for the transmission and acquisition of knowledge. Furthermore, a pupil's proficiency in, and competence with, particular language structures is often regarded as an indicator of their potential for doing well in educational terms. However, educationalists appear to work with a very narrow definition of the kind of language which is appropriate for a person to be 'successful' in school. As we shall see, this has a particular effect on the educational experiences of ethnic groups, but especially Blacks, and women.

The members of some groups, for example Asians, Italians, or Chinese, clearly have a completely different language system to that of standard English. These differences cannot only be systematically itemized and analysed by linguists, they can be unequivocally heard and appreciated by lay persons, including teachers. The educational issue, for the speakers of such languages is, therefore, the need to teach them English as a second language. For Afro-American or Afro-Caribbean children, the problem has been perceived very differently. They frequently speak not an entirely different language, nor standard English, but a variety variously referred to as 'patois', 'creole' or 'dialect' which is distinguishable in terms of both grammar and phonetics. Patois is treated as a form of non-standard speech, akin to the restricted code discussed by Basil Bernstein, and supposedly also lacking the formal properties for the organization of thought and expression. It is therefore regarded as deficient as an education medium. Teachers consider patois to be a form of sloppy broken English entirely inferior to the 'correctness' of Received Pronunciation. In addition, because it is associated with the poorer and lower-class members of society, patois, like restricted code, lacks the prestige afforded to those considered to have a 'nice voice' or to be 'well spoken' (Edwards, 1979).

The educational consequences of treating patois as an inferior and inadequate form of English have been considerable. In America, a large number of intervention programmes were designed for children variously described as 'verbally deprived', 'culturally disadvantaged' or 'culturally deprived'. Most compensatory programmes in Britain were devised on a purely *ad hoc* basis. But despite the differences in official approach to 'the problem' in the two countries, the response in the classroom has been very much the same: patois speakers have been categorized as lazy when they experience writing problems, illiterate when they find it difficult to read aloud and educationally subnormal when they 'fail' on tests which require competence in standard English and knowledge of white styles of life (Coard, 1971; Edwards, 1979; Giles, 1977; Taylor, 1981). Such designations have implications which are racist in two significant ways.

Firstly, there is no direct evidence that patois is an inferior form of English. Indeed, some researchers have argued that patois is a dialect system with its own complex internal structure and coherence. It is as useful a form for performing logical operations and expressing abstract thought as any other language system (Edwards, 1979). Education treats black children in a particularly racist fashion when it fails to acknowledge these important aspects of their speech. Thus, despite the fact that the children regard themselves as English speaking, teachers consider that they use an unsystematic form of slang. It is hardly surprising then that, amidst such confusion, black pupils become disenchanted with schooling and the education goodies which it consistently fails to offer them. It is not so much that black children need to be made aware that education is being conducted in a second language; they know that already. Rather, white teachers need to be aware of the richness of patois and the problem of moving between it and standard English.

Secondly, because speech is such an important marker of social and ethnic boundary, different kinds of language can be used to make all sorts of educational judgements about a speaker. Attitudes to language and speaker are, therefore, closely related and views about the inadequacies of a language may be transformed into self-fulfilling prophecies concerning those who use it. Thus, when a teacher fails to recognize the nature of the difficulties experienced by black children in the classroom, she/he may conclude that they are stupid and unintelligent. She/he develops a stereotype of inferiority, low ability, and lack of potential which tends to govern her attitude and behaviour towards them. The teacher expects such children to perform poorly and the children, feeling threatened and confused by the difficulties that confront them, are even less likely to meet the required standards. This, of course, reinforces the teacher's preconceived ideas and so the racist cycle is reproduced and perpetuated (Edwards, 1979). It is not, therefore, the inadequacies of their language structure which constitute an educational problem for black children since, as we have emphasized, patois is as adequate a speech system as any other form. Rather, it is the stigmatization of patois, and its users, which has placed a continual question mark over black children and their ability. To remove patois from its cultural milieu and treat it as bad English is racist. Failure to take account of patois within the educational process is to make that process itself biased. Moreover, it has to be acknowledged that patois will not die out, as some commentators initially forecast, since it is still used in the homes and among the friendship groups of the black population, while also becoming institutionalized through reggae music. As such it is an intrinsic component of black culture. For schools and educationalists to ignore this significant aspect of black life is, we contend, part of the generally unsympathetic cultural context in which Afro-Caribbean and Afro-American peoples are expected to live.

In the same way that black languages are stereotyped as inferior, so too female speech is regarded as deficient. In the early days of researching gender differences in language behaviour, two separate forms of analysis were undertaken: the way in which women themselves used language and the way language referred to and portrayed women (Lakoff, 1975). It was suggested, for example, that women were hesitant and used qualifications when speaking; that they used 'hedge' words of various kinds; that they retained a large stock of words particularly relevant to female interests; that they tended to use 'empty adjectives' and unnecessary intensifiers. In addition, it was maintained that many words, when applied to females, take on a special meaning which is derogatory to women as a group. The conclusion of such work was that women's language was a deficient version of men's, and that its various inadequacies helped to reinforce women's inferior position in society. This mirrors the arguments concerning the language of ethnic groups, in its attribution of deficiency. Women's language is inferior when compared to that of males, which is already assumed to be the important yardstick and the superior form. Similarly, patois has been found wanting when compared to the supposed superiority of white standard English. Additionally, in the same way that black speakers are ascribed inferior characteristics on the basis of their 'disordered' language form, so too women are characterized as inadequate on the grounds of deviant language practice. For example, it is assumed that thay find it difficult to make decisions and are uncertain about the views they hold because of their particular speech patterns.

The parallels between the assumptions and literature concerning the language structures of Blacks and women can be extended even further. For just as it is possible to question the racist assumptions relating to patois, so feminists have begun to challenge the sexism embedded in existing accounts of female language. Their research reveals that many of the assertions about women's speech have as little foundation in reality as those concerning the deficiencies of patois. For women there exists what Spender has referred to as a 'rule of semantic derogation', whereby all words acquire negative and often sexual connotations when associated with females (Spender, 1980). Because it is assumed that the world is male, unless proven otherwise, women are labelled in negative terms as 'not the real thing'. As de Beauvoir explains: '. . . man represents both the positive and the neutral, as indicated by the common use of *man* to designate human beings in general; whereas woman represents only the negative, defined by limiting criteria, without reciprocity.' (de Beauvoir, 1972, p.15).

One of the effects of the negativity assigned to women, both in terms of how they are defined within language and in their roles as speakers, is the general asymmetry between male and female involvement in conversation and communication. Feminists have commented on the tendency for women to take a back seat in discussion. They yield to male interruptions, take on the role of listener and generally speak less, despite the prevailing stereotype (Spender, 1980). These general aspects of women's participation in speech are particularly significant within the specific context of education. In school, boys are able to utilize their greater involvement with the spoken word to ensure that the mixed sex classroom is a man's world. Thus, they receive the lion's share of the teacher's attention, even when in the minority; taunt the girls, often without punishment; and receive praise for challenging the teacher, when similar behaviour from girls evokes rebuke (Spender, 1982; Spender and Sarah, 1980; Stanworth, 1981). On the other hand, girls are often reticent about speaking in class and are disinvolved in the discussions which take place. Their marginalization in the classroom and the fact that they demand, and receive, less attention from teachers helps to foster the view that boys are the more capable and dominant sex. Moreover, many teachers use sexist remarks to control and discipline pupils or to forge a sense of chummy cameraderie with them. Male control of language in these ways conveys implicit sexist messages to the girls concerning their lack of importance and status in comparison to their male peers. However, it is not simply sexism which is being transmitted here, nor just the benign signalling of the existence of two complementary gender roles. Rather, girls are learning that the relations between the sexes are power relations where men are dominant and in control, while women are subordinated and inferior. As one researcher puts it: 'Classroom interaction — the way in which pupils and teachers relate to each other — does not merely transmit beliefs about the superiority of one sex over the other, but actively serves to give such beliefs a concrete foundation in personal experience.' (Stanworth, 1981, p.47).

Attitudes and Assumptions: Teacher Expectations and Pupil Self-Identity

We have already suggested that the ways in which language is spoken and used by pupils plays an important part in the expectations that teachers may develop about children's potential for educational 'failure' or 'success'. However, language is not the only foundation upon which such expectations may be built. Attitudes to various aspects of pupils' lives, such as their behaviour, cultural backgrounds, interests and 'natural differences' also contribute to the construction of images concerning the sort of schooling required by women and ethnic groups. These images are significant, since not only are they premissed on certain common sense assumptions about the differences between blacks and whites, male and female, but they are also likely to effect the kind of learning experience children have in the classroom. Commentators refer to the latter as the 'self-fulfilling prophecy'. Children who are expected to perform well in class and in examinations do, in fact, perform well. Moreover, even those children who defy the educational stereotype, by being 'successful' in some way, are still regarded in a less favourable light by their teachers (Milner, 1983). Although children may inhabit the same educational space, it cannot be assumed all are treated in a similar fashion or that schooling affects them in like ways.

West Indian children, for example, are more likely to be regarded and treated as if they always behave aggressively, unresponsively or in a restless fashion. Accordingly they tend to be seen as presenting special educational and disciplinary problems. (Taylor, 1981). As discussed in chapter 4, black culture is viewed in a stereotyped way and cultural difference tends to be treated as a deficit, particularly in relation to educability. For many teachers, the black family is considered as unable to provide the conditions for, or as actually inhibiting, the successful educational progress of the West Indian child (Coard, 1971; Edwards, 1979; Giles, 1977). Since schools often underrate West Indian academic potential, they are more likely to stereotype Blacks as having superior physical capabilities and consequently have high expectations of their likely performance in such activities as sport, drama, and dance. Thus, there is a tendency to encourage their involvement in school sports and music (Carrington, 1983; Stone, 1981). Occupying Blacks in such areas may be seen as a way of keeping what appears to be an increasingly disaffected group loyal to the school, by providing them with some activities and subjects which they will view as 'relevant'. However, there is increasing concern that schools are promoting the failure of black pupils by channelling them away from the academic mainstream. It is well known, for instance, that West Indian parents believe that their children's school performance is affected and held back by the negative expectations teachers have of them (Stone, 1981; Taylor, 1981). Moreover, the 'sports and music' curriculum can be regarded as a form of social control aimed at 'cooling out' Blacks by using their anticipated interests to contain or neutralize disaffection caused by lack of educational success. Such a curriculum may also provide a justification for giving those pupils in non-academic streams a 'watered down' form of schooling. It is for these kinds of reasons, that teachers' expectations are an important factor in the educational career of the black child. They help to create, however inadvertently, an environment in which Blacks are assumed not to have and treated as if they lack, the ability and potential to 'achieve' in the conventionally accepted sense.

Different assumptions and expectations concerning males and females also affect the classroom environment for women. For example, girls are expected to be more conforming, fussy, dependent, and neat in both appearance and presentation of work than boys, who are stereotyped as more explorative, independent and untidy. This can help to create different educational experiences and standards as when boys are praised for sloppily presented work for which girls would be chastised (Clarricoates, 1980; Delamont, 1980; Stanworth, 1981; Spender, 1982). An affinity to home and domestic life is seen as the cultural milieu for girls, however bright, while for boys the world of work and relative familial detachment is taken as the norm. Whereas marriage and parenthood seem to figure prominently in teachers' visions of the futures for their female pupils, these feature only peripherally in their expectations of boys' prospects. Additionally, since girls are regarded as more interested in domestic and expressive matters, they are perceived by teachers as lacking the authority and assertiveness required for many occupations and careers. Such assumptions about the centrality of the family for women's lives means that teachers, especially the males, are reluctant to make girls prime candidates for attention in the classroom and means their educational achievement seems less pressing (Stanworth, 1981). These expectations, based on beliefs about the respective behaviour, culture, and interests of males and females, clearly affect how teachers respond to girls and boys within school. Moreover, they may contribute to the conflict experienced by those women who, although educated to a fairly high standard, find that there is little in the world of paid employment for which they are suitably qualified or trained.

It has not been our intention here to present a full review of the extensive literature, produced on both sides of the Atlantic, concerning the nature and impact of teacher expectations on ethnic groups and women. Rather, our purpose is to point out the similarities in the evidence and in particular the way in which the treatment of male and female, black and white, seems to be based on an assumption of 'natural difference'. Thus, Blacks are seen as commonsensically and naturally different from whites as are girls from boys. We are not maintaining that teachers necessarily operate with notions of biological difference or genetic inferiority, although the widespread coverage given to the views of Jensen and Eysenck on these matters suggests that, for some, they may constitute background information from which attitudes and views are formed. But, the expectations and associated behaviour which many teachers employ, however unwittingly, seem to give these differences an immutable, if not actually inherent status. Although they may discuss black pupils' difficulties in terms of their general social disadvantage, teachers harbour beliefs about and act towards them in ways which are clearly premissed on the assumption that they are 'different' from their white peers. Commenting on this, the Rampton Committee (on the education of ethnic groups) write: 'We are convinced from the evidence that we have obtained that racism, both intentional and unintentional, has a direct and important bearing on the performance of West Indian children in our schools.' (Rampton, 1981).

For girls, teachers who volunteer that they treat the sexes in an uncompromisingly equal fashion can be found using gender differences as a form of classroom management and control (thus emphasizing the assumed differentness of boys and girls and inculcating rivalry or antagonism between them), and discussing female pupils and staff as sexual objects in the staff room (Clarricoates, 1980; Delamont, 1980). Of course, teachers are not alone in the views which they hold about ethnic groups or gender, nor do their beliefs and actions exclusively account for the educational experience of Blacks and females. Nevertheless, the expectations which they take into the classroom are important, because of the climate of evaluation which they create around black and female pupils. Teachers' assumptions and actions, particularly when they are racist or sexist, cannot fail to give added meaning and legitimation in pupils' eyes to other aspects of the education system where they are treated in a discriminatory way. We therefore concur with Milner when he writes that: 'The central role of the teacher in the child's educational experience makes teacher attitudes and expectations the very fulcrum on which that experience pivots.' (Milner, 1983, p.191).

So far we have concentrated on the ways in which teachers' assumptions and attitudes effect their actions towards women and the children of ethnic groups. Additionally, researchers have given considerable atention to how women and Blacks develop views about themselves, with apparently significant educational consequences. For example, the lack of achievement of Afro-American and Afro-Caribbean children in school has been attributed to their poor self-identity, low self-esteem and consequently diminished educational aspirations. We have already questioned, in chapter 3, the validity of conclusions drawn from those studies which purport to demonstrate that children from ethnic groups show a marked preference for the values and culture of the dominant group. We also suggested that even if it could be 'proved' that such children harboured these feelings, this would tell us nothing about their views of either themselves or their culture. It would also say little about their educational ability or potential. Yet, many educationalists have asserted a connection between racism, social disadvantage, negative self-evaluation, and school failure. They maintain that black children must be given the opportunity within schools to enhance their self-concept, for example through multicultural education, which will result in a more positive attitude towards school and a subsequently improved academic performance (Bagley and Coard, 1975; Milner, 1975).

There are two major responses to these sorts of arguments. Firstly, there is an increasing amount of evidence which disputes the claim that black school children have negative self-images; instead it is argued they have positive feelings about both their parents and associated home life. In addition, such research dismisses the idea that there is any relationship between black self-concept and aspiration. Stone goes further when she argues that since black pupils hold such negative attitudes towards teachers, it is unlikely that anything could be done within the classroom to alter successfully their self-identity and esteem. Moreover, in Stone's study, experience of multicultural education appeared to depress, rather than heighten, black pupils' educational ambition and their feelings about schooling in general (Stone, 1981). It is possible to argue either that the results of attempts to measure the relationship between self-concepts and educability are contradictory, or that no such interconnection has been found. Either way, extreme doubt must be cast on the notion that schools should concentrate on improving the self-image of ethnic children as a way of increasing their academic success.

A second response to the identity arguments has been to contend that the self-esteem and self-worth of Afro-American and Afro-Caribbean children has, in any case, improved during the last ten years or so. For example, Milner has recently cited the increasing racism to which Britain's black communities have been subjected and the development of black consciousness and political organizations as a reason for this. Young West Indians now have positive and alternative images of their own group with which to identify. In this context, the development of Rastafarianism, together with black music and culture in general, has been most important. Reggae, for example, has become a focus for low-achieving Blacks in schools and is a significant factor underlying their strong black identity (Milner, 1983). Although Milner argues that there have been obvious changes in black identity, he is not able to go on from this to argue for an increase in black educational achievement. The figures simply do not allow such a claim to be made. This rather undermines the whole argument for the educational significance of self-esteem. If identities become more positive without any corresponding changes in school 'success', perhaps we should be looking elsewhere for explanations of why Blacks generally perform so poorly in schools. Also, it is difficult to go along with Milner's views on the changes that have occurred. Whilst it is clear that Rastafarianism and reggae have had an enormous impact on black youth, this is not, as Milner seems to believe, some spontaneous cultural development in response to white racism on the part of a group that was previously culturally impoverished. Rather, as we have continually argued, an alternative black culture and identity has always existed within all contemporary cultures in which African people exist. This culture has been completely ignored by all social scientists writing on black children, their self-conceptions and schooling. As Stone maintains: '. . . during the time that social scientists have been busy "proving" that black people have negative self-images based on white stereotypes, blacks have been busy living in accordance with their own world-view.' (Stone, 1981, p.86).

A vast amount of money and energy has been spent trying to

demonstrate Blacks' own culpability in their educational under-achievements. We suggest that researchers might have been better employed investigating some of the more obviously racist and discri-minatory aspects of the education system — some of which have been discussed in this chapter. In our view, much of the research on self-identity has been implicity racist, however well intentioned, because in focusing on the supposed deficiencies of individuals, it has helped to detract from consideration of the nature and quality of the education that black children can expect to receive in schools. Educational achievement is related to the teaching and facilities which are offered, and the organization of classrooms and schools, not to questions of self-concept. It is interesting that the black community acknowledged this some time ago and as a consequence set up Saturday supplementary schools in an attempt to teach black pupils the basic educational skills they were partly denied.

Attention has also been directed at the self-identity problems and conflicts experienced by women, as a way of explaining their under-achievement within education. As long ago as 1946, Kamarovsky in America reported that female students pretended to be intellectually inferior when talking to males by playing down any educational 'success'. More recently, it has been suggested that girls harbour more doubts about their ability and future potential than boys and are more likely to judge any achievements as due to luck or sheer effort, rather than their ability (Dweck, 1977; Stanworth, 1981). Girls, it seems, tend to underestimate their capacities and compe-tence, whereas boys are more likely to have an inflated impression of their capabilities. Feminists have attempted to explain this situ-ation by emphasizing girls' position as a negative reference group for boys, particularly in mixed sex classes and schools. This is seen as the product of the confusion girls experience in having to fulfil two conflicting roles. On the one hand, they must attempt to meet the accepted criteria of educational 'success'. On the other, the demands of feminity require that, especially in relation to boys, they are passive and not too bright. This is referred to as the 'fear of success' syndrome, where women think men will be frightened away from them if they appear too intellectual (Horner, 1976).

Although the literature on female self-identity and education is far less extensive than that related to Blacks, it still tends to assume that women's image of themselves, as different or inferior to men, is attributable to low self-esteem. In our view this has not been convincingly demonstrated. Obviously, for example, many girls do see themselves as incapable of undertaking numerate and practical tasks. It is clear also that boys benefit *materially* (through the acquisition of jobs and skills) and *ideologically* (through the possession of prestige and status) from being good at these sorts of things However, the notion that girls have low self-esteem because of this implies that their self-conceptions relate purely to educational 'success' or 'failure' in comparison with males. But just as we have argued that Blacks have a cultural history from which they gain positive identification, so too girls have a culture of femininity within which they can develop self-esteem. They can, and do, take pride in aspects of femaleness — having a boyfriend, fashionable clothes, domestic achievements, and later on marriage and motherhood. The fact that we may not like these aspects of female culture, or even regard them as oppressive, does not constitute grounds for denying that, for many women, they are a major source of positive self-evaluation. Just as Blacks acknowledge their subordination in the white man's world, but gain support from their own black community, so women regard themselves as inferior to men, but still have resources from which to take pride in their identity.

A second but connected point here relates to the controversy surrounding mixed versus single-sex schooling. Just as Blacks have found white schools lacking and have set up their own Saturday supplementary schools, feminists have seen co-education as one of the factors hindering girls' progress. Broadly speaking, it is argued that single-sex education improves women's chances of taking non-traditional subjects and gaining qualifications. Away from males, they find more positive role models and are less inhibited. Boys, on the other hand, appear to perform better in a co-educational setting. If this *is* correct (and the evidence is not conclusive), then we are forced to wonder whether the reason has less to do with girls' 'fear of success', than with boys' feelings of superiority and dominance which, as we have already indicated, are prevalent in the mixed sex classroom and appear to create a more favourable learning environment for boys. Perhaps their superordinate position *vis à vis* girls actually facilitates boys' motivation and hence their achievements. To the extent that girls lose out, boys inevitably gain. If the sexist nature of education is to be more fully understood, we believe that it is crucial for this latter part of the equation to be properly explored and analysed.

Pupil Resistance and Oppositional Cultures

Apart from the discussion of self-identity, our tenor of writing so far has implied that the reproduction of racism and sexism in education takes place in a fairly rigid, uncompromising and mechanistic fashion. Children in school receive a constant bombardment of images and messages which they unquestioningly internalize and which contribute to the dominance of white over black, male over female. Black and female inferiority are daily reconfirmed in the classroom and in this way schools mirror and reinforce the situation in the world outside. However, it would be naive to believe that things are quite that simple.

Firstly, there are inevitable contradictions in the messages schools transmit. For example, as we have already seen, despite the prevailing view that Blacks' underachievement is due to their cultural deficiencies, education allows them to be 'successful' in areas such as sport and music, which are paradoxically products of the very cultural backgrounds that are so derided. Similarly, although the school continually emphasizes gender differences, it denies girls certain of the the props of femininity which are so important in the world outside, such as fashion, romance, and sexuality. This, of course, is all the more significant since displays of masculinity are permitted to boys (Willis, 1978). These sorts of contradictions indicate that the nature of racial and gender domination, and the processes through which they operate, are themselves internally contradictory and not necessarily consistent or homogeneous.

Secondly, as we have previously argued, no human being passively and unquestioningly internalizes the attitudes and values of others or mechanistically mirrors their behaviour (see chapter 3). Individuals interpret and give meaning to their situation. They are not deterministically socialized and reproduced in the simple image of those around them. This approach allows for the possibility of opposition and resistance and clearly various devices of this nature are used by pupils in school. However, the meaningful development of resistance strategies is complicated by the particular location of subjects in terms of 'race' and gender. Hence, the specific forms of opposition generated by whites and blacks, males and females are likely to be rather different.

The paradigmatic study of an anti-school culture is, of course,

Willis' account of white male underachievers (Willis, 1978). Willis describes how, as far as the 'lads' are concerned, education is for 'earholes' and has little relevance for them. They are therefore likely to truant, avoid school work, and dress in unacceptable ways. The most explicit dimension of their counter-school culture is opposition to authority which involves the apparent inversion of accepted educational values such as diligence, deference, and respect. Such opposition is mounted in any number of small ways which become an almost ritualistic part of daily school life. Willis' argument is that the lads' resistance to schooling serves, paradoxically, to turn them into the appropriate recipients of manual working-class jobs. However, it is clear from his own reasoning that the resistance which leads to such an occupational destiny is couched not in class but in sexist, and to a lesser extent, racist terms. Thus the lads' oppositional strategies are structured by their position in a wider culture of machismo, wherein a premium is put on a form of life which emphasizes physicality, strength, and being able to 'handle' oneself. These are the sorts of qualities through which a 'real' man demonstrates his manhood. Such an oppositional culture is, of course, sexist because the lads' sense of their own superiority is continually enacted against the supposed inferiority of women who are regarded as either sexual objects or domestic comforters. It is also racist since they clearly differentiate between, and hold derogatory views about, other groups on the basis of colour. Such views are used daily, in Willis' study, to justify the intimidation of or physical attack upon other Asian or West Indian pupils. The anti-school culture of white poor-achieving males therefore is not simply formulated against education *per se*, but is also hostile to women and ethnic groups. To the extent that the lads continually define themselves in terms of their contrast to such groups, their opposition is also a vehicle for the reproduction and legitimation of male and white supremacy.

West Indian boys have also developed ways of challenging and resisting the assumptions and practices of schools. However, they have more culturally specific weapons at their disposal. Some writers have maintained, for example, that their appropriation of music and sports activities is a way of opposing the stereotypes of failure with which they are labelled (Carrington, 1983). To Blacks, this can be a way of delineating their own specific territory within school and encouraging cultural pride, rather than simply constituting a form of accommodation and a means of control, as we have previously argued. Other commentators have emphasized more directly confrontational strategies. For example, speaking patois in the classroom is not simply a way of excluding or defying persons in authority, it also symbolizes the undermining of school culture and creates a sense of solidarity and collective identity between black pupils and against whites (Edwards, 1979).

Related to this is the significance in schools of Rastafarianism which, in its philosophy, provides the basis not just for black consciousness and pride but also a clear analysis of the oppression of Blacks in white society, Babylon. Rastafarianism demonstrates to its followers that education is a waste of time, since the whole of white society is structured to prevent black success. Opposition is therefore registered by 'dropping out', truanting and the creation of an alternative black culture. Black pupils' refusal to work in school can, therefore, be seen as symptomatic of their resistance to the world of whites. Furthermore, it has been argued that the opposition which black youth exhibit in school is training for the struggle outside, as seen in the 1981 Brixton and other riots (Dhondy, 1982). Hence, unlike their white counterparts, West Indian males do not develop resistance strategies with purely negative consequences. From the point of view of Blacks themselves, their lack of interest in education can also contain positive, political elements.

Opposition to education is not however the sole prerogative of males, for women also have ways with which to counter meaningfully the school influence. One aspect of their activities, similar for black and white girls, is the essentially individualistic form which their opposition takes. Whereas white and West Indian boys display their antagonism in a collective manner, deriving from their participation in particular youth cultures, this is not the case for girls. Part of the explanation for this lies in women's apparent absence from youth cultures, which seem to be largely male affairs. Thus girls, according to the literature, take on the role of 'hangers on' or 'side-kicks' to men, always somewhere around on the periphery, never to the centre of the stage. All youth cultures, whether white, Asian or black are masculinist. Consequently a girl's involvement in them tends to be individualized. She is either there because of her relationship to a specific male, or involved in the invisible bedroom culture of listening to pop music, swooning over stars or practising the use of make-up, never accompanied by more than one or two friends. In neither instance do the activities lend themselves to the creation of a collective identity or group solidarity. This should be taken into account when looking at the development of girls' hostile views of school.

There is now a good deal of documentary evidence which suggests that for white girls, except those most 'successful', school is dull, irrelevant, and boring (McRobbie, 1978; Sharpe, 1976; Spender, 1982). The expectations regarding their futures on the part of teachers and the girls themselves focus on marriage and a family, with perhaps a little part-time work. They dream of leaving school, romance, and marriage. They talk about their crushes, their idols and the latest fashion trends. Their aim is to have their own man to care for, so they may set up a home of their own. Since education, achievement, and qualifications are so unimportant to them, any opposition such girls develop will be in the context of those elements of their lives which they define as significant, namely romance, caring, and sexual display. Thus within the classroom, exaggerated feminine behaviour or emphasis on sexuality may not just indicate acquiescence to the social expectations of what it means to be female. It can also signify opposition to school which continually tries to control expressions of femaleness in the the interests of management and discipline (McRobbie, 1978). For instance, some girls may use ploys such as fluttering their eyelashes or suggestive and flirtatious behaviour to undermine the authority of a male teacher (Anyon, 1983). Others may speak to male teachers as if they are small boys or trade good conduct for information about a teacher's private life (Davis, 1983). The point about these, and other ways in which girls can undermine the order of a classroom, is that they are premissed on an understanding of the major qualities of femininity. They can use the resources of such femininity to destroy a teacher's authority and control, since it challenges the decorum and etiquette of female behaviour customarily expected within schools. Although these ploys are mainly individual acts of defiance, and lack the collective foundation of many of the male strategies, this should not be taken to undermine the fact that, in particular situations, they can be a powerful and effective weapon of disruption.

It has recently been suggested that West Indian girls are more motivated towards educational achievement and likely to gain better examination results and qualifications in comparison to their white female peers (Driver, 1980; Fuller, 1980 and 1982). This has been explained in terms of the significance of work to West Indian females, a larger proportion of whom are in paid employment than in the case for either the white or Asian populations. Black girls, so it is said, are brought up to expect to work and also have a plentiful supply of female role models who are employed outside the home. Accordingly, their specific cultural background of being black and female gives particular meaning to the opportunities which are available via schooling. One aspect of this is the notion that their own particular self-worth can be demonstrated through the possession of educational qualifications (Fuller, 1983).

However, although some West Indian girls may be ambitious, this does not mean they necessarily conform while in school. They are likely to comply with the demands of teachers in terms of the completion of homework and school work only. For the rest of the time, as Fuller's research suggests, their behaviour is clearly designed to exasperate the teaching staff, without jeopardizing their overall educational chances. They therefore express opposition to what is regarded as the boring and trivial routines of school by means of numerous minor irritations and disruptions, such as reading magazines or doing homework during class. The emphasis is on the importance of having fun and 'a laugh', whilst accepting the relevance of school only in terms of the academic benefits it may be able to provide. It can therefore be argued that the experience of being black and female can lead to a particular educational response. Whereas the opposition of black males is frequently a highly visible aspect of a more general black youth culture, the female version is not collective and solidaristic in its approach. In a similar vein to white females, black female resistance is developed through various strategies of veiled insubordination. The difference is, as we have seen, that for black women this is less likely to lead to the total rejection of schooling and educational success.

We have suggested that schools are not total institutions, as much of the educational literature implies. There are various ways in which pupils can, and do, demonstrate their hostility and antagonism to the education system. These are best examined in terms of opposition, rather than deviance as is often the case, since they signify ways of challenging schooling rather than defective socialization into its mores. Moreover, the strategies deployed should be considered not just in terms of schools themselves but also with reference to the various youth sub-cultures. We also maintain that the kinds of resistance adopted differ according to 'race' and gender. However, there are three further complicating issues which must now be introduced.

Firstly, there are problems with the way in which we have been using the terms 'resistance' and 'opposition'. This is because we have failed to distinguish between action which is intentionally oppositional, and that which is is simply 'larking about' or 'playing up' the teacher. In fact, most of the instances discussed here appear to fall under the latter rubric, although some of the aspects of black male hostility are clearly formed by political commitments, whether consciously or unconsciously, and may well develop further in that direction. Similarly, the spectre of unemployment for white lads, and the futility of various government training schemes may elicit a more significant revolt from them in the future. It is important, however, that we do not treat the various strategies discussed in this chapter as necessarily similar, in terms of either their disruption of or consequences for the educational process.

Secondly, it must be emphasized that even when antagonism is expressed or resistance strategies devised, the likelihood of their accommodation and the recuperation of schooling in its extant form is high. The opposition of Willis' lads, for example, does nothing to change the education system itself and, as we have seen, provides a vehicle for the continual justification of white male oppression of women and ethnic groups. Similarly, the material destiny of most West Indian males is affected neither by the 'music-sport' curriculum, nor by withdrawing from school, although we should not underestimate their significance in establishing black pride and consciousness. With or without opposition to school, racism ensures that most black youth is destined for the lower echelons of the job market and, increasingly, unemployment. For white girls, the very use of traditional elements of femininity as a distracting tactic in school serves to further reinforce them in their traditional feminine roles. To act out the scripts of flirtation and sexuality is to rehearse and reconfirm the significance of these forms of behaviour for women. The use of femininity as an oppositional stance in schools, therefore simply aids its reproduction, along with the connotations of sexism and inferiority which go with it. For white underachievers, both male and female, together with black males, acts of opposition simply serve to reconfirm their low achievements and expectations, at the same time as boosting sexist and racist ideas which are already prevalent within school. Only black females have devised ways of expressing hostility, whilst retaining educational advantages. We are forced to conclude, therefore, that the educational system is fairly resilient in its accommodation to antagonism and opposition. We must also ask whether the reproduction of sexism and racism is not actually promoted by the kinds of resistance strategies which have been examined. If this is the case, it is a paradox of the utmost enormity.

Finally, we must not underemphasize the fact that most young people, whether black, white, male or female, do not oppose school, except for the odd bit of truancy, the missed lesson, the muttered abuse or the small act of defiance. Such modes of 'resistance' may seem major forms of revolt to their perpetrators, but in reality they offer the educational machine little significant challenge.

In an institution where the acts of 'revolution' are so minor, and even more serious strategies of resistance so easily accommodated, the impact of the ideologies and practices we have previously described remains. Rather than being a social 'leveller', the education system is still a powerful, and even respectable, bastion of racism and sexism. It is partly through the activities of schools that the reproduction of racism and sexism is confirmed and achieved.

6   Ideology and Masculinity

In this penultimate chapter we make explicit our view about the nature of masculinity upon which some of our previous arguments have been based. In our discussion of socialization we found it difficult to discover an unambiguous linkage between racism and sexism. In very broad terms, we implied that socialization mediates oppression. Here our argument will be that what is mediated is an ideology which takes for granted the reality of gender and 'race'. It is our contention that the way in which gender and 'race' are socially constructed (in Western societies at least) is dependent to a large degree on the practice of domination. The practice of domination in one sphere is never insulated from its practice in another sphere. Those who exploit workers do not have much difficulty in exploiting black groups. Those who dominate their wives and children at home have no difficulty in dominating people at work. What we are saying here is that oppression is indivisible. Where there is oppression of women, we find oppression of out-groups; where we find economic oppression, we discover sexism and racism. Furthermore, all forms of oppression are expressed and reproduced at the ideological level as though they were natural processes.

We are suggesting oppression always involves a degree of objectification. In the case of women objectification means (as Mackinnon observes) that men

> *create* the world from their own point of view, which then *becomes* the truth to be described . . . *Power to create the world from one's point of view is power in its male form.* The male epistemological stance, which corresponds to the world it creates, is objectivity: the ostensibly noninvolved stance, the view from a distance and from no particular perspective, apparently trans-

parent to its reality. It does not comprehend its own perspective, does not recognise what it sees as subject like itself, or that the way it apprehends its world is a form of its subjection and presupposes it. The objectively knowable is object. Woman through male eyes is sex object, that by which man knows himself at once as man and subject. What is objectively known corresponds to the world and can be verified by pointing to it (as science does) because the world itself is controlled from the same point of view. (Mackinnon, 1982, pp.23–24)

Accordingly, what men understand as a natural relationship between themselves and women disguises the actuality of their power. Objectification allows them to define themselves as a powerful and natural force operating on a world of things, as some kind of transcendental subjectivity moulding intractable nature into a desired form. The notion of masculinity as mastery over nature, as a heroic force struggling against the otherness of nature enables us to glean the essential component of the objectification process. It also enables us to understand how the practice of domination over things is related to domination over people.

Of course, we are not claiming that objectification is some master historical process. All we are doing is to suggest that if we can identify a masculine ideology, then it will be characterized by assumptions about the potency of male subjectivity in a world of objects. From this point of view, masculinity is an ideology of domination. In order to make this argument more cogently, we must systematize our discussion. We have to pose the question, How is it that both sexism and racism appear to be encapsulated within the same framework of ideological discourse? — that is, in simpler language, How is it that both sexism and racism appear to treat women and out-groups as if they are objects? There are five dimensions of ideology which are relevant to our purposes:

1 ideology as commonsense;
2 ideology as naturalization;
3 ideology as lived experience;
4 ideology as unconscious;
5 ideology as collective.

Ideology as Commonsense

By this is meant the way in which people appear to absorb uncriti-
cally the stock of images and beliefs about their social and cultural
world. Every society has a reservoir of folk-tales, myths, stories
about sex, gender, strangers, and out-groups which are part of a
common currency of social interaction. Moreover, these stories are
not merely absorbed as though they had some kind of artificial
status — they come to be accepted as having reality, as being only
commonsense. Thus, in Britain today there are all sorts of stories
which whites tell each other about the culture and behaviour of
Jamaicans, Pakistanis, and others. There are stories about their
sexual habits, stories about their personal conduct, stories about
their personal hygiene, stories about their intellectual and physical
capacities, etc. And there are stories that men tell each other about
women. You only have to go into a pub on any day of the week to
hear men talking about women as sexual objects. Everywhere men
repeat stories about female illogicality and intuition. The mythology
of sexual differences is passed on from man to man as if it was
received truth.

Commonsensical knowledge is the ground on which most people
make their judgements about 'race' and gender. Commonsense is
what everybody knows — everybody knows that women are emotional, that certain groups are inferior/avaricious/depraved/anti-
social etc. It is stereotypical — it exaggerates, distorts and over-
generalizes; moreover, it naturalizes unequal treatment and
discrimination.

Ideology as Naturalization

In so far as commonsensical knowledge is acquired through
socialization, through media dissemination, and through schooling,
it appears to have some kind of unshakeable reality. It is absorbed
and internalized without ambiguity; it is not questioned because it
appears to be natural knowledge. In other words, what everybody
knows about 'race' and gender is perceived and experienced as
having the quality of inevitability and universality. Racist and sexist
beliefs are given the same status as scientific knowledge. Thus, the
statement 'all Jews are greedy' is given equal standing with the

scientific generalization 'water boils at one hundred degrees centi-grade'. Furthermore, racism and sexism are saturated with 'scientific' knowledge. What everybody is supposed to know can be supported by scientific evidence. Accordingly, if Blacks perform badly at school, then the racist sees this as confirmation of the scientific evidence that she/he has read in her/his newspaper, or obtained from a 'respect-able' source such as a sociobiology text. The category of the natural, therefore, has an almost sacrosanct status in Western thought; furthermore, it dominates everyday thinking about a whole variety of themes, such as private property, competition, the nuclear family, 'race', and gender.

Ideology as Lived Experience

When we talk of racism and sexism as being 'commonsense' and as being 'naturalized', we are not referring to abstract concepts but are stressing the social potency of ideology, that is, ideology as a consti-tuent part of everyday living — how racism and sexism enter into the way in which people conduct their lives.

For the racist, beliefs are not only cognitive categories or stereotypes — they represent a way of making sense and reacting to a range of social experiences. Ideology, in this sense, is not simply imposed from the outside by some super-powerful socialization agency; on the contrary, it is used by people to define their own lives and to understand the struggles and conflicts of the world they live in. In encountering Blacks, Jews, and other groups, the white worker does not interact with them in a pre-determined manner, (although he/she has perhaps internalized and absorbed racist stories and commonsensical accounts through socialization) — rather, he/she reproduces racism as a means of coping with the exigencies of the moment. It is easier to live with unemployment if you can account for it in terms of what appears to be an accessible explanation. In living our everyday life we tend to look for the most obvious and available explanations — we do not 'demystify' what is in front of our eyes, when what is in front of our eyes is apparent (so we believe) to everybody. Even when there is readily available information about the causes of unemployment, an unemployed person will not necessarily accept that information because it does not fit in with his/her experience.

For a sexist, while we may infer the influence of gender role typing and the influence of early childhood experience on his behaviour, this does not tell us why and how he uses gender typifications in everyday life. Thus a white male brought up in Europe or the United States uses his commonsensical views of gender to come to terms with the realities which he encounters. In the home he observes women as domestic workers, as mothers; in the public sphere he sees women in subservient occupational roles; on the television screen he sees women displayed as objects. In fact everywhere he is overwhelmed by a barrage of images of women which enables him to organize his gender behaviour in sexist terms.

Both racism and sexism are not external forces operating on people — they are rather, dynamic aspects of the way in which they encounter, experience, and interpret the world. What we are saying here is that ideology does not merely reflect the world, but that it is used to live in that world.

Ideology as Unconscious

One implication of saying that ideology is lived experience is that both racism and sexism may be seen as aspects of the person's sense of self, that is, they are unconscious. By saying they are unconscious we are not, in this instance, making any claims about repression or the mechanisms of the psychoanalytic unconscious. What we are saying, however, is that racism and sexism are so sedimented in people's consciousness that it is almost impossible for them to see the world in any other way. Now we are aware that when we use the word sedimented, we are in danger of lapsing into determinism (into a strong socialization position), but sedimented does not only mean internalization — it also means living one's life in terms of ideological imperatives. A racist lives his/her life as a racist because the world she/he lives in is structured in terms of racism. Racism is such a 'normal' part of political and social life that the racist cannot help defining the world in racist terms.

There is a further connotation of unconsciousness in relation to ideology. This is the notion that ideology is locked into 'character structure'. In becoming a fascist, racist, sexist, authoritarian, and so forth, the individual is the plaything of ideological currents which shape her/his psyche. The content of the unconscious is determined by the repressive power of ideologies as mediated by various socializing agents. This is illustrated by Reich's discussion of the historical and personality consequences of sexual repression (Reich, 1975b). The implication of this is that the unconscious is the repository of repressed ideological forces which profoundly influence the manner in which the person relates to categories such as 'race', class, gender, etc. In other words, ideology is embedded into the psyche and body as some kind of material force.

Now although we may believe that this idea of the unconscious as a storehouse of repressed ideological content has a certain persuasiveness, it is not our primary concern here. Certainly we must accept the argument that ideology can have personality consequences, but we cannot conclude from this that ideology is simply a function of psychodynamic processes. Hence, when we talk about ideology as unconscious we are mainly referring to unreflexive, unexamined ways of thinking about and acting towards social objects, such as classes, genders and out-groups; we are talking about the collective naturalization of common sense in the psyche.

Ideology as Collective

It is obvious that ideology is collective, but in asserting this we reject the view that racism as an ideology is a mirror of some determining base. This is not to deny that racism may be rooted in the conditions of existence of a particular class or group, but it is to say that even when this is so, this does not subsume all we can say about it as a collective phenomenon. Indeed, there is no necessary correlation between racism and the structural location of any class or group. While it is certainly true that racism may sometimes be a legitimating strategem of a ruling group (Cox, 1970), or that it may be 'appropriated by a class for its own ends' (Miles, 1982, p.80), we cannot assent to the proposition that racism *per se* is always the ideology of a particular class. In Britain racism does not belong to the working class, nor does it belong to any other class. We would argue that racism as an ideology is sedimented in British society as a whole. By this we mean that racist assumptions and beliefs are entrenched in the state, the family, the educational system. In talking about sedimentation, we are therefore pointing to the way in which racism is collectively reproduced in social consciousness.

More importantly, we would want to argue that racism is not simply a collective cognitive orientation. British society is racist because it *discriminates* against Jamaicans, Indians, and others. Racism as an ideology implies racism as a practice. Moreover, racism is practised in a multiplicity of sites; the landlord who turns away a prospective black tenant, the building society which rejects a request for a loan by a black applicant, the teacher who defines immigrant children as culturally deprived are all instances of the collective sedimentation of racism in British society. Note, we are not maintaining that this collective sedimentation is *immanent* in culture. Racism is sedimented in culture because it has a history. In the United States it cannot be understood without an understanding of the history and structure of slavery. In Britain, its contemporary manifestation must, to a considerable degree, be seen in terms of the aftermath of colonialism. But this is not tantamount to saying that racism is the ideological baggage, the 'hand-me-downs' from the past — it is not simply the accumulation of traditional stereotypes; it is also an ideological form which has meaning for the way in which people try to cope with the contradictions and ambiguities of their everyday life. At the same time, as we have argued, racism is also a practice. The practice of racism is an exercise in power. To talk about the 'sedimentation of racism in social consciousness' is to talk about the readiness of these people to engage in some kind of discriminatory action against these groups.

At this juncture it seems appropriate to concretize our discussion of the collective aspect of ideology by focusing on 'masculinity'.

Masculinity as an Ideology

If we could represent men as a collectivity, then what options are available in the literature which help us to define men's collective interests in terms of a common identity and ideology?

As Chauvinism

One option is to define masculinity as chauvinism in the same way as American Blacks defined white racism as white chauvinism. This implies that all men are exposed to a socialization experience which turns them into male supremacists. They inevitably internalize beliefs and feelings which naturalize their commitment to the subordination of women. In general, this view of masculinity is given a trans-cultural and trans-historical profile. Men as oppressors always adopt an ideology which elevates masculinity and devalues femininity (Millett, 1969).

If we take this view at its face value, then we would expect that chauvinism must indeed be universal, that masculinity was always defined in the same way, that men were always unambiguous about their sexuality, about their authority, and about their relations to women. We would expect to be able to trace the universal nature of masculinity in all contexts, that is, we should be able to discover some quintessential masculine identity in societies ranging from Japan to contemporary California. The trouble is that when we start looking for universals, then we are back with essentialism of both the psychological and biological kind. We are back with the argument about male aggressiveness and strength. In other words, when we postulate a universal male chauvinism, this is another way of talking about universal male psychology. It does not enable us to understand the historicity of masculinity, nor does it allow us to take account of the variety of ways in which masculinity is expressed.

So, if we reject the idea of a general ahistorical masculine ideology related to a universal male identity, then presumably an alternative option is the one which locates masculinity within given structural locations. Here, in very crude terms, the argument is that specific kinds of social formation or modes of production have definite linkages to the relationship between men and women. Furthermore, these relationships are given institutional form in appropriate household and familial arrangements. In developmental terms, we get arguments which state that the status of men and women is dependent on the kind of role they play in the productive process. Hence, there are attempts to correlate the emergence of patriarchal forms of authority with the transition from nomadic to agricultural modes of production. In most cases, the rise of male domination is associated with private property. The male access to and control of a community's surplus is seen as the cornerstone of their domination over women, and their consequent construction of a legitimating and commonsensical ideology of male supremacy.

What this argument suggests is that private property gives men authority, not only over the economic surplus, but also over the labour and reproductive capacities of women. Masculinity, from this point of view, is a historically produced and reproduced ideology which gives men the 'right' to dominate women. The implication here is that only with the abandonment and the overthrow of property rights will men lose their aggressive masculinity. Of course, as we have stated it, this argument is far too simplistic. There are far more sophisticated versions of this thesis. However, for the moment we are only interested in describing it as an alternative to the idea of a universal masculine ideology. (We certainly, as will become clear, do not subscribe to this sort of approach.) This alternative assumes that masculinity is ultimately reducible to the particularities of structural location. Hence masculinity in China is not the same as masculinity in Borneo or in Sweden. Furthermore, bourgeois masculinity is different from working-class masculinity. Masculinity is infinitely variable. What is regarded as being manly and assertive in one context, is regarded as bogus in another. In other words, this alternative makes masculinity relative, just as it makes gender in general relative. How men define themselves depends on where they find themselves. But this apparent diversity of masculine ideologies and identities does not obscure the fact that men stand in a dominant relationship to women in most of the diverse settings. Although there is sufficient anthropological documentation of the variety of ways in which masculinity is expressed, the mere fact of diversity does not mean that men do not control the economic and political resources of that society. It is this power and control that partly conditions their 'chauvinism', their view of themselves as 'lords' of creation.

As Politics

From this viewpoint chauvinism may be seen as the ideological expression of male domination of the public and private spheres. Hence, the inference to be drawn is that masculinity is a measure of the power of men in most extant societies. Historically, it relates to the development of modes of production which secured male control over economic surpluses, and their control and disposal of the 'means of production'. Furthermore, there is the implication that men, because of their internalization of an ideology which confirms and reinforces their dominant status, tend to devalue women's work and their reproductive functions, while simultaneously regarding their own work as being critically important and necessary. Consequently, masculinity is equated with the public sphere. To be a man in most contexts is to be a person who does important things outside the domestic sphere. The world of politics, power, work *(sic)* is the world of men's dominion. It is here that the 'business' of the world is done. What men do in the public sphere is make the decisions and do the work that makes society possible. Put differently, we could say that if there is a masculine ideology, then one of its main dimensions is the belief in the functional necessity of the right of men to control and shape the public world of politics and work.

This is not the place to engage in a lengthy analysis of the 'private and the public', but we cannot ignore its relevance for contemporary debate. And it is precisely because men in Western history have assumed the role of 'speaking' for the whole species that makes us see this 'speech' as ideological. It is ideological because it assumes that what men say and do arbitrates experience and reality. But what men say and do is related to the power they have over property and persons. And indeed, politics as we know it has been practised and elaborated by men. From Plato to the present day, politics (in the Western context at least) has been a male prerogative. Politics is the male game par excellence. To be a man is (in theory) to be in a position to ensure that the world of women is confined and separated from any possibility of power sharing and decision making.

> Because women have, throughout much of Western history, been a silenced population in the arena of public speech, their views on these matters, and their role in the process of humanization, have either been taken for granted or assigned a lesser order of significance and honour compared to the public, political activities of males. Women were silenced in part because that which defines them and to which they are inescapably linked — sexuality, natality, the human body (images of uncleanness and taboo, visions of dependency, helplessness, vulnerability) — was omitted from political speech. Why? Because politics is in part an elaborate defense against the tug of the private, against the lure of the familial, against evocations of female power. The question to be put, then, is not just what politics is for but what politics has served to defend against. (Elshtain, 1981, p.15–16)

For Elshtain, politics, to a large extent, is there to defend men's power and domination against the encroachment of women — it is a defence against the intrusion of the personal into the heady business of running the state and the economy. The public sphere is invented and constructed in order to maintain the illusion of men's inherent right to dominate the private sphere. So, in a sense, it could be argued that men have a collective interest in maintaining the distinction between the private and the public because, in so doing, they justify their continued hold on the trappings of power.

But politics is not only about the defence of the public sphere against infringement from the private sphere — it is also about the way certain collectivities coerce other collectivities. In short, it is about the way in which people in general dominate or are dominated by others. If men as a collectivity dominate women, then we cannot say that they achieve this domination simply by the device of dividing the world into the public and the private. What we are saying here is that domination of women by men is to be found alongside the domination of men over other men. Men compete with other men — they engage in power struggles, they fight wars, they exploit entire populations, not simply to maintain the distinction between the public and the private. The question we have to ask, therefore, is whether masculinity is not only about the domination of men over women, but also about the domination that *some* men have over everybody else?

As Competitiveness

In a previous chapter we discussed the problem of masculinity from the point of view of improper socialization and flawed male identity. Male aggressiveness is attributed to some fundamental lack, some inadequacy in their psychological make-up when compared with women. Hence, from this perspective, history may be described as a monumental attempt by men to compensate for their inadequacies by coercing the world in their image. Not only do they exact a terrible price on women, but they also fight each other in order to demonstrate their manhood. Other men are perceived as a threat to their possession of women and property. Such a view is 'essentialistic' — it seems to situate masculinity in the recesses of the unconscious. Both sexism and racism are explained by the male's need to prove himself by dominating others and nature.

Other versions of the competitiveness thesis attempt to locate it in particular socio-historic settings. The argument here is that men only become competitive when they have secured property and control over surpluses which they protect from the encroachment of other men, who themselves have similar control over property. Competition, from this point of view, is a battle over scarce resources where scarce resources may be defined in terms of women and property. The belief and perception that other men are possible threats to one's ownership rights over women is sufficient to account for the phenomenon of sexual possessiveness and racism. Other men (nations, tribes, races) are elevated to the status of the 'enemy'.

In this respect, Hoch talks about the contamination of European culture by images of the bestiality of Blacks, Jews, foreigners, etc. White masculinity is tested by the unfair competition of the super-masculine males of the 'barbarians' who are supposed to rape and seduce white women to demonstrate their superior virility.

> The notion of interracial conquest as an ultimate test of heroic masculinity was quite visible in late nineteenth century asser-tions that the struggle between white Europe and dark Africa represented only an inevitable competition between the races, male survival of the 'fittest'. In such struggle the most shatter-ing (though rarely admitted) assertion of virility often lay in taking control of the other group's females — most obviously in the institution of slavery — and at all costs excluding them from access to one's own. Defence of manhood demanded, above all, the defence of the white goddesses of civilization against the dark, sex-crazed barbarians at the gates, and such fears provided the most explosive fuel for interracial hatreds, lynching and war. (Hoch, 1979, p.47)

Racism, in this view, may be understood as the resentment that white males feel toward 'dark-skinned' outsiders who are considered to be potentially more sexually potent than white males. Perhaps it would be more accurate to say that the fear of out-group male virility is perceived as an implicit threat which can only be met if the white male is prepared to assert his own virility. To be a man is to be able to prove oneself on the sexual battleground, where the enemy is waiting to challenge one's sexual prowess (Stember, 1976).

Sexual competitiveness, then, is defined in more or less the same terms as economic competitiveness. Indeed, sexual and economic competition are conflated. In the struggle for competitive advan-tage, men fight wars and compete against each other to obtain goods

and women. To the victor go the spoils. Ideologically, this is trans-
muted into a belief in the superior masculinity of the winners. The
history of colonial conquest, from this viewpoint, can be recon-
structed as the triumph of white manhood over the bestiality, the
savageness of the colonized. If one's rivals are defined as animals, as
bestial, then it makes it so much easier to employ tactics against
them which one would not presumably countenance against one's
own group.

Yet the enemy may not only be conceived of as outsiders or aliens.
The enemy may be found on one's own doorstep, so to speak. The
implicit taboo in Western societies against marriage and sexual
contact across class lines is still very much an aspect of class-defined
behaviour. Although the romanticism of the penniless working-class
girl who marries into the aristocracy had a great appeal to a large
public, the reality was very different, especially in terms of the
images that the middle class had of working-class sexuality. Thus,
those who have strong power positions in a society are always ready
to believe that those who do not are only waiting to rape and pillage.

This conflation of sexuality and economic competitiveness has
been explored through two versions of masculinity as the ideology of
the male ruling class. Firstly, there is the version which defines *all*
men in terms of a competitive masculinity deriving from their collective control and ownership of property and their claims to exclusive
sexual and reproductive rights over women, and secondly, there is
the version which sees competitive masculinity as reflecting the
interests of a *particular* ruling groups of men who impose their
ideology on everybody else. In either case, the assumption is that
men will come into conflict with each other in order to hold on to
what they possess. In both cases, sexuality and property are closely
intertwined. Men fight other men to protect what they believe is
theirs. In both cases we are therefore presented with the view of men
acting as collectivities with collective ideologies.

This kind of analysis runs counter to those which emphasize
economic class as being the relevant factor in ideological formation.
Certainly, Marxism does not define men as a collectivity. What
constitutes a class for Marxism cuts across gender and 'race'. Men
and women are working-class, or they are bourgeois. They are given
a class position only in relation to the productive process. Both
sexism and racism are consequences of the primary class
antagonisms associated with the extant mode of production. What

the masculinity thesis asserts, on the other hand, is the equal status of patriarchy where patriarchy is conceived of in terms of the relative power of men and women with respect to property and sexual access. Men, from this point of view, at some point in time achieved dominance. Capitalism as a mode of production merely articulated the dominance in a new form — it did not alter its reality. The implication is that in dominating women, in treating them as possesions, or in claiming sexual rights over their bodies, men also acquired the capacity to control other men, that is, they defined other men as appropriate targets for colonization and conquest. Hence, history is male-constructed. It is 'HIStory' of wars, conquests, colonizations, exploitation, and slavery. Masculinity, conceived historically, is the accumulative celebration of male domination. History celebrates the male conquest of the natural world — it defines the male as the maker of 'HIStory'. 'Men make themselves' while simultaneously dominating nature and other 'inferior' and 'weaker' people. Competitive masculinity is, by this account, a consequence of the conflation of sexuality and economics. This conflation is most clearly articulated in systems of exploitation like slavery and spectacularly expressed in contemporary fascism and racism.

As Culture

There is another aspect of the masculinity thesis which appears to have an older pedigree, namely, the notion that 'culture' *per se* is masculine. In its crudest form this kind of thinking is to be found in the self-congratulatory male enumeration of male technological, cultural, and political achievements. In all this women do not appear. The assumption is that they do not appear because it is not their 'nature' to be technological innovators. In other words, there is an implicit belief in the duality of culture and nature. Men are the creators and mediators of culture — women are the manifestation of nature. The implication is that men develop culture in order to understand and control the natural world, while women being the embodiment of the forces of nature, must be brought under the civilizing control of men. Because of their central role in childbirth and child rearing, women are considered to be not suited for the task of culture building.

This duality of culture and nature is not confined to the

distinction between men and women. it is also used to distinguish between so-called higher nations or civilizations, and those deemed to be culturally backward. The notion of the black 'beast' is contrasted with the civilized complexity of European civilization. Non-European peoples are conceived of as being nearer to nature than Europeans. Hence, the justification or, at least, the partial justification for slavery and colonialism was often couched in the language of guardianship. White slavers and colonists described themselves as the bringers of a modicum of civilization to poor, benighted savages. They saw themselves as the trustees (benevolent or otherwise) of uncivilized beings 'who needed a firm hand to guide them out of the straightjacket of instinct and bestiality' (Fredrickson, 1981, p.3–53).

This duality of nature and culture has recently been used by a number of writers in an attempt to account for the apparent universality of male domination across cultures. The argument here is premised on the belief that all societies somehow devalue women and, by extension, also devalue other cultures:

> Returning now to the issue of women, their pan-cultural, second-class status could be accounted for, quite simply, by postulating that women are being identified or symbolically associated with nature, as opposed to men, who are identified with culture. Since it is always culture's project to subsume and transcend nature, if women are considered part of nature, then culture would find it 'natural' to subordinate, not to say oppress them. Yet although this argument can be shown to have considerable force, it seems to oversimplify the case. The formulation I would like to defend and elaborate on . . ., is that women are seen 'merely' as being *closer* to nature than men. (Ortner, 1974, p.73)

Ortner is at pains to stress that it is the cultural definition of women as being closer to nature that is important for the self-definition of men as culturally innovative. The argument is that most, if not all, cultures make this distinction, but they do so in terms of symbolic construction. The difficulty is, that once we start dividing the cultural world into the categories of the natural and the cultural, we inevitably lapse into a form of essentialism in which the binary opposition of men and women is given the status of a cardinal principle of social life. Furthermore, in opposing culture to nature we assume that what is cultural is not natural, that is, we assume that culture is some supra-human category which relentlessly impresses nature in its own image. Certainly, there are male viewpoints of this cultural reification which have dominated European thinking. The identification of the intellect and rationality with the 'male' in history has been a common enough theme in philosophy and literature. The imperious 'he' is rooted in Western discourse to such an extent that even when an attempt is consciously made to avoid its use, we either have to invent a new language, or have to deconstruct our present usage. Language, written and spoken, is saturated with 'masculinity'. Not only do men make history, but they write and speak that history. It is only recently that feminist writers have begun to reclaim and reconstruct women's past.

Just as Western discourse is male-centred in that it presents 'masculinity' as superior and qualitatively different to 'femininity', so is it culturally ethnocentric. The distinction between 'black' and 'white' is superimposed upon the distinction 'savage' and 'civilized'. These distinctions have a long history in the contact between Europeans on the one side, and Africans and Asians on the other side. Initially the differentiation between Christian and heathen did not necessarily imply any racist conception (Frederickson, 1981), but the perception of the difference in behaviour and culture did lead explorers, colonists, traders, and other European adventurers to report back to their European homelands about the 'savagery' and 'barbarism' they encountered in Africa, Asia, and the Americas. But, as Frederickson points out, Europeans did not encounter the rest of the world without pre-conceptions of what they would find. There already was implicit in European culture an association of blackness with bestiality and evil. This association initially did not have contemporary racist undertones, but it was readily adaptable to the circumstances of Western colonial conquest:

> the medieval belief in the existence of sub-human 'wild-men' and monsters influenced Europeans' perceptions of the savages they encountered or expected to encounter in remote parts of the world. The literature of the sixteenth and seventeenth century on exploration and travel is filled with comments likening American Indians, Eskimos, or 'Hottentots' to wild beasts. In 1586, the English explorer Thomas Cavendish described some Brazilian Indians as being 'as wild as ever was a

buck or any other wild beast'. As sophisticated an Englishman as Sir Walter Raleigh was credulous enough to believe that there were natives in Guinea who 'have eyes in their shoulders, and their mouths in the middle of their breasts'. Because of their use of click sounds as part of their language, a general impression existed that the 'Hottentots' of the Cape were so bestial that they lacked the ordinary power of human speech. Whatever the conventional religious doctrine may have been, such accounts of creatures who seemed more animal than human must have raised doubts in the minds of many Europeans as to whether they really shared 'one blood' and a common ancestry with many of the types of men being brought to their attention by the explorers and travellers of the late Renaissance' (Frederickson, 1981, p.11)

While contemporary racist discourse is not so crude as this, we still come across media presentations of Third World cultures which, to say the least, portray these cultures as if they are bestial and sub-human. News of war in Africa is treated from the perspective of horrified, civilized (white) commentators who give the impression that they are not really surprised by the events they report. After all, what does one expect of 'primitive' human beings?

In very simple terms, the distinction between culture and nature is a way of saying that there are differences between groups of people. But the perception of differences is not a mere categorical and perceptual device — it is also evaluative, implying that these differences are indicative of relative merit. The differences between men and women are given the status of moral categories in which men assign to themselves civilized worth. Moreover, evaluation of differences assigning some kind of superiority to one group *vis à vis* another group is not only an exercise in moral ascription — it reflects differences of power. So the perception of inferiority in out-groups in terms of the culture-nature dichotomy is not a refraction of 'polarity' built into the structure of human society, but is symptomatic of the structure of social inequality and the manner in which this inequality is sedimented ideologically. To distinguish betwen men and women, or black and white, in terms of culture and nature is, therefore, related to how a group perceives and acts towards groups it oppresses or dominates.

To sum up, we have noted the tendency of Western 'intellectual' and 'popular' thought to classify the world in dichotomous terms.

We cannot concern ourselves with the epistemological implications of this tendency, except in so far as it supposedly effects the relationships between men and women and whites and blacks. This distinction is part and parcel of the commonsensical image that those who oppress have about themselves and the oppressed. However, we are not contending that men as a collectivity define themselves as the standard-bearers of culture and rationality. All we are saying is that Western definitions of masculinity appear to celebrate male 'civility' while simultaneously denigrating the natural as the province of women, and wild and savage out-groups. (Of course, when we speak of Western conceptions of masculinity, we are thereby presuming a lot. For example, can we equate the masculinity of middle-class and working-class men? Do they share the same views about culture and rationality? Indeed, is there any commonality of interest and ideology between men whose respective circumstances and experiences are so removed from each other?)

So, in discussing masculinity as chauvinsim, politics, competitiveness, and culture, we get the impression that we are dealing with a very elusive concept. We can understand the attraction of subsuming masculinity under the umbrella of some essentialist explanation. It is simple enough to discover masculinity in the behaviour of men and then to trace it back to their biological and instinctual make-up. 'Essentialism' makes the task of explanation very easy indeed. Yet, in rejecting essentialism, we still have to account for the fact that concepts and ideologies of masculinity are prevalent in Western consciousness. We have already intimated at the beginning of this chapter that these concepts are related to the objectification process.

The Objectification Process

Objectification as a process is dramatically illustrated by slavery. Obviously, classical slavery was different from the Caribbean and North American plantation system. However, in all systems, the slave's relation to his/her owner was one in which the owner's power was absolute (Patterson, 1982). It is this notion of absolute control that allows us to speak about objectification. Slavery, in this sense, can be construed in the same way we construed sexual objectification at the beginning of this chapter. Just as sexual objectification negates a woman's subjectivity, similarly, so does slavery define a slave as incapable of having an intentional life. The point here is not that the slave was dehumanized, but that the slave-owner treated her/him as though she/he was dehumanized.

Slave women in particular were treated as if they were completely deficient in human status. Not only did the owner make complete use of their labour power, but they subjected them to the most vicious sexual abuse. A black slave woman was fair game for any white male (Hooks, 1982). Although not all plantation owners and their overseers were rapists, there can be no doubt that rape was a common enough phenomenon to create an indelible impression on black women and their descendants. The abolition of slavery did not materially modify the way white men regarded black women. Their 'blackness' continued to define their sexuality. Moreover, their 'blackness' was a symbol of a thing-like condition.

Traditionally, objectification has been associated with production. For Marx, production was logically prior to objectification. Or, to put it another way, without production there could be no objectification. History can be seen as the history of production in which human beings constantly objectify the natural world in order to control and master it. In mastering nature, they enter into social relationships which lead to the domination of one group of human beings by another. Accordingly, all forms of domination are derived from production. Gender and racial oppression by implication are aspects of the objectification process set in motion by production. Moreover, with the advent of a capitalist mode of production, the objectification process informs the entire fabric of social and personal relationships. At the beginning of this chapter we asserted that 'oppression in indivisible'. We realize economic exploitation is closely linked with gender and 'race' oppression, but this is not equivalent to saying that they are thereby reduced to each other. While it is certainly true that sexual objectification in most Western societies is couched in the language of the market, this does not in any way account for its particularity. It does not account for the 'male epistemological stance' which apprehends the world as if it is an object to be worked upon. Whatever the origin of sexual objectification, we can testify to its presence among large numbers of Western men. The reproduction of this objectification is mediated through the press, television, cinema, but more significantly, it is continuously reinforced by the mundane interactions of men in their football clubs, their pubs, their workplaces, etc., in their constant production of sexual images which reduce women to bits and pieces. This reduction is generalized — it is not only found on the factory floor, but is powerfully present in the board-room and at the tennis club. And, of course, it is part and parcel of academic games*man*ship.

The reduction of women to sexual objects is also a central dimension of the male comedian's performance. The dirty joke is juxtaposed with the racist joke. But the comedian is not exceptional — all he does is to make a living out of racism and sexism, whereas most other men live their racism and sexism as if they are unremarkable aspects of everyday life. Masculinity as an ideology takes for granted the naturalness of gender divisions, and accepts without question the division between nature and culture, and it celebrates the potency of man the 'maker'. In saying that most men live their lives as racists and sexists, we are merely pointing to the way in which male consciousness is dominated by the objectification process. While we may agree with those theorists who argue that a capitalist society is especially congenial to objectification, we part company with them when they claim that objectification is always an effect of production. It is our contention that objectification can be prior to production. Or, to put it differently, it is domination (oppression) which objectifies the world. Domination always involves the objectification of the dominated; all forms of oppression imply the devaluation of the subjectivity of the oppressed.

Although, for example, we can construe slavery as one extreme means among many of exploiting labour, this in itself does not help us to understand the extreme objectification of the slave. The practice of slavery does not only entail the slave's dehumanization, it also depends on the pre-definition of certain categories of people as worthy of exploitation. Thus, as we have noted, long before European powers embarked on their colonial enterprises, we find images of the savage and negative beliefs about 'blackness' in European thought and culture. While in principle, anybody could be enslaved, the definition of blackness already contained within it a presumption about the non-human status of black people. In a sense, the history of colonialism can be seen as the history of the practice of objectification.

Objectification of the subject race seems to be as ubiquitous as reduction to the animal world. It consists in a denial of the right to self-regulation or the capacity for self-regulation. In its

ultimate form, members of the subject race are equated with
objects, with things; deprived of autonomy in many spheres,
they are regulated by the dominant race. The fullest
expression of this state is to be found in chattel slavery. Depes-
tre refers to the process of zombification, the zombie, according to Haitan myth, being a person . . . from whom one has
stolen spirit and reason, and to whom is left only the force of
work: he describes the history of colonization as a process of
the generalized zombification of man. In a milder form, the
reduction to the non-status of objects is also to be found, in
appreciable measure in the South African Government's regulation of African labour, as indicated in such conceptions as
the 'canalisation' of Native labour, or the concept of 'redundant' labour, or in the systematic control of the flow of labour,
along the lines of the marketing of commodities. (Kuper, 1974,
p.13–14)

Zombification might seem to be too strong a term to use when
describing how dominating groups regard those they oppress, but it
catches nicely the reduction that takes place in these situations. A
constant theme in the West's incursion into Africa, the Americas,
and Asia has been the brutality which marked its treatment of
indigenous populations. This brutality cannot be explained simply
as an unavoidable consequence of conquest, nor can it be seen as a
by-product of exploitation of labour. The objectification of colonized
people is underpinned by an ideology which facilitates the brutal
practice of domination. It is this ideology of objectification which we
call masculinity. Masculinity, as we understand it, is that ideological form which informs any kind of oppression.

In this respect, one of the strongest tenets of some recent femininst
analysis of male dominance is their claim that dominance depends
on 'compulsory heterosexuality' (Rich, 1981). The sexual act itself
secures the basis of male power. In a sense, the sex act is the primal
power relationship — it is the prototype on which all other power
relationships are built. Men use women's bodies to establish the
primacy of their own pleasure, while simultaneously forcing women
to accept the inevitability of their sexual dependence. Marriage,
from this point of view, is the institutionalization of male penis
power, but it is more than this; it is also the social recognition that
men have colonized women in the same way as they colonized the
non-European world. White men (all men) stand in the same

relationship to women as colonists stand to the colonized. Now this is a very strong analogy. It assumes that the subjection of women in heterosexual relationships is mirrored by the subjection of the colonized in the colonial world. By objectifying women, men have a working model for the domination of other men and women.

> The first division of labour, in pre-history, was based on sex: men hunted, women built the villages, took care of the children, and farmed. Women collectively controlled the land, language culture, and the communities. Men were able to conquer women with the weapons that they developed for hunting when it became clear that women were leading a more stable, peaceful, and desirable existence. We do not know exactly how this conquest took place, but it is clear that the original imperialism was male over female: the male claiming the female body and her service as his territory (or property).
>
> Having secured the domination of women, men continued this pattern of suppressing people, now on the basis of tribe, race, and class. Although there have been numerous battles over class, race, and nation during the last 3000 years, none has brought the liberation of women. While these other forms of oppression must be ended, there is no reason to believe that our liberation will come with the smashing of capitalism, racism, or imperialism today. Women will be free only when we concentrate on fighting male supremacy. (Bunch, 1975, p.29)

The colonization thesis implies a historical reconstruction of a male victory over women. It situates the beginnings of objectification in the subjection of the female body. Accordingly, from this perspective, the male epistemological stance has its origins in men's appropriation of women as sexual possessions.

Now, while this argument is persuasive, it does not in our view fully catch the nature of objectification. Objectification involves more than the subjection of the female body. Fundamentally, it is rooted in the human assertion of power over nature. It is men who, for a variety of reasons, come to see themselves as being the tamers of nature, as the vanguard fighting scarcity. In their subjection of nature they simultaneously begin to subjugate other human beings. The masculine ideology is the ideology of objectification. As such, it naturalizes the distinction between subject and object. In so doing, it distinguishes between the agency of man the maker, and the passivity of nature. The pacification of nature involves the pacification of women, as well as the subordination of other men perceived as potential rivals. Hence, from our perspective, masculinity as an ideology elevates the primacy of technique, rationality, and power. In objectifying nature, men lay the foundation for the objectification of all social and personal relationships. It is in this sense that we believe that racism and sexism belong to the same discursive universe, because they both are premissed on the objectification of other human beings.

Obviously, we are not making any claims about the inevitability of the masculine ideology. What we are claiming is that racism and sexism are sedimented in our society, and this sedimentation depends to a large degree on the reproduction of a masculine ideology. We say 'in our society' in a restricted sense. How racism and sexism were expressed in Asian and African contexts before the intrusion of European colonialism and capitalism is, of course, a moot point. If we talk about racism and sexism in China before European contact, for example, we have to be very careful to pay full regard to the specificity of Chinese history and society. It is easy enough to discover parallels with European contexts, but this can be a dangerous exercise. Yet, in most historical societies, it is not difficult to find evidence of hierarchical structures in which domination is the rule of the game. Moreover, despite some important exceptions (e.g. the Mbuti people and others), we find men in dominating positions. Men dominate (control) the economy, they make the central political decisions, as well as playing a pivotal role in the domestic and kinship systems. This is not news. We are maintaining that hierarchy and domination, in any setting, must, by definition, imply objectification. We are so used to the discourse of oppression being couched in terms of capitalism, multi-national corporations, colonialism, imperialism, etc., that we find it hard to conceive of domination except in terms of the operation of market forces and the interests of particular classes. While we do not necessarily reject this picture, we argue that domination and hierarchy are not simply defining features of class society. They may be *prior* to class society, or they may exist after class society:

> To use the words hierarchy, class, and State interchangeably, as many social theorists do, is insidious and obscurantist. This

practice, in the name of a 'classless' or 'libertarian' society, could easily conceal the existence of hierarchical relationships, and a hierarchical sensibility, both of which — even in the absence of economic exploitation or political coercion — would serve to perpetuate unfreedom. (Bookchin, 1982, p.3)

What Bookchin refers to as the hierarchical sensibility, we call the masculine ideology. The masculine ideology only comes into existence when men confront nature as an adversary. It permeates the entire fabric of social relationships. In our society it is distorted by the operation of the class system and the general commodification of social and personal life. Theorists such as Horkheimer and Adorno (1973) have talked about 'instrumental rationality' to describe the objectification process at work in industrialized societies. While we have some sympathy with aspects of their analysis of Western capitalism, our view of objectification emphasizes, more than theirs does, the critical importance of *male* instrumental rationality. Our argument is that in appropriating nature, men appropriated women as objects. The masculine ideology always implies domination. Put more strongly, we could say that the 'rape of nature' is parallelled by the subordination of women.

Conclusion and Recapitulation

In this chapter, we have argued that both racism and sexism belong to the same discursive universe. By this we mean that they both are constituted by the objectification process. The objectification process is intimately related to the appropriation of nature by men. As such, objectification involves domination and hierarchy, which is reproduced as the masculine ideology.

In the course of our discussion, we were faced with the problem of masculinity as the collective ideology of men. Now while agreeing that ideology is a collective phenomenon, we do not believe that it merely articulates the interests of a particular class or group. This is not to say that racism as an ideology may not serve the interests of a class in given circumstances, but it is to say that racism cannot be reduced to class interests alone. In our view, racism is the sedimentation in Western culture and society of a hierarchical view of human relationships originating in the objectification process. Historically, objectification and hierarchy are twin-born in that they are both aspects of the subjugation of nature. We accept those feminist arguments that the subjugation of nature is accompanied by the subjugation of women. The transition from a relatively non-hierarchical matricentric community to a fully fledged patriarchal social structure seems to be a central theme in the development of Western society. Not only is male power institutionalized in this context, but it is given the status of a naturalized commonsensical inevitability.

> Even before man embarks on his conquest of man — of class by class — patriarchal morality obliges him to affirm his conquest of women. The subjugation of her nature and its absorption into the nexus of patriarchal morality forms the archetypical act of domination that ultimately gives rise to man's imagery of a subjugated nature. It is perhaps not accidental that nature and earth retain the female gender into our own time. What may seem to us like a linguistic atavism that reflects a long-gone era when social life was matricentric and nature was its domestic abode may well be an on-going and subtly viable expression of man's continual violation of woman as nature and of nature as woman. (Bookchin, 1982, p.21)

In other words, the subjugation of women is continuously re-enacted in the male subjugation of nature and other men. There is a further consequence of all this, namely masculinity as an ideology becomes generalized in society. Those who are objectified, who are dominated, come to see the world through male eyes. The 'male epistemological stance' becomes everybody's stance. Women and other objectified groups define their own realities through the perspective of their oppressors. Hence, the naturalization of 'race' and gender is collectively sedimented in the consciousness of oppressors and oppressed. What we have to understand is how this sedimentation takes place, that is, how it becomes entrenched, confirmed, challenged, and reinforced, not only across generations, but also across classes and other groups. And this is what the chapters on socialization, the family, education, and class endeavour to do.

Before we conclude this chapter, there is an important point to be made. In the socialization chapter we criticized the strong socialization thesis. We do not believe that human beings are always at the mercy of determinate social forces. Similarly, we do not accept the notion of an 'over-objectified' view of social relationships. Our argument that racism and sexism are constituted by the objectification process does not imply that the 'objectified' simply become things. Objectification implies a continuous attempt by some human beings to dominate and control others. But this in no way means that those who are at the receiving end of this process merely sit passively on the sidelines of history and allow others to oppress them. Despite the enormous forces ranged against them women do not become objects, nor for that matter, do oppressed minorities. In Hegel's paradigmatic discussion of the master-slave relationship, the slave is not the master's absolute 'other'. The slave is more than capable of rejecting her/his objectification. Indeed, the slave does not confirm the master's craving for recognition. Put differently, the oppressed are always capable of subverting objectification by insisting on their status as intentional beings.

7   The Reality of Oppression

We have called this final chapter 'The Reality of Oppression' because it is clear that most academic accounts of racism and sexism demote their significance as specific forms of oppression, by reducing them to manifestations of some other underlying cause or mechanism. As we have suggested in the first chapter, various strategies are employed by writers to explain racism and sexism in terms which deny that they can be treated as forms of domination and control in their own right. Those who claim the reality of their oppression as women or Blacks are told that this reality is illusory. If a woman asserts that she is oppressed by male employers because she is a woman, she is told that, in fact, her subordination is defined by her position as a worker. Certainly women are used as cheap labour but this is not tantamount to encapsulating their 'exploitation' under the rubric of a 'labour theory of value'. Similarly, it is not much comfort to those subjected to vicious racist violence, to be told that this violence is symptomatic of the perpetual crisis of capitalism. We are re-emphasizing here a point made consistently throughout this book, namely that the experience of oppression cannot be reduced to one simple formula. To put it another way, we are committed to both the reality of what the oppressed have to say about their experience of domination, and to the significance of racism and sexism as independent and irreducible forms of oppression.

The Reductionist Denial of Oppression

When social and scientific commentators in the West deny the reality of 'racial' and sexual oppression they tend to do so by adopting, as if they have general validity, concepts and theories constructed within specific and limited contexts. Thus they treat arguments developed in one sphere as though they can explain the circumstances and relationships in another. These projections take three major forms: the anthropomorphic, the Western, and the masculine projections.

By the *anthropomorphic projection* we mean the tendency to read biological evidence in terms of categories which are specifically human. For example, researchers may account for animal behaviour in terms of the existence of dominance hierarchies, or discuss the nature of insect societies with reference to the idea of a rigid division of labour. The problem with attributing human forms to animals in this way is that it can easily provide a justification for the supposed naturalness or inevitability of certain social relationships and arrangements. Thus, studies of the sexual conduct of some of the lower primates conclude that the male of the species is promiscuous and a rapist. This then serves as a biological legitimation for supposedly similar behaviour on the part of 'man'. In other words, the projection that animal and insect societies are organized in ways that resemble those of people, is used to infer the existence of an inherent and immutable underpinning to the activities of humans. Bookchin puts this point nicely.

A snarling animal is neither 'vicious' nor 'savage', nor does it 'misbehave' or 'earn' punishment. . . . By making such anthropomorphic judgements about natural phenomena, we deny the integrity of nature. Even more sinister is the widespread use of hierarchical terms to provide natural phenomena with 'intelligibility' or 'order'. What this procedure does accomplish is reinforce human social hierarchies . . . as innate features of the 'natural order'. Human domination is thereby transcribed into the genetic code as biologically immutable — together with the subordination of the young by the old, women by men, and man by man. (Bookchin, 1982, p.27)

Bookchin's point is clear. Hierarchy, dominance, aggression, promiscuity, 'race', gender, class are human constructions. Animals therefore cannot dominate and oppress one another, only humans treat other humans in this kind of way. It is thus inappropriate to explain how and why we oppress each other by using biological evidence that is already contaminated by anthropomorphic notions. Racist and sexist events have no meaning in animal societies, except in so far as people claim that they do. Any attempt to understand such practices as rape or hostility towards out-groups with reference to supposedly similar behaviour in non-human groups is fraught with difficulties, if not completely illegitimate.

By the *Western projection* we mean the way in which Western social science, philosophy, and psychology have claimed priority for specific kinds of categorization and analysis. In their accounts and investigations of Asian, African, Australasian, and American societies, Western writers have automatically assumed that their models and methods of approach are just as applicable as they are in the West. For example, in searching out sexual oppression in non-literate societies, the temptation is to treat it in a similar way to that of Western societies. Like the anthropomorphic projection, the Western projection judges other social and cultural contexts in terms of its own cognitive and analytical categories. We are not simply referring here to the ethnocentrism which exists in Western thought and culture. Rather, we are maintaining that 'Western scientific discourse' is universalized as the yardstick of understanding and investigation. Accordingly, when commentators consider instances of oppression in other contexts they immediately try to assimilate these instances to a general theory of oppression which is assumed to have universal applicability. However, the very concepts of oppression and exploitation may not have any relevance in pre-literate and pre-colonial societies. So, for example, when we locate hierarchy among the indigenous Australian population, this may be a projection of Western social processes. Note we are not arguing that oppression is a feature of Western societies alone, but that its form may differ according to culture or historical period. It is incorrect to claim that what constitutes oppression in Lagos and, Rhiad, is necessarily similar to what constitutes oppression in Moscow, New York, and London. Nor are we suggesting that Western forms of domination have not affected traditional modes of control. Western colonialism has had such a significant impact on African societies, for example, that it is not at all easy to disentangle the indigenous from the exogenous dimensions of oppression. But we cannot assume that all colonized and oppressed people define their oppression in the same way as Western social and political theory. What appears to be class exploitation to Western observers, may be conceived as national oppression by the colonized society. Thus, it might appear to British and American theorists that the white minority in South Africa has a class relationship to the black majority, although, the majority itself does not define the situation in this way. For them, the crucial dimensions are 'race', colour, and white supremacy. From the perspective of Western social analysis such indigenous theorizing is regarded either as misconceived and tradition-bound, or as a form of false consciousness. The Western projection is, therefore, blind to the concrete experience of oppressed nations, groups and minorities. Its assimilation of women's oppression under the aegis of universal explanatory schemes also renders it insensitive to the various ways women are oppressed in different societies and contexts.

When we talk about the *masculine projection* we also discover the tendency to define the world from the perspective of a particular group — in this case white men. In our discussion of masculine ideology, we used McKinnon's phrase 'the male epistemological stance' to delineate the coherence of this ideology. We argued that it is related to the male objectification of female sexuality which facilitates the construction of a view of the world in which man is active subject and woman is passive object, defined and controlled as such by males. Furthermore, during our examination of the education processes, we also indicated that whereas men are taken as representing the positive or neutral aspects of social life, women are regarded as signifying only its negative elements. Thus, because it is assumed that the social world is essentially male, men are able to create and interpret this world from their own point of view. Our perceptions of 'reality' are in fact male orientations, because our conceptualizions are made on the basis of male priorities defined from the perspective of men. It is this kind of partial knowledge which is presented and accepted as the received truth. It is this sort of biased approach which informs many academic accounts of racism and sexism for, of course, the masculine ideology has racist as well as sexist connotations. Our previous discussion has already emphasized this in its assertion that the development of the masculine ideology had specific connections with the racism of European history and culture. Its relationship to the rest of the world has been, and still is, one of aggressor. However, this is not to suggest that the masculine projection is the prerogative of white Western males alone. Evidence from other societies, the Islamic for example, indicates that this type of projection is paramount. Nevertheless, it is so naturalized and taken for granted in Western culture and society, that it is only with the greatest of difficulty that people are able to see it for what it is.

It is only with the advent of recent feminist scholarship that we are able to recognize the pervasiveness and universality of male definitions of the world. The feminist critique of Marxist and other reductionist accounts of women's oppression is thus concerned with demystifying masculine knowledge as objective knowledge. In doing this, feminism is concerned to give credence to the 'concrete reality' of women's experience of oppression, which male theorists tend to rule out of court. By 'concrete reality' we mean the acknowledgement that domination occurs in personal, everyday encounters, as well as at the collective and institutional levels. We are also referring here to the immediate and direct experience of men as oppressors. This is to say that women's oppression cannot be attributed to other forces which may be simply mediated or transmitted through males. Rather, men are unambiguous agents of women's subordination. It is these aspects of the phrase 'concrete reality', its emphasis on the everyday and the non-mediated experience of oppression, which we regard as important for the understanding of racism, as well as sexism.

Our objection to reductionism then, is not simply to make an academic point. Rather it is to allow the oppressed some kind of say in the way their oppression is theorized. Inevitably, we will be accused of giving too much consideration to the actors' points of view, to the participants' definitions of the situation. There is an orthodoxy in social science which devalues the testimony of those engaged in social relationships. This orthodoxy claims an almost inviolate objective epistemological access to the world. Consequently, those who resist this 'objectivity' find themselves defined as being 'subjectivists' or 'romantic idealists' who refuse to come to terms with the brute reality of social and personal life. We find it very hard to have any sympathy with this point of view. In maintaining that racism and sexism cannot be reduced to another more primary level of causation, we have not given up the task of serious analysis. On the contrary, we are pointing to serious absences, lacunae, in the traditional accounts of oppression.

When feminist theorists point to the inappropriate way in which male-dominated scholarship has conceptualized the relationship between men and women, and when they emphasize the masculine projection in both society and scholarship, they are not engaging in a game of 'one-upmanship'. Historically, women have been oppressed and they continue to be oppressed. The initial promise of socialism as the royal road to women's liberation has been found wanting, because the terms of this liberation were defined by men. Similarly, the claim of Marxism that it provided oppressed nations and groups with an adequate means of liberating themselves has foundered on its commitment to the Western projection. In trying to account for oppression purely in terms of concepts developed for the explication of European capitalism, Marxism has seriously misunderstood and underestimated 'nationalism' and traditional forms of domination. Moreover, it has seriously ignored the existence and sedimentation of racist themes in European society and culture.

> European Marxists have . . . mistaken for universal verities the structures and social dynamics retrieved from their own distant and more immediate pasts. Even more significantly, the deepest structures of 'historical materialism' . . . have tended to relieve European Marxists from the obligation of investigating the profound effects of culture and historical experience on their science. The ordering ideas which have persisted in Western civilization . . . have little or no justification in Marxism for their existence. One such idea is racialism: the legitimation and corroboration of social organization as natural by reference to the 'racial' components of its elements. Though hardly unique to European peoples, its appearance and codification, during the feudal period, into Western conceptions of society was to have important and enduring consequences. (Robinson, 1983, p.2)

Robinson is reiterating the point we have already made in chapter 2 about the reduction of racism to class ideology. What disappears completely in such approaches is any consideration of the vast range of events and experiences which are subsumed under the concept racism.

Clockwork Oppressors?

Most accounts of domination deny the existence of active agents who 'do' the oppressing. It is not men who oppress women, rather it is the 'mode of production', a 'programmed genetic trait', or the 'system of patriarchy' which is responsible. Similarly, racism is explained in terms of the 'logic of capitalism' or the inevitability of 'kin altruism'. Reductionist theories, therefore, treat those who oppress as though they are clockwork oppressors, wound up by some inexorable determining mechanism which resides in the 'system'. Whites do not oppress Blacks, it is the 'system', the logic and laws of historical development which force them to do so. Clockwork oppression thus assumes a world without agency or purpose, where both oppressors and oppressed are engaged in a continuous round of stimulus-response relationships in which sexism and racism are seen as simple reflexes or preprogrammed responses to objective situations. Whites and men are thereby absolved from involvement in, and accountability for, oppressive acts. In addition, because racism and sexism are always attributed to other forces for which men and whites are the mediators, racial and sexual oppression disappear as forms of domination in their own right. They become mere manifestations of some hidden, underlying base.

Our argument in this book has been that oppression cannot be conceptualized in such abstract terms. Oppressors and oppressed often confront each other in 'concrete' situations. When a white middle-class teacher makes a snide remark about a black pupil to a colleague, this remark is not a rhetorical device — it is made by one real person to another. Teachers and pupils are not, simply role players with predetermined scripts. It is 'this teacher' who makes a racist or sexist remark. Similarly, even in an extreme case like the incineration of millions of people in the ovens of Auschwitz and Dachau, we cannot simply point our accusatory finger at 'totalitarianism' or 'monopoly capitalism'. In confronting their murderers, victims did not encounter eviscerated abstractions. When facing lynch mobs in Alabama or Tennessee, black people did not come up against a theory of society. What they faced were real people who defined the world in racist terms. These real people were whites. Of course, we have to try and understand and explain why these particular whites were doing what they were doing. We are not for one moment suggesting that oppression is contingent and situationally specific. Historically, we know that it is more than likely that some people will lynch others in the *ante bellum* South. We know that white policemen in Brixton or Toxteth are more likely to stop black people than they are to stop their white counterparts. We also know that male violence against women is not a random factor. But this is precisely the point. It is men who rape women. It is whites who discriminate against Blacks. It is heterosexuals who oppress lesbians and homosexuals.

Our purpose here is not to claim that single individuals are necessarily responsible for their racist or sexist practices, (although we would not want to completely deny such a claim), but to establish the obviousness of the fact that human actors in specific social contexts can and do oppress each other, not roles, genes, or modes of production. The obviousness of this fact may seem to be unproblematic. Yet it is almost impossible to unpack its implications. To say that individuals oppress each other is to imply that oppression is the result of human agency. The racist teacher is not merely reproducing a racist ideology. He/she is an active agent in the reproduction of that ideology. While we may agree that his particular teacher's racism does not seem to be any different from that of other teachers, it is she or he who is being racist. At the same time, the pupil who may be on the receiving end of a racist remark does not simply react as a representative of a group. It is she/he who experiences the pain or humiliation. Hence, at one level oppression is extremely personal, and at another level the personal is political. All racist and sexist practice involves a power relationship in which the subjectivity of personal experience is intertwined with the objectivity of collective and political relationships. By this we mean that oppression is simultaneously an individual and collective phenomenon. But because of this collective dimension, we find it impossible to argue that expressions of anti-fascist or anti-sexist sentiments or attempts to structure personal relations in a non-dominating way can acquit either men or whites from responsibility for oppression, however genuine and sincere their views may be. To the extent that society is constructed on racist and sexist lines, men and whites accrue advantages, however unintentionally, which are denied to others. For, example, men have the freedom of the streets at night, while women are constrained by fear of attack. Even though an individual man may constitute no threat to a particular woman, his presence is oppressive to her because she has no way of distinguishing his intentions from those of a potential sexual attacker or rapist. Similarly, as whites, we benefit from the general acceptability of our skin colour and from the cheap goods and services produced in Britain, America, and the non-Western world by workers who are particularly exploited because they are black.

Multi-dimensionality and Objectification as the Paradigm for Oppression

Our disenchantment with theories of clockwork oppression, with their denial of agency and the realities of racism and sexism, does not mean that we have accepted without reservation the notion that different forms of oppression have no relationship to each other. In fact, we find it almost impossible to conceive of a society in which economic dominance and exploitation are not somehow linked to 'race' and gender oppression. However, our argument is that we cannot find evidence for the primacy of any one kind of domination over another. Living in a society in which the capitalist mode of production has, to a large extent, tended to permeate the very fabric of our consciousness, it is obviously very easy to lapse into an explanation which seems to offer a clear-cut view of all social relationships. But it is this very fact which is suspect, because it incorporates within it a monumental presumption about the universality of a particular epistemology and mode of analysis. The generalization of capitalist social relations to most parts of the world has disguised and distorted pre-capitalist forms of oppression. Admittedly, capitalism may have given these forms a more 'economistic' mode of expression, but it is not responsible for their existence.

We are not trying to make a case for the empirical autonomy of different oppressive modes; we believe that there is no way in which the practice of oppression in one sphere can be insulated from its operation in another. In our discussions of the multi-dimensionality of black woman's oppression in South Africa, we did not thereby indicate that economic exploitation, gender and 'race' oppression could merely be aggregated to provide an overall profile of her situation. What we did imply was that her situation cannot be reduced to any one single domain. However, at the same time, we recognized that being 'black' and a 'woman' in South Africa gives a particular specificity to her position. Accordingly, we have to make certain strategic choices about what we emphasize as being critically relevant to a particular context. It would seem to us that when South Africa is taken to exemplify an extreme form of capitalist exploitation, based on the operation of a cheap labour policy, commentators lose sight of an entire range of ideological and social practices. We come back to our earlier point about the mediation of oppression. Those who accept the class argument in the South

African case, have chosen to ignore other forms of oppression as being crucial. But from the oppressed's perspective it is racism which is critical. While we are certainly not claiming that oppression is not mediated, we are asserting that mediation by itself does not constitute oppression. We are stressing this point because we want to underscore our belief that oppression is not reducible to a singular mode. The analysis of racism in South Africa, for instance, must proceed as if we take its mode of expression seriously. Apartheid is not simply the consequence of a cheap labour policy. The systematic separation of people at social, cultural and personal levels is not inherent in the logic of capitalist development.

Similarly, the particular forms that male domination take cannot be mediated in class terms. The extreme objectification of women in a large number of societies does not lend itself to a class analysis. No amount of sophisticated social investigation can explain the hierarchical nature of gender relationships, without taking into account that the protagonists, men and women, confront each other as oppressors and oppressed. Although we agree that a particular mode of production may change the terms of gender relationships to a certain extent, we do not accept the proposition that it therefore defines sexual objectification. As we indicated in the ideology chapter, sexual objectification derives from the male claim to female sexuality, to her body, to her reproductive capacities. This assumption of rights is made independently of his or her class position. It is a claim which is reproduced across generations as the masculine ideology, an ideology which takes for granted the normalcy of the distinction between the cultural and the natural, and the primacy of male subjectivity. Sexual objectification is an expression of a power relationship in which men dominate women. How men achieve power over women, of course, has to be documented empirically and historically. It is our contention that gender hierarchy is a historical phenomenon which arises in specific contexts. The fact that it appears to be universalized in all extant societies does not entitle us to read history retrospectively, to give it the status of an inevitable and immutable phenomenon. Its apparent universality today does not mean that this has to be the case in the future.

We have asserted our commitment to the notion that all forms of oppression must be understood in social and historical terms. All oppression is constructed for and by human beings. The power relation implicit in sexual objectification is not symptomatic of the biological differences of men and women. Rather, it is an articulation of human praxis and intentionality. It is, in other words, a social relationship which is only meaningful to human beings. As we have already argued, animals do not oppress animals. It is only human beings who learn the rules which enable them to 'do' oppression and to socialize their children to accept the naturalness of gender, 'race', and class distinctions. Thus, when we claim that sexual objectification is paradigmatic of all oppression, we are merely reiterating the point that all oppressive practices are related to each other. This is because each acts as a form of articulation or mediation for, and thereby forges links with, the others.

We are, of course, talking here about the practice and not the origin of particular types of oppression. The multi-dimensionality of oppression is, therefore, not a function of a supreme organizing principle, but is based on a similarity of oppressive practice and method. What relates gender to 'race' to structures of economic dominance is not a common reductive mechanism, but the modality through which oppression is accomplished. All three forms of domination are achieved through various processes of objectification. We are not suggesting that the nature of this objectification is the same for gender, 'race', and economic oppression; neither that the activities of objectifying are identical. In fact we have strongly asserted that they cannot be reduced to each other in this way. Rather, we are maintaining that whenever we insist a particular set of relationships is oppressive, we are definitionally talking about objectification.

The examples of National Socialist Germany and plantation slavery in North America serve to illustrate our point. In both these cases there is no great difficulty in seeing an affinity between sexism and racism, and this is because both these systems contain, in the starkest possible form, the core of the objectification process at work. In both cases, we discern a highly developed structure of inequality and hierarchy. In both cases, men appear to absolutely control the means of production and the instruments of political control, as well as the means of reproduction. In both cases, there is an attempt to elevate white women and denigrate the status of Jewish or black women. In both cases, the enemies of society are defined as barbarians and sexual beasts. In both cases, there is a horror of and fascination with homosexuality and lesbianism, which are seen as representing the ultimate antithesis of Aryan and white masculinity.

In both cases, there is an overwhelming emphasis on masculinity as a moral force legitimated and sanctioned by both history and nature. Of course, Nazi Germany and plantation slavery societies are highly attentuated examples, but they illustrate in a dramatic way how the practice of oppression is never confined to any one arena. Opression is multi-dimensional because its operation in one domain is easily transferable to another. It is multi-dimensional because the activity of domination is premissed on the objectification of the oppressed. One form of domination serves as a paradigm for another. This is why we agree with those feminist writers who argue that patriarchy can serve as a model for all oppression. Or perhaps it would be more accurate to say that it is in the 'sex-gender' system that we can discern the objectification process at work in its basic form (Rubin, 1975). In objectifying women, men provide us with a model for the objectification of all social relationships. This is not to say that oppression is always modelled on patriarchy, but it is to suggest that there is a profound similarity in the way in which oppression is accomplished by man over woman, and how it is achieved in other relationships. In summary then, the oppressive practices which occur in one sphere are never entirely encapsulated or contained within that sphere alone.

The Personal and Oppression

In our discussion of the family we argued that familial relationships could not simply be defined in terms of the needs of the economy. In other words, they could not be regarded as mere instruments for the transmission of oppression constructed elsewhere. The family, in our view, is the major sphere in which the domination of men is secured at the expense of women. The family, from this perspective, is the intimate testing and proving ground for the generalization of male oppression. It is at the personal level, in the face to face encounters between men, women, and children that the intrinsic political qualities of gender relationships may be caught. Each family situation provides the site for a kind of political practice which results in the subservience of the personal to the political. Personal and intimate relationships between men and women are therefore never conducted in entirely encapsulated or privatized spheres in which the currency of interaction is pure 'mutuality' or 'reciprocity'. Rather,

family life is carried out in the context of established gender typifications and the pervasiveness of the masculine ideology. Each family
fights its battles in terms of its own version or definition of these.
Thus each family, as a site, allows men to oppress in their own way.
Oppressive practice cannot be regarded as an activity which is a
social hangover from a dead past. On the contrary, it involves the
active engagement of participants. These views are captured in the
feminints slogan, 'the personal is political'.

When the assumption that the personal is not immune from the
political became so important in the discourse of feminism, it was
taken to mean that the family, the subjective sphere, is the ground
upon which the subjection of women is accomplished. The inference
to be drawn from this premiss is that the personal becomes subject
to the will of the oppressor. Our examination of the 'strong socialization thesis' made it clear that one of the main aspects of its view of
human behaviour is the passivity of the socialized. From the oppressor's point of view, the object of political practice is to break the
resistance of the potential victim. However ideally, this object
should not be secured by the use of force. Instead, the victim should
somehow be persuaded that her/his best interests can be served by
acquiescing to the demands of the oppressor:

> What the exploiter needs is that the will and intelligence of the
> victim be disengaged from the projects of resistance and escape
> but that they not be simply broken or destroyed. Ideally, the
> disintegration and mis-integration of the victim should accom-
> plish the detachment of the victim's will and intelligence from
> the victim's own interests and their attachment to the interests
> of the exploiter. This will effect a displacement of dissolution of
> self-respect and will undermine the victim's intolerance of
> coercion. With that, the situation transcends the initial para-
> digmatic form or structure of coercion; for if people don't mind
> doing what you want them to do, then, in a sense, you can't
> really be *making* them do it. In the limiting case, the victim's will
> and intelligence are wholly transferred to a full engagement in
> the pursuit of the dominating person's interests. (Frye, 1983,
> p.60)

Thus, it is only when the victim comes to want the same things as
the oppressor, that we can properly speak of the victory of the
oppressor. The strong socialization theory, with its mixture of Freudian and behaviourist themes, assumes that the early training of

people makes them want and perform the things that society wishes them to do. Their subjectivity becomes the plaything of social forces outside their control. Ultimately, this is to assume that people somehow want to be oppressed, because it is the least painful of alternatives available to them. In a sense, it could be argued that women assent to male domination because they have been convinced (conditioned) that it is in their best interests to do so.

Of course, as just stated, this process seems to be too conscious and rational. In Freudian arguments, there is no question of the victim *choosing* to accept the oppressor's point of view. The oppressor's definition of the situation is internalized as part and parcel of the Oedipal resolution. Thus, almost inevitably, the way women regard themselves will be a consequence of intra-psychic processes which highlight their sense of inferiority in comparison with men. Juliet Mitchell, for example, has claimed that the resolution of the Oedipal conflict marks woman's unconscious internalization of her view of herself as a male exchange object (Mitchell, 1974). More importantly, the point is that from Freudian perspectives, the oppression of women begins in the unconscious, in the continuous re-enactment of the Oedipal drama in family sites. Because of the power of 'repression', the subjection of women is accomplished, so it is argued, almost automatically.

We have already examined some of the problems relating to a view of oppression which sees it as an exemplifying process by means of which 'instinct' is overcome by 'culture'. The main problem arises out of the assumption that repression is a universal and ahistorical process. Yet to understand how 'the victim comes to want the same things as the oppressor', we must somehow come to terms with the process by means of which victims experience themselves as objects. In this connection, while we have serious reservations about Freud's view of society, his analysis of female sexuality and his pessimism, we cannot ignore the emphasis he places on the 'body' as a site of oppression. Thus, when we say the personal is political, we are suggesting that the body is also politicized. It is the sphere in which consequences of oppression are most readily felt. How an individual experiences his or her body will depend, to a large degree, on the 'others' in the immediate environment, who continuously monitor and interpret his or her bodily processes. To an extent, the body is society's creature. It will live through the image of those who watch, nurture, punish, and reward it. The body becomes an 'it' when it is experienced as a thing among things. Sexual objectification turns a woman's body into an 'it', but sexual objectification is not immanent in or necessary to the sexual relationships of men and women. It is a power relationship with a history. Although it is impossible to say that sexual objectification started in this time at that place, we would argue, along with Bookchin, that it is only with the emergence of hierarchy that we can begin to discern the beginnings of male domination (Bookchin, 1982). Hierarchy is a social concept and practice, with its basis lying in the meaning given to the division of activities between men and women in society. Only when men come to believe that what they do is more important than women's contribution, do we discover the outline of hierarchical social relationships. It is at this juncture, that men begin to perceive women as subject to their power, and consequently as being their property, their possessions, their objects. The history of sexual objectification then, is as old as hierarchy. There was no hierarchy until:

> Man staked out a claim for the superiority of his work over woman's; later the craftsman asserted his superiority over the food cultivator; finally the thinker affirmed his sovereignty over the workers. Hierarchy established itself not only objectively, in the real, workaday world, but also subjectively, in the individual unconscious. Percolating into virtually every realm of experience, it has assimilated the syntax of everyday discourse — the very relationship between subject and object, humanity and nature. Difference was recast from its traditional status as unity in diversity into a linear system of separate, increasingly antagonistic powers — a system validated by all the resources of religion, morality, and philosophy. (Bookchin, 1982, p.63)

It is when hierarchy establishes itself subjectively that women begin to define themselves in terms of the 'male epistemological stance', and to experience their bodies as if they did not belong to them. It is hierarchy that politicizes the unconscious and transforms the body into an object that can be manipulated. Although we do not agree with Mitchell's argument that the unconscious is an autonomous domain for the acquisition and reproduction of ideology, we believe that oppression cannot be fully understood unless we have some notion of how hierarchy reproduces itself in the body (Mitchell, 1974).

This point can be illustrated by the way in which heterosexuality, as a political and social force, defines the parameters of male and female sexuality. In so doing, it also defines the unacceptability of homosexuality and lesbianism. Homosexuals and lesbians, until very recently, have been pariah and outcast objects in Western society. Their pariah status derives to a significant extent from the refusal on the part of the heterosexual establishment to acknowledge their existence as appropriate sex objects. Hierarchy presupposes that those one dominates do not possess the same characteristics as oneself. To imply that one can have sexual relations with somebody sexually like oneself, is to admit to the possibility that the potential homosexual partner has the same rights and power as you do. But this is precisely the point. Because sexual relations between men and women are political, in the sense that they are symptomatic of hierarchy, then sexual relations between men or between women are potentially subversive of that hierarchy. Consequently, some of the most vicious forms of discriminatory and oppressive pressure are directed against gays and lesbians. Compulsory heterosexuality, to use Rich's term, is so pervasive that those who resist its demands often discover that they do so at a terrible cost (Rich, 1981). In surrendering to 'straight' society, the lesbian or homosexual acknowledges hierarchy, that is they objectify their bodies in the same way as their oppressors do. The price of survival is to become what your oppressors want you to be.

The Politics of Resistance

Of course, from the above argument it would appear that oppression always wins the day, that hierarchy is so endemic in Western society that the objectification process can never be subverted. However, this is to assert that oppressive practices entail an all-inclusive reductive mechanism — the very approach which, in this book, we have been seeking to deny. Our argument is that although oppression does have terrible personal and social consequences for the oppressed, it does not, and cannot, achieve its aims completely. It is precisely because women do not accept their objectification without resistance that we do not subscribe to a view of the family and 'personal relationships' as being the scene of woman's 'historical defeat' by men. The battle for the control of the personal is not pre-ordained and there is no certainty that men will always emerge as complete victors. Indeed, it could be argued that the re-emergence of feminism as a significant political force has made this outcome less inevitable than past pessimistic pronouncements might have led us to believe.

Similarly, the unconscious does not simply become the repository of an external ideological content which determines an individual's structural and personal location in the social world. If the personal *is* political, then this implies the possibility of conflict, struggle, and change. In order for victims to surrender absolutely to the whims and desires of their oppressors, there has to be a state of affairs in which the dominators have total control over those they subordinate. It might be argued that this is or has been the situation in prisons, concentration camps, totalitarian societies, Stalin's Russia, Nazi Germany or South Africa. However, this would be to dismiss out of hand the reality of resistance. Total control (so far) only exists in dystopian views of the future. Nowhere is oppression so complete that human intentionality and puposefulness are reduced to nothing.

Resistance to oppression is, therefore, such a crucial component of historical and social processes that it makes no sense to talk about the defeat of human agency and struggle. From the standpoint of the theorist or the social observer, the power of the oppressor may appear so overwhelming that it seems unavoidable that the oppressed conform and abandon any attempt to rebel. Certainly, at one level, there is a great deal of evidence to support the view that the dominated appear to do and think whatever their superordinates wish them to. Accordingly, it is clear why the 'dominant ideology thesis' has proved so popular among some social scientists. The argument that the masses are not forcibly controlled by a ruling class or group, but are seduced into accepting their rule by the 'engineering of their consent' seems to do away with the necessity for talking about the nakedness of power and social control. However, even if we partly accept the view that resistance may be undermined and bought off by 'rewards' and 'promises', we do not hold that this in any way demonstrates the passivity or defeat of those objectified and oppressed. The past and present histories of the strategies developed by various ethnic groups to counter racism are too numerous and replete with pride and political consciousness for us to be able to endorse such claims.

Perhaps it is because so many oppressed groups have simulated conformity, by offering a smiling face of acceptance to their oppressors, that commentators have been misled into assuming that oppressive practices always eventually break their victims. In discussing objectification and domination, therefore, we must be very careful not to deny completely the objectified person his or her subjectivity. Such a presumption is implicit in the Western and masculine projections which study, from the standpoint of their own situated subjectivity, 'others' whose particular subjectivity is rejected. But oppression can never be simply defined as though it was merely an acting out of the wishes and power of the oppressors, for it is a two-way process in which both parties are engaged in a continuous struggle to establish the terms of their existence. To be sure, at the moment, the dice appear to be loaded against a great proportion of the world's population, both women and ethnic groups, but this does not mean they are the inevitable playthings of ineluctable forces. The asymmetry of power is an historical phenomenon and, as such, is capable of being subverted.

Bibliography

Adamson, Olivia, Carol Brown, Judith Harrison, and Judy Price 1976: Women's oppression under capitalism. *Revolutionary Communist*, 5.

Adorno T.W., Else Frenkel-Brunswik, Daniel J. Levinson, Sanford R. Nevitt 1968: *The Authoritarian Personality*. New York: W.W. Norton.

Amos, Valerie, and Pratibha Parmar 1981: Resistances and responses: the experiences of black girls in Britain. In Angela McRobbie and Trisha McCabe, (eds), *Feminism for Girls*. London: Routledge and Kegan Paul.

Antonis, Barbie 1981: Motherhood and mothering. In *Women in Society*. London: Virago.

Anyon, Jean 1983: Intersections of gender and class: accommodation and resistance by working-class and affluent females to contradictory sex-role ideologies. In Stephen Walker and Len Barton (eds), *Gender, Class and Education*. Lewes, Sussex: Falmer Press.

Ardrey, R. 1966: *The Territorial Imperative*. London: Collins.

Atkinson, Ti-Grace 1974: *Amazon Odyssey*. New York: Links Books.

Bagley, C., and B. Coard 1975: Cultural knowledge and rejection of ethnic identity in West Indian children in London. In G.K. Verma and C. Bagley (eds), *Race and Education Across Cultures*. London: Macmillan.

Barker, Martin 1981: *The New Racism*. London: Junction Books.

Barrett, Michèle 1980: *Women's Oppression Today*. London: Verso.

Barrett, Michèle and Mary McIntosh 1982: *The Anti-social Family*. London: Verso.

Beechey, Veronica 1977: Some notes on female wage labour in capitalist production. *Capital and Class*, 3, Autumn.

Bell, Colin, and Howard Newby 1976: Husbands and wives: the dynamics of the deferential dialectic. In Diana Leonard Barker and Sheila Allen (eds), *Dependence and Exploitation in Work and Marriage*, London: Longman.

Berk, Richard A 1980: The new economics: an agenda for sociological research. In Sarah Fenstermaker Berk (ed), *Women and Household Labour*, Beverley Hills: Sage Publications.

Billig, Michael 1976: *Social Psychology and Intergroup Relations*. London: Academic Press. Quoted in David Milner 1983: *Children and Race: Ten Years On*. London: Ward Lock.

Billig, Michael 1982: *Ideology and Social Psychology*. Oxford: Blackwell.

Bland, Lucy, Charlotte Brunsdon, Dorothy Hobson, and Janice Winship 1978: Women 'inside' and 'outside' the relations of production. In Women's Studies Group, Centre for Contemporary Cultural Studies, *Women Take Issue*. London: Hutchinson.

Blumer, Herbert 1965: Industrialisation and race relations. In Guy Hunter (ed), *Industrialisation and Race Relations*. London: Oxford University Press.

Bodmer, W.F., and L.L. Cavalli-Sforza 1976: *Genetics, Evolution and Man*. San Francisco: W.H. Freeman.

Bookchin, Murray 1982: *The Ecology of Freedom*. Palo Alto: Cheshire Books.

Britten, Nicky, and Anthony Heath 1983: Women, men and social class. In Eva Gamarnikow, David H.J. Morgan, June Purvis, and Daphne E. Taylorson (eds), *Gender Class and Work*. London: Heinemann.

Bruegel, Irene 1978: What keeps the family going? *International Socialism*, 2,1.

Bunch, Charlotte 1975: Lesbians in revolt. In N. Myron and C. Bunch (eds). *Lesbianism and the Women's Movement*. Oakland, California: Diana Press.

Carby, Hazel V 1982a: Schooling in Babylon. In Centre for Contemporary Cultural Studies, *The Empire Strikes Back*. London: Hutchinson.

Carby, Hazel V 1982b: White woman listen! Black femininsm and the boundaries of sisterhood. In Centre for Contemporary Cultural Studies, *The Empire Strikes Back*. London: Hutchinson.

Carrington, Bruce 1983: Sport as a side-track. An analysis of West Indian involvement in extra-curricular sport. In Len Barton and Stephen Walker (eds), *Race, Class and Education*. Beckenham, Kent: Croom Helm.

Castles, Stephen, and Godula Kosack 1973: *Immigrant Workers and Class Structure in Western Europe*. London: Oxford University Press.

Centre for Contemporary Cultural Studies 1982: *The Empire Strikes Back*. London: Hutchinson.

Chodorow, Nancy 1978: *The Reproduction of Mothering*. Berkeley, California: University of California Press.

Clark, K.B. and M.P. Clark 1939: The development of consciousness of self and the emergence of racial identification in negro pre-school children. *Journal of Social Psychology*, 10.

Clarricoates, Katherine 1980: The importance of being Ernest . . . Emma . . . Tom . . . Jane. The perception of gender conformity and gender deviation in primary schools. In Rosemary Deem (ed), *Schooling For Women's Work*. London: Routledge and Kegan Paul.

Coard, Bernard 1971: *How the West Indian Child is Made Educationally Sub-Normal in the British School System*. London: New Beacon Books.

Cock, Jacklyn 1980: *Maids and Madams*. Johannesburg: Rowan Press.

Cockburn, Cynthia 1981: The material of male power. *Feminist Review*, 9 Autumn.

Coleman, Marshall 1982: *Continuous Excursions*. London: Pluto Press.

Comer, Lee 1974: *Wedlocked Women*. Leeds: Feminist Books.

Coward, Rosalind 1983: *Patriarchal Precedents*. London: Routledge and Kegan Paul.

Cox, Oliver Cromwell 1970: *Caste, Class and Race*. New York: Monthly Review Press.

Davis, Angela 1981: *Women, Race and Class*. London: Women's Press.

Davis, Lynn 1983: Gender, resistance and power. In Stephen Walker and Len Barton (eds), *Gender, Class and Education*. Lewes, Sussex: Falmer Press.

de Beauvoir, Simone 1982: *The Second Sex*. Harmondsworth: Penguin.

Deem, Rosemary 1978: *Women and Schooling*. London: Routledge and Kegan Paul.

Delamont, Sara 1980: *Sex Roles and the School*. London: Methuen.

Delmar, Rosalind 1976: Looking again at Engels' 'Origin of the Family. Private Property and the State'. In Juliet Mitchell and Ann Oakley (eds), *The Rights and Wrongs of Women*. Harmondsworth: Penguin.

Delphy, Christine 1977: *The Main Enemy*. London: Women's Research and Resources Centre Publications.

Delphy, Christine 1981: Women in Stratification Studies. In Helen Roberts (ed), *Doing Feminist Research*. London: Routledge and Kegan Paul.

Dhondy, Farrukh 1982: Teaching young blacks. In Farrukh Dhondy, Barbara Beese, and Leila Hassan (eds), *The Black Explosion in British Schools*. London: Race Today Publications.

Dobash, R. Emerson, and Russell Dobash 1980: *Violence Against Wives*. London: Open Books.

Driver, Geoffrey 1980: *Beyond Underachievement: Case Studies of English, West Indian and Asian School-Leavers at Sixteen Plus*. London: Commission for Racial Equality.

Dweck, Carol S. 1977: Learned helplessness and negative evaluation. *Educator*, Vol. 19, 2.

Easlea, Brian 1981: *Science and Sexual Oppression*. London: Weidenfeld and Nicholson.

Edwards, V.K. 1979: *The West Indian Language Issue in British Schools: Challenges and Responses*. London: Routledge and Kegan Paul.

Eisenstein, Zillah R. 1979: Developing a theory of capitalist patriarchy and socialist feminism. In Zillah R. Eisenstein (ed), *Capitalist Patriarchy and the Case for Socialist Feminism*. New York: Monthly Review Press.

Eisenstein, Zillah R. 1982: The sexual politics of the new right: understanding the 'crisis of liberalism' for the 1980s. In Nannerl O. Keohane, Michelle Z. Rosaldo, and Barbara C. Gelpi (eds), *Feminist Theory: A Critique of Ideology*. Brighton: Harvester Press.

Elshtain, Jean Bethke 1981: *Public Man, Private Woman*. Oxford: Martin Robertson.

Engels, Frederick 1972: *The Origin of the Family, Private Property and the State*. New York: Pathfinder.

Evans, Mary 1982: In praise of theory: the case for women's studies. *Feminist Review*, 10, Spring.

Firestone, Shulamith 1972: *The Dialectic of Sex*. London: Paladin.

Foreman, Ann 1977: *Feminity as Alienation*. London: Pluto Press.

Foucault, Michel 1979: *History of Sexuality*, Vol. 1. London: Allen Lane.

Fredrickson, George M. 1981: *White Supremacy*. New York: Oxford University Press.

Freud, Sigmund 1977: *On Sexuality*. Harmondsworth: Penguin.

Fromm, Erich 1942: *The Fear of Freedom*. London: Routledge and Kegan Paul.

Frye, Marilyn 1983: *The Politics of Reality: Essays in Feminist Theory*. New York: Crossings Press.

Fuller, Mary 1980: Black girls in a London comprehensive school. In Rosemary Deem (ed), *Schooling for Women's Work*. London: Routledge and Kegan Paul.

Fuller, Mary 1982: Young, female and black. In Ernest Cashmore and Barry Troyna (eds), *Black Youth in Crisis*. London: George Allen and Unwin.

Fuller, Mary 1983: Qualified criticism, critical qualifications. In Len Barton and Stephen Walker (eds), *Race, Class and Education*. London: Croom Helm.

Gabriel, John and Gideon Ben-Tovim 1978: Marxism and the concept of racism. *Economy and Society*, 7, 2, May.

Gardiner, Jean 1977: Women in the labour process and class structure. In Alan Hunt (ed), *Class and Class Structure*. London: Lawrence and Wishart.

Genovese, Eugene 1975: *Roll Jordan Roll: The World the Slaves Made*. New York, Pantheon.

Giles, Raymond 1977: *The West Indian Experience in British Schools*. London: Heinemann Educational.

Gill, Dawn 1983: The contribution of secondary school geography to multiracial education: a critical review of some materials. *Multicultural Education*, 10, 3, Summer.

Gilroy, Paul 1982: Steppin' out of Babylon — race, class and autonomy. In Centre for Contemporary Cultural Studies, *The Empire Strikes Back*. London: Hutchinson.

Goffman, Erving 1968: *Asylums*. Harmondsworth: Penguin.

Goffman, Erving 1979: *Gender Advertisements*. London: Macmillan.

Goldberg, Stephen 1977: *The Inevitability of Patriarchy* London: The Temple Press.

Goode, W.J. 1971: Force and violence in the family. *Journal of Marriage and the Family*, 33, November.

Grabb, E.G. 1979: Working-class authoritarianism and tolerance of outgroups: a reassessment. *Public Opinion Quarterly*, 43.

Graham, Hilary 1982: Coping: or how mothers are seen and not heard. In

Scarlet Friedman and Elizabeth Sarah (eds), *On the Problem of Men.* London: The Women's Press.

Gutman, Herbert G. 1976: *The Black Family in Slavery and Fredom, 1750–1925.* New York: Vintage Books.

Hartmann, Heidi 1979: The unhappy marriage of Marxism and feminism: towards a more progressive union. *Capital and Class,* 8, Summer.

Hoch, Paul 1979: *White Hero, Black Beast.* London: Pluto Press.

Hodge, John L., Donald K. Struckman and Lynn D. Trost, 1975: *Cultural Basis of Racism and Group Oppression.* Berkeley, California: Two Riders Press.

Holland, Ray 1977: *Self and Social Context.* London: MacMillan.

Holliday, Laura 1978: *The Violent Sex: Male Psychobiology and the Evolution of Consciousness.* Guerneville, California: Blue Stockings Press.

Hooks, Bell 1982: *Ain't I A Woman.* London: Pluto Press.

Horkheimer, Max and Theodore Adorno 1973: *Dialectic of Enlightenment.* London: Allen Lane.

Horner, Matina 1976: Towards an understanding of achievement related conflict in women. In Judith Stacey, Susan Béraud and Joan Daniels (eds), *And Jill Came Tumbling After: Sexism in American Education.* New York: Dell Publishing.

Imray, Linda and Audrey Middleton 1982: Public and private: marking the boundaries. Paper presented at the Annual Conference of the British Sociological Association, 5-8 April.

Jacoby, Russell 1977: *Social Amnesia.* Hassocks: Harvester Press.

Jordan, Winthrop D. 1968: *White Over Black: American Attitudes Towards the Negro.* Chapelhill: University of North Carolina Press.

Jordan, Winthrop 1974: *The White Man's Burden.* New York: Oxford University Press.

Joseph, Gloria 1981: The incompatible *menage à trois:* marxism, feminism and racism. In Lydia Sargeant (ed), *The Unhappy Marriage of Marxism and Feminism.* London: Pluto Press.

Kamarovsky, Maria 1946: Cultural contradictions and sex roles. *American Journal of Sociology,* 52, 3. November.

Kelly, Alison (ed), 1981: *The Missing Half.* Manchester: Manchester University Press.

Kuhn, Annette 1978: Structures of patriarchy and capital in the family. In Annette Kuhn and Ann Marie Wolpe (eds), *Feminism and Materialism.* London: Routledge and Kegan Paul.

Kuper, Leo 1974: *Race, Class and Power.* London: Duckworth.

Kuper, Leo 1981: *Genocide.* Harmondsworth: Penguin.

Lacan, Jacques 1982: The Meaning of the Phallus. In Juliet Mitchell and Jacqueline Rose (eds), *Feminine Sexuality.* London: Macmillan.

Lakoff, Robin 1975: *Language and Woman's Place.* New York: Harper and Row.

Lasch, Christopher 1977: *Haven in a Heartless World*. New York: Basic Books.

Lawrence, Errol 1982: In the abundance of water the fool is thirsty: sociology and black 'pathology'. In Centre for Contemporary Cultural Studies, *The Empire Strikes Back*. London: Hutchinson.

Leacock, Eleanor Burke 1981: *Myths of Male Dominance*. New York: Monthly Review Press.

Lewis, Jane 1981: Women lost and found: the impact of feminism on history. In Dale Spender (ed), *Men's Studies Modified*. Oxford: Pergamon Press.

Lieven, Elena 1981: 'Subjectivity, materialism, and patriarchy' In Cambridge Women's Studies Group, *Women in Society*. London: Virago.

Littlewood, Roland, and Maurice Lipsedge 1982: *Aliens and Alienists*. Penguin: Harmondsworth.

Lown, Judy 1983: Not so much a factory, more a form of patriarchy: gender and class during industrialisation. In Eva Gamarnikow, David H.J. Morgan, June Purvis and Daphe E. Taylorson (eds), *Gender, Class and Work*. London: Heinemann.

McArthur, Tom (ed) 1981: *Longman Lexicon of Contemporary English*. Harlow: Longman.

McDonough, Roisin, and Rachel Harrison 1978: Patriarchy and relations of production. In Annette Kuhn and Ann Marie Wolpe (eds), *Feminism and Materialism*. London: Routledge and Kegan Paul.

MacDonald, Madeline 1980: Schooling and the reproduction of class and gender relations. In Len Barton, Roland Meighan and Stephen Walker (eds), *Schooling, Ideology and the Curriculum*. Lewes, Sussex: Falmer Press.

Mackinnon, Catherine A. 1982: Feminism, marxism, method and the state: an agenda for theory. In Nannerl O. Keohane, Michelle Z. Rosaldo and Barbara C, Gelpi (eds), *Feminist Theory*. Brighton: Harvester Press.

McRobbie, Angela 1978: Working class girls and the culture of femininity. In Women's Studies Group, Centre for Contemporary Cultural Studies, *Women Take Issue*. London: Hutchinson.

Malos, Ellen 1980: *The Politics of Housework*. London: Allison and Busby.

Miles, Robert 1980: Class, race and ethnicity: a critique of Cox's theory. *Ethnic and Racial Studies*, 3, 2, April.

Miles, Robert 1982: *Racism and Migrant Labour*. London: Routledge and Kegan Paul.

Millett, Kate 1969: *Sexual Politics*. London: Rupert Hart-Davis.

Milner, David 1975: *Children and Race*. Harmondsworth: Penguin.

Milner, David 1983: *Children and Race: Ten Years On*. London: Ward Lock Educational.

Mitchell, Juliet 1974: *Psychoanalysis and Feminism*. London: Allen Lane.

Morris, Desmond 1966: *The Naked Ape*. London: Jonathan Cape.

Moynihan, Daniel 1965: *The Negro Family in the United States: The Case for National Action*. Washington: U.S. Government Printing Office.

Myrdal, Gunnar 1944: *An American Dilemma: The Negro Problem and American Democracy*. New York: Harper and Row.

Ortner, Sherry B. 1974: Is female to male as nature is to culture? In Michelle Zimbalist Rosaldo and Louse Lamphere (eds), *Women, Culture and Society*. Stanford: Stanford University Press.

Parsons, Talcott, and R. Bales 1956: *Family: Socialization and Interaction Process*. London: Routledge and Kegan Paul.

Patterson, Orlando 1982: *Slavery and Social Death*. Cambridge, Massachusetts: Harvard University Press.

Patterson, Sheila 1965: *Dark Strangers*. Harmondsworth: Pelican.

Phizacklea, Annie 1982: Migrant women and wage labour: the case of West Indian women in Britain. In Jackie West (ed), *Work, Women and the Labour Market*. London: Routledge and Kegan Paul.

Phizacklea, Annie, and Robert Miles 1980: *Labour and Racism*. London: Routledge and Kegan Paul.

Poggi, Dominique, and Monique Coormaert 1974: The city: off-limits to women. *Liberation*, July/August.

Poster, Mark 1978: *Critical Theory of the Family*. London: Pluto Press.

Proctor, Chris 1977: Racist textbooks. In John Raynor and Elizabeth Harris (eds), *Schooling in the City*. London: Ward Lock.

Rampton, A. 1981: *West Indian Children in Our Schools*. London: HMSO.

Rex, John 1973: *Race, Colonialism and the City*. London: Routledge and Kegan Paul.

Rex, John 1983: *Race Relations in Sociological Theory*. London: Routledge and Kegan Paul.

Rex, John, and Sally Tomlinson 1979: *Colonial Immigrants in a British City*. London: Routledge and Kegan Paul.

Reich, Wilhelm 1975a: *The Mass Psychology of Fascism*. Harmondsworth: Penguin.

Reich, Wilhelm 1975b: *The Invasion of Compulsory Sex Morality*. Harmondsworth: Penguin.

Rich, Adrienne 1981: *Compulsory Heterosexuality and Lesbian Existence*. London: Only Women Press.

Robinson, Cedric J. 1983: *Black Marxism*. London: Zed Press.

Rosaldo, Michelle Zimbalist 1974: Women, culture and society: a theoretical overview. In Michelle Zimbalist Rosaldo and Louise Lamphere (eds), *Women, Culture and Society*. Stanford: Stanford University Press.

Rubin, Gayle 1975: The traffic in women: notes on the 'political economy' of sex. In Rayna R. Reiter (ed.), *Toward an' Anthropology of Women*. New York and London: Monthly Review Press.

Sciama, Lidia 1981: The problem of privacy in mediterranean anthropology. In Shirley Ardener (ed.), *Women and Space*. London: Croom Helm.

Select Committee on Race Relations and Immigration 1977: *The West Indian Community*. London: HMSO.

Sharpe, Sue 1976: *Just Like a Girl*. Harmondsworth: Penguin.

Sivanandan, A. 1976: Race, class and the state: the black experience in Britain. *Race and Class*, XVII, 4, Spring.

Smith, Dorothy 1975–76: Women, the family and corporate capitalism. Berkeley Journal of Sociology, XX.

Spender, Dale 1980: *Man Made Language*. London: Routledge and Kegan Paul.

Spender, Dale 1982: *Invisible Women*. London: Writers and Readers Publishing Cooperative.

Spender, Dale and Elizabeth Sarah (eds) 1980: *Learning to Lose*. London: The Women's Press.

Stanley, Liz and Sue Wise 1983: *Breaking Out: Feminist Consciousness and Feminist Research*. London: Routledge and Kegan Paul.

Stanworth, Michelle 1981: *Gender and Schooling*. Women's Research and Resources Centre.

Stember, Charles II 1976: *Sexual Racism*. New York: Elsevier.

Stone, Maureen 1981: *The Education of the Black Child in Britain*. London: Fontana.

Tajfel, Henri 1978: *The Social Psychology of Minorities*. London: Minority Rights Group.

Taylor, Monica J. 1981: *Caught Between: a Review of Research into the Education of Pupils of West Indian Origin*. Windsor: NFER-Nelson.

Tilly, Louise A., and Joan W. Scott 1978: *Women, Work, and Family*. New York: Holt, Rinehart and Winston.

Tolson, Andrew 1977: *The Limits of Masculinity*. London: Tavistock.

Trigg, Roger 1982: *The Shaping of Man*. Oxford: Blackwell.

Turnbull, Colin 1982: *The Forest People*. London: Chatto and Windus.

van den Berghe, Pierre 1978: Race and ethnicity: a sociobiological perspective. *Ethnic and Racial Studies*, 1, 4.

Wellman, David 1977: *Portraits of White Racism*. Cambridge: Cambridge University Press.

Westergaard, John, and Henrietta Resler 1975: *Class in a Capitalist Society*. London: Heinemann.

Willis, Paul 1978: *Learning to Labour: How Working Class Kids get Working Class Jobs*. London: Saxon House.

Wilson, Edward 1975: *Sociobiology: the New Synthesis*. Cambridge, Massachusetts: Harvard University Press.

Wolpe, Anne-Marie 1977: *Some Processes in Sexist Education*. London: Women's Research and Resources Centre.

Zaretsky, Eli 1976: *Capitalism, the Family, and Personal Life*. London: Pluto Press.

Index